BREAKING
RANKS

*the text of this book is printed
on 100% recycled paper*

BREAKING RANKS

Norman Podhoretz

A POLITICAL MEMOIR

HARPER COLOPHON BOOKS
HARPER & ROW, PUBLISHERS
NEW YORK, CAMBRIDGE, HAGERSTOWN, PHILADELPHIA, SAN FRANCISCO
LONDON, MEXICO CITY, SÃO PAULO, SYDNEY

A hardcover edition of this book is published by Harper & Row, Publishers.

BREAKING RANKS. Copyright © 1979 by Norman Podhoretz. All rights reserved. Printed in the United States of America. No part of this book may be used or reproduced in any manner whatsoever without written permission except in the case of brief quotations embodied in critical articles and reviews. For information address Harper & Row, Publishers, Inc., 10 East 53rd Street, New York, N.Y. 10022. Published simultaneously in Canada by Fitzhenry & Whiteside Limited, Toronto.

First HARPER COLOPHON edition published 1980.

ISBN: 0-06-090816-5

80 81 82 83 84 10 9 8 7 6 5 4 3 2 1

For Midge

CONTENTS

PROLOGUE

A Letter to My Son

Dear John:

The other day, reminded by some passing remark that I used to be a radical—indeed that I visibly and enthusiastically participated in the swing to radicalism in the early 1960s—you asked me with astonishment in your voice whether I had ever really believed "all that stuff." The thought of your father in connection with "all that stuff" evidently strikes you as a contradiction in terms. No wonder. All your conscious life you've known me as an opponent of the New Left and the counterculture and their various descendants in the liberal culture. For all your precocity you could never fully understand why I always seemed to be against everything everyone else in the world—your teachers, your classmates, your friends—seemed to be for. I would try to explain whenever you asked me, but it was all so complicated and you were just too young to take it in. You're a little less young now, however, and maybe the time has come for a fully detailed account.

I'll begin by answering your question of the other day. Yes, once upon a time I really did believe in all that stuff. In fact, I played a not inconsiderable part in spreading it around, beginning with a number of articles I wrote in the late fifties and then, much more importantly, through Commentary *after I became its editor in 1960. But the minute I say even that much, one of those complications arises that you were until recently too young to understand. Because all that stuff was both the same as it is today and entirely different. That is, the ideas were more or less the same, but the context, the circumstances, the background were all different, and this had the effect of giving a different feel to those ideas than they have today.*

For one thing, they were new when I first encountered them. They were also daring and a little dangerous: they could get you into trouble. Not so much, I hasten to add, with the FBI or the House Un-American Activities Committee as with one's fellow intellectuals.

You see, in the late fifties the important forces in the intellectual world—magazines like Partisan Review, Commentary, and Encounter, and writers like Lionel Trilling, Hannah Arendt, Reinhold Niebuhr, Arthur Koestler, Sidney Hook, Leslie Fiedler, Saul Bellow, etc. etc. etc.—were against radicalism. That doesn't mean (as again you've been led to imagine) that they were on the Right or that they were conservative in the sense, say, that William F. Buckley, Jr., and The National Review were. On the contrary, they were all liberals. This was even true of Encounter, which turned out to have been subsidized secretly by the CIA up until the late 60s. But (still another complication) the CIA was itself a liberal organization. Yes, yes, I know, it did illiberal things. Nevertheless the people who ran it were liberals. For example, the officer who headed the division that was responsible for Encounter had come to the CIA from a high position in the United World Federalists, than which nothing could have been more liberal. In any case, whatever its connection with Encounter may have been, the CIA had no connection whatsoever with Partisan Review or Commentary, even though both of them had a point of view similar to Encounter's. I've already said that it was a liberal point of view, and it was; but if you really want to understand it, you have to think of it more in terms of what it was against than of what it was for. And what it was against was Communism.

The reason the anti-Communism of those liberals has to be stressed is that—to complicate matters still further—there were also liberals in America who were not anti-Communist—who were, to tell the truth, favorably disposed toward the Communists. They weren't Communists themselves, but they were generally sympathetic to the Communists. These liberals—fellow travelers, they were called—thought the Communists were on the same side as they were, only more zealous and more impatient (faults for which they could easily be forgiven, and even admired and envied).

The Communists, for their part, had no such illusions. To them liberalism was nothing more than the political ideology of the bourgeoisie and therefore marked for destruction in the revolution ahead. But around 1935, when Stalin began to get worried about the growing military power of Nazi Germany, he decided that he had better move toward an alliance with the "bourgeois" democracies—specifically the United States, Britain, and France—in case of war with Hitler. At that point the Communist parties in those three countries, all of which took their orders from Moscow, changed their line. In America (and there were similar developments in Britain and France) they dropped all talk of revolution, they represented themselves as patriots (the slogan of the American Communist party was "Communism Is Twentieth-century Americanism"), and they began encouraging the idea that they were nothing more than "liberals in a hurry." As for the Soviet Union, it was portrayed as a democratic country and Stalin as a benevolent figure leading his people out of the backwardness of czarist times toward a richer, fuller, and happier life.

Nobody knows how many American liberals were fooled by propaganda like this. But enough of them were, certainly, to make a difference. For example, the two leading liberal weeklies in America, The Nation *and* The New Republic, *became loyal apologists for Stalin, constantly printing pieces that praised his many accomplishments and denouncing as reactionaries and fascists anyone who called those accomplishments into question or tried to expose the bloodiness and repression behind the smiling façade. No one today denies that Stalin murdered millions of peasants who resisted his plan to expropriate their land and organize them into collective farms where they would all become employees of the state. But the fellow-traveling liberals (not to mention the "liberals in a hurry") of the 1930s denied it and vilified as liars and worse those who tried to tell the world what was happening. Nor does anyone today deny that the Soviet Union under Stalin was a police state in which all political opponents were either murdered or imprisoned in the Gulag Archipelago, a vast network of concentration camps that, according to Solzhenitsyn's estimate (he, as you know, spent eleven years in* the Gulag himself), eventually offered gruesome hospitality to an estimated sixty million people. Yet the fellow travelers of the 1930s denied this too and denounced reports of it as fascist propaganda.

Who were these "fascists" and "reactionaries"? You might think they were rich businessmen or sinister capitalists like the character played by Edward Arnold in Mr. Smith Goes to Washington, that old Frank Capra movie you've seen so many times on television. But you would be wrong. Mostly they were intellectuals, and a lot of them had once themselves been Communists who had joined the party in the belief that it stood for social justice and democracy and who had then eventually come to know better. Many others had never been Communists but were members of rival socialist parties who also opposed Communism (or Stalinism) as a betrayal of the ideals in which they all as followers of Marx claimed to believe.

As time went on, a few of these anti-Communists of the Left moved all the way over to the Right and became what it is fair to call conservatives. One such, an ex-Communist, was Whittaker Chambers, who became famous when he accused Alger Hiss of having been a Communist spy while occupying an important position in the State Department. Another was James Burnham, who had been a follower of Leon Trotsky, Stalin's defeated rival, and then wound up as an editor of The National Review and a defender of Joe McCarthy. A third was Will Herberg, who had belonged to a tiny subdivision of the Communist movement, the Lovestonites, and eventually became an influential Jewish theologian as well as an important political conservative. And there were others of whom you've probably heard, among them the novelist John Dos Passos, who was a radical when he wrote U.S.A. and then became a conservative in later years, and the critic Max Eastman, who began by translating the works of Trotsky from Russian into English and ended by writing articles for the very conservative Reader's Digest.

But if some anti-Communists of the Left became conservatives, most of them did not. Some became, or remained, socialists; others became liberals. For example, Jay Lovestone, the leader of the little group to which Will Herberg had once belonged, wound up working for the liberal trade-union movement. Sidney Hook, the author of one of the first important books on Marx written by an American and one of the fiercest and most consistent critics of Communism, continued through thick and thin to regard himself as a socialist. And so did Philip Rahv and William Phillips, the two chief editors of Partisan Review who (like the magazine itself) remained sympathetic to radicalism in one form or another after their break with the Communist party in the early thirties.

All these people had one thing in common. Whether they became conservatives, socialists, or liberals, their ruling passion tended to be a hatred of Communism and a suspicion of Communists. Having been Communists themselves, or having seen and dealt with Communists at close range, they had all come away from the experience with the conviction that Communism was a great evil—as great an evil as Nazism and possibly even greater.

There were those who came to feel this way as early as the 1920s when reports of repression and brutality first began circulating in the West—many of them brought out by refugees who had themselves participated in the making of the Russian Revolution in the fond hope that it would bring socialism and democracy to their country. For others the turning point was the Moscow Trials, when Stalin purged and murdered many of his associates on false charges of treason; and for still others the break came when in 1939 Stalin signed a pact with Hitler. Can you imagine the shock that was caused by this incredible event? How could Stalin have done such a thing? Explanations and rationalizations were of course offered and a surprisingly large number of people accepted them. But for many others, this was the end of the line. Not even Hitler's invasion of the Soviet Union two years later, and the fact that Stalin was now allied with the democratic world in the fight against fascism, could repair the moral damage that signing a pact with Hitler had done to Stalin's reputation and to the reputation of the Communists in America and elsewhere who had justified the pact as a necessary maneuver.

What the anti-Communist intellectuals were saying, in short, was that Communism in the Soviet Union had led not to justice, equality, and freedom but to a system of dictatorial control as thoroughgoing as any the world had ever seen. In fact, except for Nazism the world had never seen anything quite like the Communist system. Older-style dictatorships were mainly interested in concentrating all political power in their hands, but they were generally willing to permit a certain amount or even a great deal of freedom in other areas of life—religion, for example, or the arts. But in these new systems—to which the word totalitarianism was beginning to be applied—everything was controlled and no freedom was allowed in any area of life. A single political party ruled the state and the state ruled all of life.

From the point of view of the anti-Communist intellectuals, one of the worst things about this system was the ruthlessness with which it suppressed freedom of thought and freedom of speech. These were, after all, the freedoms that concerned them most closely as intellectuals; and in fact one of the main reasons why so many intellectuals were attracted to Communism in the first place was their belief that in a Communist society people like them—educated people, cultivated people—would be better off than they felt themselves to be under capitalism. In America, for instance, everything was, or seemed to be, run by businessmen. Intellectuals had no status, no power, no money. At worst they were ridiculed and sometimes harassed; at best they were tolerated and ignored. But in a "socialist" society where private property was abolished and the pursuit of profits put to an end, people who cultivated the nonmaterial values would become more and more important, and art and thought would flourish as they never had before. Marx himself had even said that under Communism factory workers would spend their leisure time reading and writing poetry.

This was the theory, but the Soviet reality was something else again. For a few brief years after the Russian Revolution, there was a cultural flowering, but soon the totalitarian darkness descended. Experimentation in the arts was suppressed in the Soviet Union no less thoroughly than in Nazi Germany. The best writers were silenced; some, like Isaac Babel and Osip Mandelstam, were murdered, and others were forced either to be still or to write according to the dictates of the party bureaucrats. Painting too was made to conform to the canons of "socialist realism" —a style that was neither socialist nor realistic, but rather an idealized and sentimental representation of approved scenes and subjects (portraits of Lenin and Stalin, workers building socialism, and so on). Great composers like Shostakovich and Prokofiev were humiliated and forced to apologize and revise their work when they violated the equivalent of these aesthetic rules in music.

Nor was it only the arts that were subjected to this kind of control. Philosophers, historians, sociologists, psychologists—all had to toe the "party line," all had to say what they were in effect told to say and to keep silent about everything else. Not even scientists were safe. A charlatan named Lysenko, for instance, was given the highest honors for "proving" that genetic changes could be induced by changes in the environment—an idea that conformed to the party line but contradicted all the scientific evidence accepted by geneticists everywhere else in the world.

Up until the end of the Second World War, what mainly concerned the anti-Communist intellectuals was the internal character of the Soviet regime. But right after the war, a new anxiety arose over what looked very much like the beginning of a campaign by the Communists to extend their control far beyond the borders of the Soviet Union itself. The victorious Russian armies, moving toward Berlin, had already occupied all the countries of Eastern Europe and, in violation of wartime pledges, had set up governments run by local Communist leaders who took their orders from Moscow and were kept in power by Soviet troops. Then, in Czechoslovakia, the only democratic country in Eastern Europe, the Communists staged a coup and all of Western Europe began to feel threatened.

To make matters even more ominous, the "popular-front" line, stressing the loyalty of the various national Communist parties to their countries of origin and their commitment to peaceful democratic change, was now dropped. "Proletarian internationalism" —that is, the principle that all Communist parties owed their primary allegiance to the Soviet Union—was back, and the fear of Czech-style coups on the one hand and outright Soviet invasion on the other became very great throughout the whole of Western Europe.

It was to prevent any such thing from happening that the United States undertook two major initiatives. It created a military alliance called NATO to defend Western Europe against the threat of a Soviet invasion. And it set up a huge system of economic aid called the Marshall Plan, which, by speeding the reconstruction of the war-torn European democracies and turning them into prosperous modern societies would (or so it was hoped) deprive the Communists in those countries of opportunities for political subversion.

Here, then, an effort was mounted by the United States and its allies to hold the line against any further advances by the Soviet Union, whether operating on its own through military invasion or indirectly through the agency of local Communist parties. This policy was known as "containment," and the struggle to which it addressed itself also had a name: the cold war.

It will not surprise you to hear that the anti-Communist intellectuals enlisted in that war on the side of the United States. But it did surprise some of them. What surprised them was not, of course, that they were against the Communists: they had been against the Communists all along, or at least for some years past. But being for the United States was a new experience to many of these people. All their lives they had thought of themselves as virtual foreigners in this country, as aliens—hence the term "alienated" was so often applied to intellectuals in America. As it happens, the community of anti-Communist intellectuals in America included a large number of Jews (and so, on the other side, did the community of fellow travelers), and no doubt this had something to do with their feelings of alienation. In those days there was still a great deal of open hostility to Jews in America and Jews were still excluded from many positions of power and influence. Even as late as the 1950s colleges and professional schools had unacknowledged but strictly enforced quotas limiting the number of Jews who could be admitted (I myself entered Columbia in 1946 under a seventeen-percent quota). Many firms would not hire Jews; many social clubs barred Jews from membership; Jews were unable to get rooms in many hotels or rent apartments in many buildings or buy houses in many neighborhoods. Even in the world of culture restrictions were still in force. At Columbia, for example, Lionel Trilling was the first Jew ever to be appointed to a professorship in the English department; and despite the fact that he had already done very distinguished work in the field, his appointment was resisted on the theory that as a Jew he lacked the background to understand English literature as fully as a "rooted" person of Anglo-Saxon ancestry quite naturally would. (This, I remind you, happened not in the Middle Ages but in my own lifetime and to a man you yourself actually knew.)

But it would be wrong to ascribe the alienation of the intellectuals in America entirely or even largely to Jewishness. For one thing, not all the intellectuals were Jewish; in fact many, and perhaps most, were WASPs from old American families whose position at the head of American society had been challenged by the rise of a new breed of Americans in the years after the Civil War. These old WASP families felt that the country was being stolen away and changed into a place that had no room for the likes of them. Edmund Wilson, who was probably the most important literary intellectual of his time, came out of just such a background, and in one of his essays he describes the difficulties his father and his uncles, educated at schools like Exeter and Andover and such colleges as Princeton and Yale and trained "for what had once been called the learned professions," experienced in trying "to deal with a world in which this kind of education and the kind of ideals it served no longer really counted for much."

Like the Jews down at the bottom of the social ladder, then, the old WASP families at the top had reasons of their own to feel alienated at a certain period in the history of this country. But whether they were Jews or WASPs, intellectuals had cause enough as intellectuals to feel like foreigners in America during that same period—the period running roughly from the end of the Civil War up through the end of the Second World War. It was during those years that America moved into the forefront of the modern world. This was the time when the West was opened up and settled, when the great railroads were built, when all the great industries were established—and many of the great fortunes. It was a time when, as Calvin Coolidge notoriously said during his term as president in the late 1920s, the business of America was business. So it was, and that meant that nothing else was valued very highly—certainly not intellectual and cultural pursuits or the "oddballs" who pursued them. Intellectuals were ridiculed and despised. They were impractical. They were effeminate. They had—in a famous American phrase—"never met a payroll."

If I've given you the impression that the intellectuals were merely passive, pathetic victims and martyrs who took all this lying down, let me immediately set things straight. They didn't take it lying down; they responded by developing a critique of America as a country in the grip of false and corrupting values. "The exclusive worship of the bitch-goddess SUCCESS," said the great philosopher William James, "is our national disease." By the worship of success, James meant the worship of money, and this diagnosis of the American condition was confirmed by practically every important American writer of the period. Not only that, but it was extended into a merciless assault on practically every aspect of the national life. There was nothing good to be said about America, except perhaps that it had a certain raw energy and vitality. For the rest, in addition to being moneygrubbing and materialistic, it lacked any of the civilized graces. It was a "bourgeois" country, a narrow-minded country, a puritanical country, a philistine country. What else could one expect when it was dominated by businessmen and run entirely for their benefit? In such a country it was a badge of honor to be estranged or alienated; it signified a stubborn devotion to the higher things in life.

So powerful were these feelings of estrangement that they persisted right into the Second World War, when some intellectuals (including a few Jews!) saw no reason to "support" America even in a fight against so obviously greater an evil as Nazi Germany. But as the war went on, things began to change. Mary McCarthy once described the happiness she experienced when, as a young writer associated with Partisan Review and sharing the stock attitudes of contempt for and estrangement from "bourgeois society," she suddenly realized one day that she cared about the outcome of the war, that she wanted the United States to win.

A few years later, in 1952, Partisan Review ran a symposium with the title "Our Country and Our Culture," and the fact that a magazine which had always stood as the very symbol of the alienated intellectual could speak of America as our country in itself said more about the changing attitudes of the intellectuals than anything the contributors to the symposium had to say. Not that what they had to say contradicted the spirit of the new sense of personal identification with America expressed in the title. On the contrary. Though very few went quite so far as Mary McCarthy had recently done in an essay for Commentary called "America the Beautiful" (with only a protective touch of irony), many of them found virtues in the country and even in its culture to which they had previously been blind.

So democratic America was "our country" now, a bulwark of freedom against both Nazi and Communist totalitarianism. Amazing as this discovery about America was, what amazed the anti-Communist intellectuals even more was how well "our country" worked. During the Great Depression of the thirties, almost everyone thought that the American economic system—capitalism, in a word—had reached a point of collapse, just as its critics, especially the Marxist ones, had always predicted it would. According to these critics, only the war had saved it by absorbing into the armed forces millions who would otherwise have been unemployed and by stimulating production through the temporary need for guns, tanks. and planes. Since these were only temporary expedients, however, the economy was bound to sink back into a depression again once the war was over. But not only did this confident prophecy fail to come true; the very opposite occurred. There was no depression after the war. Instead there was prosperity—more of it than anyone had ever seen before either in America or anywhere else; and more people were getting a share of this prosperity than anyone had ever thought possible under either capitalism or any other economic system.

Henry Wallace had been considered a visionary when he said (as vice-president under Roosevelt) that there would be sixty million jobs in America after the war; but during the fifties that goal was reached, and the number was growing all the time.

Included among these—and this probably came as the greatest surprise of all—were jobs even for intellectuals. It had always been difficult in the past for intellectuals to earn their living as intellectuals. Of those who lacked inherited wealth, a small number had been able to support themselves by teaching or by contributing to the handful of magazines which provided a market for serious writing. Everyone else either gave up or was forced to do intellectual work in the hours left over from an unrelated job (one of the great American poets of our time, Wallace Stevens, was a lawyer for an insurance company; another, William Carlos Williams, practiced medicine) or had to manage (like several of our best novelists, including William Faulkner and F. Scott Fitzgerald) by doing hack work for the movies and the popular magazines. This situation also began to improve in the years after the Second World War. As prosperity increased, more and more young Americans were being sent to college, which meant that more and more people had to be hired to teach them, and this in turn meant the opening up of a large new source of jobs for intellectuals.

But the expansion of higher education did more than provide teaching jobs for the intellectuals. It also helped to create a much larger public for serious writing (and for the arts in general) than had ever existed before. "Quality paperbacks"—that is, inexpensive reprints of literary classics, many of which had scarcely been available before even in expensive editions—now began to flood the bookstores. Difficult contemporary works (by authors like James Joyce, T. S. Eliot, and William Faulkner) which had previously been of interest to only a minuscule number of readers also began attracting a relatively large audience, while several younger writers like Saul Bellow and Mary McCarthy, whose work had previously been confined to the "little" magazines, were now suddenly appearing on the best-seller lists and being courted by magazines catering to very large audiences.

Thus America was becoming "our country" to the anti-Communist intellectuals not just in the sense that they now had a stake in its political system and because they also for the first time had a stake in its economic system; there was the equally astonishing fact that America now had a reciprocal stake in them. The old contempt for intellectuals so characteristic of an earlier day was gradually giving way to a new regard for "brains" and education and the people who had them. Whatever the reasons for this development may have been, intellectuals were more and more looked up to instead of down upon, and were more and more being sought out for advice and guidance by the government, by foundations, and even by corporations. In short, from having been virtual outcasts and pariahs, the intellectuals were becoming a respected group in American society.

To all this the anti-Communist intellectuals responded by moving—to borrow the title of a book later written about American fiction in the postwar period—"beyond alienation" and toward a new sense of identification with and sympathy for the country of which they were now an increasingly important part. If in the past they had been anti-Communist (or anti-Soviet—it came to the same thing at a time when all Communists everywhere were controlled by the Soviet Union) and uncertain about America, they were now anti-Communists and committed to America. They continued, most of them, to think of themselves as men of the Left or as liberals, but liberals who differed from the fellow-traveling species in their ideas about the Soviet Union.

Even Delmore Schwartz, who as late as the Partisan Review *symposium of 1952 had insisted on the continuing relevance of the idea of alienation, and on the need to maintain the "critical nonconformism" which had traditionally characterized the intellectual's attitude toward American society, began experiencing a change of mind. Here is how he put the case in a lecture on "The Present State of Modern Poetry" delivered in 1958:*

Since the Second World War and the beginning of the atomic age, the consciousness of the creative writer, however detached, has been confronted with the specter of the totalitarian state, the growing poverty and helplessness of Western Europe, and the threat of an *inconceivably destructive war which may annihilate civilization and mankind itself. Clearly when the future of civilization is no longer assured, a criticism of American life in terms of a contrast between avowed ideals and present actuality cannot be a primary preoccupation and source of inspiration. For America, not Europe, is now the sanctuary of culture; civilization's very existence depends upon America, upon the actuality of American life, and not the ideals of the American Dream. To criticize the actuality upon which all hope depends thus becomes a criticism of hope itself.*

Now if you want to understand my own political development, the first thing you have to bear in mind is that it was on these attitudes toward Communism on the one side and America on the other that I cut my teeth as a young intellectual. It was from here that my odyssey to radicalism began, and it was back to a remarkably similar set of attitudes that my gradual revulsion from radicalism eventually took me.

To be sure, where I stand today is not precisely where I stood twenty-five years ago. How could it be when so much has happened both to the world and to me in the course of those extraordinarily unsettling years? But there is no way I can truly explain the differences both gross and subtle, both large and small, without telling the whole story of how and why I went from being a liberal to being a radical and then finally to being an enemy of radicalism in all its forms and varieties.

That I define my present position in such negative terms does not mean that it is a wholly negative position; not at all. But I do so because I still have trouble finding a positive political label for myself. The label I usually use when I am forced to use one at all is centrist or centrist liberal; the label almost everyone else uses in describing me or the general point of view I hold is "neoconservative." But whatever its most appropriate name, my present position is very hard to describe in terms of abstract propositions or doctrines. There too the whole story has to be told.

It is that story I want to tell in this book. Obviously I want to tell it because I would like you to understand who and what I am. But I also believe that in the story of my own radicalization and deradicalization, and of what I saw going on around me in the *process, there is a larger story about the political culture of this country that needs to be faced and absorbed if we are ever to recover our health as a nation after the fevers and plagues of the two decades just past. I have a rather different conception of the nature of those fevers and plagues—and therefore of the possible cures—than is generally accepted by the conventional wisdom of the moment. But once again, I can only explain by telling the whole story.*

BREAKING RANKS

1

When I arrived at Columbia College in 1946 I was not quite seventeen years old, and to the extent that I cared about politics at all (and I did, though not as much as I cared about literature), my views were the standard views of those American liberals who were suspicious of America and sympathetic to the Soviet Union. That was only natural: where I came from and went to school that kind of liberalism was the dominant orthodoxy. But by the time I graduated from Columbia four years later, I had been converted into a passionate partisan of the new liberalism—the kind that was at once pro-American and anti-Communist.

Those years have often been described as the start of a long period of apathy on American college campuses—they are the years in which the "silent generation" is supposed to have been born. The truth, however, is that at Columbia, at least, an endless and vehement political debate went on between the Stalinists and their fellow travelers on the one side and the anti-Communist liberals on the other, and the "silence" was at a high decibel level. The main difference between this period of political ferment and the one which had preceded it in the thirties and the other which would follow it in the sixties was that in my time the radicals, for once, wound up on the losing side. Whereas the anti-Communist liberals were full of the dynamism, élan, and passion that so often accompany a newly discovered way of looking at things, the fellow travelers could marshal nothing but boring clichés and tired arguments that were being drained of plausibility with every passing day. To me, mainly observing from the sidelines (I was too busy trying to read every great book ever written to keep up with *The New York Times,* as you had to do if you wanted to participate in these arguments), it was simply no contest. And as if this were not enough to win me over, most—not all, but most—of the professors at Columbia I admired (Lionel Trilling, F. W. Dupee, and Richard Chase, for example) were liberals of the pro-American, anti-Communist variety.

After graduating from Columbia, I went on to do graduate work at Cambridge, and I think that even if I hadn't already become a liberal of this type myself, the sheer ignorance and bigotry toward America that were so commonplace in England in the early fifties would have turned me into one. Be that as it may, I can hardly count the number of hours, days, weeks of my three-year stay in England that were taken up with arguments about America—what it was like, and what was happening there. Yes, McCarthy was very bad, but the country was not going fascist. Yes, there was a lot of advertising but the reason millions of Americans were buying cars and washing machines and other such appliances was that they really wanted these things, not that they had been "brainwashed" into believing they did. But no, Americans were not more "materialistic" than Europeans; if anything, they were less so in many different ways. Yes, there was a great deal of violence in America, but fistfights and gun duels did not go on all the time in the streets. No, not all American women hated sex, nor were all American men ridden with status anxieties and suffering from ulcers. Yes, there was such a thing as an American culture and an American intellectual life. Yes, America was a better place, an infinitely better place, and in every possible way, than the Soviet Union: how could any rational person doubt it?

It was during those years in England and two subsequent ones in the army that I began writing professionally, mainly for scholarly literary journals like *Scrutiny* and *Essays in Criticism* in England and more general intellectual magazines like *Commentary* and *Partisan*

Review in America. When, in December of 1955, I was discharged from the army, I got a full-time job as an assistant editor at *Commentary,* where I remained for the next two years while writing fairly regularly for *Commentary* itself and a number of other magazines, including *The New Yorker* and *The Reporter.*

Though the great majority of my published pieces during those years were on literary subjects, and though I rarely dealt with politics as such, almost everything I wrote reflected the influence of the new, revisionist liberalism of the fifties in one way or another. But only indirectly. As a literary critic I believed in the doctrine that a work of art lived or died by the laws of its own being—aesthetic laws—and I believed that it must not be judged by any other standards, whether moral or political. A poem or a novel might contain offensive sentiments (anti-Semitism, for example) or it might celebrate evil behavior (even including murder), but it could still be a great work from a strictly literary point of view, and it was the responsibility of a serious critic to make his judgments on the basis of literary values alone.

At the same time, as a disciple of Lionel Trilling, with whom I had studied at Columbia, and of F. R. Leavis, with whom I had studied at Cambridge, I also believed that the only kind of criticism really worth writing was the kind that began rather than ended with the making of aesthetic judgments. Trilling once spoke of standing at "the bloody crossroads" where literature and politics meet, and that was exactly where I wanted to take my stand as a critic too. They were bloody, those crossroads, because blood had often actually been shed in the clash between literature and politics. Writers had been killed by politicians for expressing certain ideas or writing in certain ways; but (what was less often acknowledged) these same politicians had often been inspired by other writers to shed the blood of their fellow writers, and millions of nonwriters as well. This, I thought, was what Trilling had intended to convey in quoting a remark by the French poet Charles Péguy: "*Tout commence en mystique et finit en politique*"— which he translated or paraphrased as "everything begins in sentiment and assumption and finds its issue in political action and institutions."

What these ideas meant to me in practice was that whenever I reviewed a new book (and it would usually be a novel) I would first try to explain why I thought it was good or bad from a strictly literary point of view, but I would then go on to say what the success or failure of the work revealed about the attitudes of the author and what those in turn revealed about the general temper of the times. It was in discussing these broader questions that I stepped directly into the bloody crossroads. I don't mean that I praised or criticized every book I wrote about on the basis of its conformity or opposition to my own political ideas. On the contrary: two of the novels I treated most harshly as a young critic were Saul Bellow's *The Adventures of Augie March* and Herman Wouk's *Marjorie Morningstar,* both of which were written (Bellow's on a much higher literary level than Wouk's) from a political perspective very close to my own. Yet each in its way seemed to me a bad novel from a literary point of view, and so that is what I had to say. Nor did stepping directly into the bloody crossroads mean that I attacked Communism and pledged my allegiance to America at the conclusion of every piece I wrote. The issues were rarely that simple or open, and the process worked more indirectly and more often than not in a variety of other ways.

For example, in an article for *The New Yorker* about Nathanael West, whose work had been (in my then minority opinion) unfairly neglected, I tried to show that the reason so obviously good a novelist had always been underrated was that his sense of life clashed with one of the great articles of faith of the "radical press"—the idea that all the miseries of the human condition could be cured by the right social and economic arrangements. This was a case of defending a writer against the politically inspired misjudgments of fellow-traveling liberalism.

Interestingly enough, West himself had been a fellow traveler in his political sympathies, but his deeper sense of life, which is what he drew on in the writing of his novels and what made him into an artist, had nothing whatever in common with the simplistic assumptions about the malleability of human nature that lay at the foundations of that kind of liberalism. Exactly the opposite was true of certain other writers and there were occasions when I tried to show how the ideas of fellow-traveling liberalism (though I never called it by that name) could lead a novelist to misjudgments of the realities of the world around him even against the evidence of his own eyes and ears. Nelson Algren, for instance, wrote about America as though it contained only two kinds of people—the exploiting (and listless) rich and the exploited (and colorful) poor—when even a glance at his own career as a best-selling novelist would have immediately revealed a truth more complicated and far more interesting than that.

Yet it wasn't only fellow-traveling liberalism that I blamed for blinding writers to the realities of the world around them. In a couple of pieces I wrote on William Faulkner I said that he too had lost touch with contemporary experience, and with what was interesting about it, because of a bias against the middle class which in his case derived from a conservative rather than a liberal point of view. And here we come to another one of those complications that makes this story so hard to get right. The conservatism of Faulkner, which he shared with many other southern novelists, poets, and critics of that period (Allen Tate, Robert Penn Warren, John Crowe Ransom, et al.), had very little in common with what is nowadays called conservatism. Today the word "conservative," whatever else it may be thought to mean, usually signifies a belief in capitalism (or, to use the current euphemisms, "free enterprise" or the "free market"). But conservatives like Faulkner and his fellow southerners were as hostile to capitalism and to capitalists as any Communist or socialist or fellow-traveling liberal. Where the southern conservatives differed from the opponents of capitalism on the Left was in believing that the agrarian civilization of the Old South (the South of the great cotton plantations, the South of the old mansions, and, it is worth bearing in mind, the South of Negro slavery) was superior to the industrialized world of the urban middle class of the North.

In criticizing this point of view, as I did in several other pieces beside the ones on Faulkner, I was still speaking as a liberal. And it was also as a liberal that I did something else in those pieces, which was to defend the secularism of contemporary middle-class society against conservative attack. Again a complication. Reading the standard accounts of the fifties, one finds that a "religious revival" was going on in the country at large, taking the form of increased church attendance and of frequent displays of public piety (no ceremonial occasion was complete, for instance, without the presence of a minister, a priest, and a rabbi). But to conservative literary people—and here I include not only writers like Faulkner and the "Southern Agrarians" but such figures as T. S. Eliot and his followers—none of this ran very deep. America, they said, was still for all practical purposes a secular society, and it still suffered, just as the West in general did (though perhaps even more, since it was so much more advanced in modernization) from a loss of the values that its entire civilization rested on and that derived ultimately from religious faith. It remained, in other words, the spiritual "wasteland" that Eliot had seen as the defining metaphor of the modern world as a whole.

I too thought that the religious revival was not to be taken seriously, but in the first major piece I ever did for *Commentary,* in the early fifties, and then again in an article for *Partisan Review,* published around the same time, I attacked the idea that secularism for most Americans involved an absence of values. My argument was that the values of a people were to be found not in the speeches they made or in their rhetorical professions of belief, but in the way they lived their lives from day to day; and if American values remained invisible to so many social critics, it was because neither those critics nor indeed our novelists— blinded as most of them were by preconceived notions about the American middle class, notions deriving in about equal measure from the Left and the Right—had ever taken the trouble to look at the way the people of this country really lived.

I also argued, and even more fiercely, against the political corollary of the antisecularist position (held, for example, by Whittaker Chambers and William F. Buckley), which was that the main difference between the Western and the Communist worlds was that they were godless and we were not. I did not, that is, accept the idea that the cold war was a war between atheism and religious faith. What in my view separated us from them was that we were free and they were not, that our political system was democratic and that theirs was totalitarian. And I consistently maintained that liberal democracy was itself a value—a value that Americans wanted to live by and that they were even willing to die for.

There was, finally, a third assault from which I found myself defending middle-class life in America, and that was the assault from Bohemia. In a series of articles about the group of writers who called themselves the Beat Generation—the leading members were of course the novelist Jack Kerouac and the poet Allen Ginsberg, but there were literally dozens of others whose names have faded into oblivion—I laced into the fantastic notion that life in the middle class was not actually a form of life at all but a kind of living death. And I tried to show through a critical analysis of their own novels and poems how ridiculous was the claim that the Beats represented a healthier and more vital alternative.

If I was speaking as a liberal in defending middle-class life against the fellow travelers on the Left and the conservative critics of contemporary society on the Right, in defending middle-class life against the Beats I was speaking more personally than politically: in a sense, that is, it was myself and my own experience I was defending rather than my political ideas.

I may not exactly have been what the Beats and people like them had in mind when they said that to choose a life of middle-class respectability was to condemn oneself to a living death. They were usually thinking of businessmen who lived in the suburbs, not of literary critics who lived on the Upper West Side of Manhattan. Nevertheless I *had* chosen a life of middle-class respectability in many essential respects. I was married and I believed in marriage; I had children and I believed in having them; I had a steady job and I believed in working hard. The notion that all this represented a form of suicide—spiritual, emotional, and sexual suicide—I knew to be simply ridiculous in my case, and I had no reason to think that it was any the less ridiculous in the case of others.

Most of the time I didn't feel defensive at all about these matters. Far from it. In that period of my life there was nothing that appealed to me less than the idea of refusing to grow up and settle down—which, stripped of all the rhetoric and all the ideology, was what Kerouac and Ginsberg and their friends stood for—and nothing that I wanted more than to take my rightful place as an adult among other adults. They feared maturity and the responsibilities it entailed as a limitation of their freedom. In fact, one of the reasons so many of them were tempted into homosexuality was that it allowed them to avoid becoming husbands and especially fathers—it was a way of never growing up, of trying to remain forever young. My ambitions ran in exactly the opposite direction. As a child I couldn't wait to grow up; as a young man I was eager to get married, and so far from unwilling was I to become a father that when I did get married it was to a woman who already had two little children for me to raise while waiting for my own to be born.

All this was obviously consistent with my political attitudes. More than that: my feelings about maturity were what might be called the nonpolitical face of those attitudes (just as, on the other side, the Beats, like the Bohemians of an earlier period and the hippies of a later, represented the nonpolitical face of radicalism).

And yet and yet and yet—something new was stirring in me. In an article I was asked to write by *The New Leader* about my own generation, having first given a sympathetic account of our idea that the real adventure of existence lay not in radical politics or in Bohemia but in the "moral life" of the individual, I found myself giving a surprisingly sour account of how these ideas were working themselves out in practice among my contemporaries:

> A great many of them married early, most of them made firm and decisive commitments to careers of a fairly modest kind, such as teaching; they cultivated an interest in food, clothes, furniture, manners—these being elements of the "richness" of life that the generation of the thirties had deprived itself of. As befitted responsible adults, there was nothing playful or frisky about these young people; their very presence and bearing announced that they were serious men and women with no time for fooling around, burdened with a sense of mortality, reconciled to the sad fact of human limitation.

Robert Nisbet, the brilliant social theorist, once said that boredom is the most neglected force in history, that it is on certain occasions as important a cause of change as the economic and political factors to which we generally pay so much more attention. One of those occasions, I believe, was the radicalization of American culture in the 1960s. And in this respect my own case turned out to be a foreshadowing of things to come.

The "restless generation" which I said in the conclusion of the *New Leader* piece was getting more and more restless as it got older because it was beginning to feel cheated of its youth, was, after all, my own; I was a part of it—always slightly detached and critical, but a part of it nonetheless. But in my case it was not "youth" in the relatively trivial sense of "sowing wild oats"—or even, despite my own reliance on the metaphor, the capacity for reckless abandon implied by taking a swim like F. Scott Fitzgerald in the Plaza fountain in the middle of the night. Whatever may have been the full truth about my contemporaries, I was not at twenty-seven anything like what a friend of mine used to call a "young fogey." I had sown more than a few wild oats before settling down at the relatively late (by the standards of that generation) age of twenty-six to a wife and family. Nor was I comfortably launched as yet on the kind of orderly academic career whose course could be foreseen in almost every detail up to the day of retirement: from graduate student to instructor to assistant professor to associate professor to full professor to professor emeritus living in one set of tasteful if somewhat modest surroundings in one academic environ or another and with solid and serious publications all along the way. Indeed, the opposite was more nearly true for me. Already, after only two years at *Commentary*, my first real job, I was on the point of quitting and I had only the faintest notion of where I was going in my professional career. On the other hand I knew very well—or thought I knew—that my possibilities were strictly limited. I could return to graduate school and get a job teaching English; or I could find something in book publishing; or conceivably I could manage as a free-lance writer. My being who I was, and conditions being what they were, I had to resign myself and accept the fact that there was nothing else to hope for and nothing else in sight. Everything was foreknown and foreclosed and it was "childish" or "immature" to think otherwise or to take a risk.

It was the possession of this knowledge that made me feel middle-aged before my time. The youth that I felt cheated of was youth in the sense of innocence, the capacity to entertain illusions about oneself as well as about life, the state of not yet having crashed up against one's own limitations as an individual or those of the human race as a whole, the stage of not yet having discovered that not everything is possible, the condition of not yet having made one's peace with things as they are in the sad and perhaps bitter recognition that this was how they had always been and how they would always be.

I don't know why I should suddenly have begun feeling so antagonistic toward attitudes I had previously delighted in, or why ideas that had so recently seemed both true and profound should suddenly have seemed boring and stale. Was it because they had come to me too easily—from books rather than from first-hand experience—and were therefore wearing thin the way any hand-me-down is bound to do after only a brief period of use?

Possibly so. But whatever the cause may have been, the consequence was a growing restlessness with an outlook that I had
adopted as my own when scarcely out of my teens and that I had
tried to live by ever since.

2

My own growing disaffection with this outlook, however, was as
nothing compared to how Jason Epstein, who was my closest
friend at the time, felt. I had originally met Jason at Columbia,
but even though we were in the same year and were both major-
ing in English, we never as undergraduates got past a nodding
and slightly antagonistic acquaintance. I belonged to a crowd that
considered people like him intellectually unworthy and he belonged to a crowd that considered people like me socially unworthy. They were right about us—we *were* socially unworthy. All
of us had come to Columbia either on scholarship or on the GI
Bill from working-class or lower-middle-class backgrounds, and
we all still bore the signs and stigmata of those origins in the
"bourgeois" (or worse—"petty-bourgeois") earnestness with
which we pursued our studies. But we were wrong about them:
they weren't stupid at all. What they really suffered from—and
what really bothered us about them—was not a lack of intelligence so much as a lack of seriousness. They were snobs, they
were dandies, and they were aesthetes. All they seemed to care
about was striking stylish poses, dressing with the right touch of
careless elegance, affecting an "aristocratic" indifference to
courses and grades and the opinions of professors. They specialized in quips, the more cutting the better, and in being as fey and
provocatively perverse as possible. And in what to us was their

most grievous offense, they took a sneering tone toward the idea
—our idea, to which we held with a religious fervor—that literature had any meaning: in their exquisite world a poem existed to
be savored and relished and not to be analyzed and understood.

I lost touch with Jason after graduating from Columbia, and
when I ran into him again five or six years later, I found that he
had changed to an amazing degree. I would have expected him
to be lolling about somewhere languidly taking in such pleasures
as a hopelessly middle-class society could afford. Possibly this is
what he would have been doing had he been rich, as I had always
assumed he was: he certainly *acted* like someone with a lot of
money. But *acted* was the word, in this as in so many other respects where Jason was concerned. He was, as it turned out,
neither rich nor, as it also turned out, lacking in ambitions very
similar to my own—which is to say that he wanted to have a career
and he wanted to have a family. And in fact he was on his way to
realizing both these ambitions long before I ever got started. By
the time I took my first job he had already been working as an
editor in a publishing house for nearly five years; and by the time
I got married, he was already celebrating his fifth anniversary and
he already had a child. Despite what his college personality suggested, then, he fit the description I was subsequently to write of
the young generation more closely than I did myself: the early
marriage, the early commitment to a career, and—something that
was true of him and never true of me—the interest in those
"elements of the 'richness' of life that the generation of the thirties had deprived itself of"—food, clothes, furniture, manners.

But what was at least as surprising as the "maturity" of Jason's
life was his new interest in politics and more specifically his commitment to the new liberalism of the fifties. At Columbia not only
had he and his friends been indifferent to politics, they had been
hostile, taking the political passions and convictions of the crowd
I associated with as yet another mark of our petty-bourgeois
crudity and crassness. Yet in this too Jason had undergone an
amazing transformation. He was, when I ran into him again, just

on the point of launching Anchor Books, the first of the new quality-paperback series that would revolutionize American publishing, and almost everything about the project breathed the atmosphere of the new liberalism. For example, the person he had hired to be his main adviser was Nathan Glazer, who, as a member of the editorial staff of *Commentary* and a prolific contributor to its pages, had been instrumental in turning the magazine (founded by the American Jewish Committee and edited by Elliot E. Cohen with more narrowly Jewish objectives in mind) into one of the leading voices of the new liberalism in the intellectual community. Among the first few books to appear in the Anchor series, moreover, were Lionel Trilling's *The Liberal Imagination,* which was probably the single most important expression of the new liberalism to have come out of the literary world, and David Riesman's *The Lonely Crowd* (in the writing of which Glazer had himself collaborated), perhaps the single most important expression of the same point of view to have come out of the field of sociology. Trilling and Riesman spoke mainly for that side of fifties liberalism which involved the newly sympathetic attitude within the intellectual community toward American society and culture. But the Anchor list included a number of works that came from the anti-Communist side of the new liberalism as well, most notably Edmund Wilson's *To the Finland Station,* a major study of the intellectual background of the Russian Revolution.

As if all this weren't enough to suggest that Jason was trying to corner the market on the new liberalism—to become, one might say, its official publisher—he appointed Melvin Lasky to edit an intellectual magazine that he launched on a short-lived career as part of the Anchor series in the mid-fifties. At the time Lasky was also editing one of a vast network of magazines published in many different countries by the Congress for Cultural Freedom, an organization of intellectuals, most of them Europeans and all of them either liberals or social democrats, who had come together to combat the influence of the Communists among their fellow intellectuals. Jason had no way of knowing that the

Congress for Cultural Freedom was getting its financial support from the CIA; even most of the people active in the organization were deceived as to where the money was coming from. But unlike some of them, who would have felt compromised by the knowledge, Jason, I suspect, would have been titillated to find himself connected with an undercover operation. In any case, he would certainly have seen nothing wrong in principle in cooperating with an agency of the American government at a time when the United States was in effect at war with an enemy as evil and as dangerous as Nazi Germany.

Neither, for that matter, would I. For me the issue never arose, but it could very easily have come up when in 1958 I found myself being looked over by the head of the Congress for Cultural Freedom, a man named Michael Josselson, for the position of the American co-editor of *Encounter.* Irving Kristol, who had held that job since the magazine was founded, had resigned and the plan was to replace him with Lasky, then the American co-editor of *Encounter*'s sister magazine in Berlin, *Der Monat.* But Stephen Spender, the "native" co-editor of *Encounter,* who was unhappy at the prospect of working with Lasky, tried to get Josselson to offer me the job instead. Spender and I knew each other only slightly, but we got along well, and, moreover, anyone was preferable to Lasky so far as he was concerned. In the end, deciding that I wanted to live in New York, not in London, I took myself out of the running, and the job went to Lasky (which it no doubt would have done even if I had pushed for it).

No one ever mentioned the CIA in any of the many conversations I had in those few weeks about the job—not Kristol, not Spender, not Josselson. Nor did I ever bring it up. I had heard the rumors—everyone had—that the CCF was getting money from the State Department or perhaps the CIA, but I was inclined to think that this idea was a romantic fantasy. Anyhow, if it was true, it would do no good to ask, since the people who knew would have had to say that it wasn't. About ten years later, when the rumors were finally confirmed, Kristol, Spender, and Lasky all denied ever having had any knowledge of the CIA connection, and Spender in particular maintained almost hysterically that he had been lied to and duped by the Congress for Cultural Freedom. Presumably, then, if I had been offered the job, no one would have told me that I was going to work for the CIA. But if I had been told, how much difference would it have made? Would I have turned it down on that account alone? Out of prudence, perhaps, but then perhaps not. And I doubt even more strongly that Jason would have urged me to turn it down just because of the CIA.

It might seem, then, that the Jason I had known in college was gone and that a new Jason—a mature and serious man with mature and serious ideas—had emerged to take the place of the flippant youth, the dandy, the snob, the aesthete of his Columbia days. Nothing of the kind: the old Jason was still there, and still very much alive. He was there in the careless extravagance with which the new Jason—whose salary was not so large but who was endowed with a very generous expense account—threw money around. He never ate except in the best and most expensive restaurants, often accompanied by large numbers of friends and acquaintances who would (just as he had calculated) be dumbfounded by the size of the check and the insouciant way he paid it. He was there in the clothes: Brooks Brothers, of course, and fantastically expensive shoes from Peel's on which he once spent another small fortune when he airmailed them to London merely to be resoled. The old Jason was there in the parties the new Jason and his wife Barbara were always throwing: parties that seemed to grow larger and more star-studded all the time (the stars in this case being literary celebrities like W. H. Auden and Edmund Wilson, whom he was getting to know through Anchor Books). As was clear from those parties, the old social snobbery was still alive in Jason too. Always there seemed to be people around whose only claim to distinction was the possession of a classy name. Dullards and dolts they usually were, but Jason would insist (invariably seconded by Barbara, whose weakness for the upper orders of society was even greater than his own) that they were interesting or charming or gifted in some mysterious way.

Conversely he loved to make fun of the intellectuals he now also associated with on a regular basis, most of whom were Jewish. He was Jewish himself (as was Barbara), he recognized that they were all talented and intelligent, he agreed with their ideas, he sought out their advice, and he published their books. Nevertheless he all but openly mocked them; he ridiculed their earnestness, their City College accents, their strenuous efforts to acquire social graces and what seemed to him the incorrigible drabness of their personal lives. Whenever he went to one of their parties, he would make an ostentatious show of how bored he was. Once he proposed writing a Gilbert and Sullivan-type operetta to be set at such a party of Jewish intellectuals on the Upper West Side and to open with a stranger entering and introducing himself with the words:

> I am the man who wrote the piece
> About the man who wrote the piece
> On David Ries-man.

On another occasion he solemnly informed the sociologist Daniel Bell that he considered the author of a satirical popular song about marriage called "Makin' Whoopee" a greater poet than T. S. Eliot, and his malicious delight knew no bounds when Bell cited this in a scholarly study as evidence of the changing attitudes toward popular culture among the younger generation of American intellectuals.

But in a way the joke was on Jason, not on Bell, because Jason really did think "Makin' Whoopee" was wonderful. "Makin' Whoopee" was at least fun, which was more than you could say for T. S. Eliot. Its cynical view of marriage was also accurate, which was more than you could say for what the ideologues of "maturity" had been telling us for so many years. Marriage and everything that went with it—the stability, the solidity, the jobs, and the children—were a trap. We were fools for having fallen into it, we were fools for having let ourselves be tricked into surrendering our freedom, and the least we could do about it was complain.

Actually, the most Jason wanted to do about it was complain—and complain and complain and complain. Though he ranted against marriage as an institution, he never got divorced, not even when everyone else around him (including most of the ideologues of maturity) seemed to be doing so. And when in the late fifties he finally quit his job at Doubleday, it was not in order to break loose and run off in high romantic style to the South Seas or the south of France, but to make a stab at getting rich by going into the publishing business for himself; and even then he prudently hedged his bet by taking another—and better—job with Random House against the possibility that the private little venture he was starting on the side might fail (which is precisely what it proceeded to do).

In all this I participated. It was I who taught Jason the words to "Makin' Whoopee," and I also collaborated on the "operetta" about the man who wrote the piece. In general, when he was being perverse and impious, I would egg him on, enjoying every minute of it and flirting in the privacy of my own mind with his outrageous ideas about many of our elders, but then protesting when he began to go too far even for secret inner flirtation.

This was particularly true of the terrible things he used to say about Lionel Trilling, against whom he had evidently harbored a deep resentment ever since college. I never found out what the source of this resentment was, and Jason would play dumb whenever I asked him, claiming there was nothing personal in it. But looking back on the quality of it today, I have no doubt that his animus against Trilling derived from wounded *amour propre*—the feeling he must have got as a student that Trilling had a low opinion of *him* (which was, as I later discovered, a not entirely inaccurate impression).

In any case, he would go on and on about how *middle-class*

Trilling was. What Jason admired, and wanted to be part of himself, was the aristocracy. When he complained of feeling trapped, it was the middle class he felt trapped in, and out of which he wanted to break loose, just as surely as Kerouac and Ginsberg did. But breaking loose into Bohemia was out of the question for Jason: if he ever went "on the road" it would have to be in a chauffeured limousine with stops at the best hotels. Since he lacked what the critic David Bazelon once called "a shrewd birth certificate," the freedom Jason dreamed of could only be had by acquiring wealth and power.

Jason's dream certainly had more appeal for me than Allen Ginsberg's, but it was not the lack of wealth and power or the wish to live the life of an aristocrat that accounted for my own growing restlessness. My problem had much more to do with ideas than with money, with writing much more than with power. I don't say this in order to claim any special virtue for myself. But the fact is that my dreams, including my dreams of power, were centered on work, and what was bothering me more than anything else in those days was that the new liberalism, the organizing principle of my life as a writer and an intellectual, was beginning to seem played out. For a long time it had been supplying me with a perspective that illuminated everything it touched. It had given me energy and direction. It had made a critic out of me. But now it was going dead. The well seemed to be running dry, and there was hardly anything left to say with the help of this perspective that I myself, and many others besides, had not already said over and over again. Yet for me at least there was still no alternative perspective in sight; intellectually there was nowhere else to go. Jason felt trapped by the life, I felt trapped by the ideas. Together we made a team.

The process of radicalization, then, started from within. But it wasn't a matter of inner need alone. Things were happening in the world out there as well that were working to weaken my attachment to the more strictly political elements of the liberal position while also helping to prepare the way for the flowering of the new radical impulses that were stirring inside.

The first shock came in 1956, a few years after the death of Stalin, when Khrushchev, his successor, delivered a speech to the Communist Party Congress in Moscow in which he talked in great detail about many of the crimes Stalin had committed against his own colleagues and against his own people, and announced that he intended to run the country in a more benevolent way. This was an immense event. It confirmed, and from the most authoritative source imaginable, the charges against Stalin that had been made all along by the anti-Communists; and of course in vindicating them, it also embarrassed and humiliated all the Communists and their sympathizers who for so many years had been maintaining that such charges were malicious lies.

But while offering aid and comfort to the anti-Communists with one hand, Khrushchev was taking it away with the other. For by suggesting that change in a more liberal direction was possible in the Soviet Union, Khrushchev was seriously undermining the theoretical foundation of the anti-Communist case, according to which only change in the opposite direction—toward tighter and tighter control—was possible in a totalitarian society. To this theory, which had been developed most fully and most brilliantly by Hannah Arendt in *The Origins of Totalitarianism,* but which was accepted in one form or another by most anti-Communist intellectuals, Khrushchev's "de-Stalinization" speech delivered a serious blow.

At any rate, that was the effect it had on *me.* To my great surprise, however, it had no such effect on most of the other anti-Communist intellectuals I knew. They saw the whole thing as a trick, a tactical maneuver; and soon they could point to the tanks Khrushchev would send into Hungary, to suppress the revolt against Communist rule that erupted there in the wake of his own speech, as evidence that nothing essential had changed in the nature of the Soviet regime.

Yet exercised though I was about the Hungarian Revolution of

1956, I still couldn't help feeling that the world had become a different place since the death of Stalin and that possibilities now existed which hadn't been there before. I still considered myself an anti-Communist, but I was less and less comfortable with the so-called "hard" anti-Communist position of many of my older friends, especially Lionel Trilling and his wife Diana. It seemed to me that they were being rigid and doctrinaire, which was all the more disheartening in people who prided themselves on their freedom from ideological fanaticism. In fact, not the least of the sins Lionel ascribed to the fellow travelers was that they had turned liberalism into an ideology, and not the least of the virtues he claimed for his own work was that it brought back the old sense of "variousness and possibility" to the "liberal imagination." But there was very little sense of "variousness and possibility" in the way Lionel talked about the Soviet Union and Communism, and none at all in the way Diana did. Lionel's anti-Communist passions were certainly as deep as hers, but in this as in so many other areas, she was blunter and more direct. Whereas he almost never wrote about politics as such except in the most general terms, she published a number of explicitly political pieces, and it was she, not Lionel, who became active in the anti-Communist American Committee for Cultural Freedom (the American counterpart of the Congress for Cultural Freedom, which, unlike the Congress, never received any direct support from the CIA).

It was also Diana who arranged for me to become a member of the board of that committee—a board that in addition to Diana herself included such prominent anti-Communists as William Phillips, Sol Levitas of *The New Leader,* the socialist leader Norman Thomas, the eminent historian of the Russian Revolution Bertram D. Wolfe, Sidney Hook, and the well-known labor journalist Arnold Beichman. But no sooner did I join the board than I began wondering what I was doing there surrounded by people most of whom were twice or even three times my age and all of whom were the products of political histories very different from my own. I did not doubt that they were right in believing that

Soviet Communism represented the greatest threat on the face of the earth to intellectual and cultural freedom, but I did find myself asking whether they were right in their single-minded preoccupation with that threat. In the past there had been many defenders of the Soviet Union to argue against, but against whom was the argument being conducted in the present? The American Communist party—discredited by its own record as a craven apologist for Stalinism and intimidated by official harassment— was in a shambles. The party was still there and still attempting to speak but no one was listening anymore, not even the fellow travelers of old.

It was around this time—the late 1950s—that I began getting to know some of these fellow travelers of old. The most prominent of them was Lillian Hellman, whom I first met, ironically, at the Trillings' in 1956. How did an old fellow traveler like Lillian Hellman come to be a guest in the home of such passionate anti-Stalinists as the Trillings? Years earlier, in their twenties, they had all been friends. Then, of course, they were driven apart by the bitter political disputes of the thirties. Even as late as 1949 the mutual enmity ran very deep. That was the year when a conference was held at the Waldorf in New York in which Lillian, along with other prominent Americans sympathetic toward the Soviet Union, joined with a delegation of Soviet artists and intellectuals to appeal for "peace" and "friendship" between the two nations. The hypocrisy of this appeal—which was part of a desperate campaign to quash the first stirrings of American resistance to Stalin's expansionist designs—so outraged anti-Stalinist intellectuals like Dwight Macdonald and Mary McCarthy that they organized a counterconference not only to refute the lies the Waldorf group was spreading about the international situation but to protest against the support given by writers and intellectuals to a regime in which cultural freedom of every kind was so ruthlessly and murderously suppressed. It was, in fact, out of this counterconference that the American Committee for Cultural

Freedom—of which Diana Trilling would later become chairman —was born.

The Trillings, then, had good reason to feel hostile toward Lillian. And she, from her side, had, as she saw it, even better reason to feel hostile toward them. Many years later, in *Scoundrel Time,* she would speak of her amazement at the fact that people like the Trillings had failed to side with her and other "radicals" when they were being hounded during the McCarthy period. She was especially bitter over the case of Dashiell Hammett, to whom she had for all practical purposes been married, and who was sentenced to six months in jail for contempt of court after refusing to answer certain questions about a Communist-front organization of which he was a trustee. The issues involved in the case were complicated, but Hammett was surely being disingenuous when he claimed to be acting as a good American citizen in defense of the privacy of his political beliefs. Almost certainly he was then—and just as certainly remained—a loyal member of the Communist party, and when he refused to acknowledge this, he was acting not out of his principles as an American citizen but in obedience to the policy of the party. If the party had ordered Hammett to proclaim proudly and defiantly that he was a Communist (which was never against the law), he would in all probability have done so. No doubt Dashiell Hammett was a brave and loyal man, but it was Communism to which he was loyal and for the sake of which he was brave, not the United States of America and not the Bill of Rights.

Probably Lillian never saw it this way, but it is hard to be sure. Not even after Hammett's death in 1961 could she ever bring herself to say simply and straightforwardly that he had been a Communist. She had never asked him and he had never told her: that was how she put it. Yet they lived together for many years and he was her mentor in all things. He taught her how to write and he certainly influenced her political ideas. If it is true that he never confirmed her suspicion that he was a member of the party, not even when there was no prudential reason to conceal it, then she must also have suspected that his membership was a very serious business indeed, and that he would as a matter of honor —of Communist integrity—always do what his superiors in the party ordered him to do. And the Lillian Hellman I knew was not so naïve as to think that what the Communist party was ordering its people to do in the days of the congressional investigations was to protect and defend the Constitution of the United States.

Perhaps, then, there was less bitterness in her toward people like the Trillings—people who really were concerned with protecting and defending the United States—than she affected to feel. On the other hand, her bitterness toward the ex-Communists who had cooperated with the congressional investigations—including former colleagues like the director Elia Kazan and the playwright Clifford Odets—was undoubtedly real and intense. She would have nothing to do with any of them, and she even chided me once when we had become intimate friends for associating with Robert Rossen who, after being blacklisted for a number of years, had finally agreed to testify about his own days as a Communist in exchange for the chance to work again as a Hollywood film director.

In any event, there she was at the Trillings' one night in 1956, not yet looking like a duchess but getting there. She had, I later learned, sought them out, saying that she wanted to be friends again, that she was ready to put their political differences aside if they were, that she was not really a political person anyway.

She often told me that she was not a political person, though I never believed it. To me she always seemed political to the core. It was not that she took a great interest in public events or followed the political world in detail. Literary people—and she was, of course, a writer above all else—are rarely political in that sense. They don't read the papers carefully, they don't know or care which bills are before Congress, and they don't—or at least they didn't in those days—generally get involved in electoral campaigns. Most of them never even bother to vote. But those who are political will respond to public events in a more or less predictable pattern. In Lillian's case the pattern was more rather than less predictable. She may no longer have been an automatic apologist for the Soviet Union, but she could always be counted upon to sympathize with the approved "radical" position of the moment. Her own radicalism was real, but it lacked content: it was a disposition, a stance, an attitude, and yet not the less persistent for its substantive emptiness.

It was in Lillian's home only a few weeks after meeting her at the Trillings' that I first met another famous fellow traveler of old, Norman Mailer. What I knew at that time about Lillian's political past I knew only at second hand, from the Trillings and a few references in print, but Mailer's fellow-traveling past I knew about at first hand. During the 1948 presidential campaign, a rally had been held on the Columbia campus in support of Henry Wallace, the candidate of the so-called Progressive party. Wallace had had a complicated career, culminating in the vice-presidency under Roosevelt, but he had bolted the Democratic party and was now challenging Truman from the Left. Although not even remotely a Communist himself—he was a midwestern isolationist at heart—Wallace had permitted the Communists to take over his candidacy so completely that in the end hardly anyone but party members and hard-core fellow travelers were supporting him. Mailer, who at twenty-five had just made a sensational debut as a novelist with *The Naked and the Dead,* was one of these fellow travelers. And so it was that I first laid eyes on Norman Mailer— he on the platform, a slight, thin, nervous figure speaking bumblingly for Wallace, I in the audience listening, appalled.

In the eight years since I had last seen him, Mailer had moved away from Stalinism but in doing so he had followed a trajectory rather different from Lillian's. From Stalinism he had gone over to a species of Trotskyism (reflected in his second novel, *Barbary Shore*), thus recapitulating the course of development which had been followed by the *Partisan Review* intellectuals in the 1930s. Like those intellectuals too, he soon lost faith in Marxism altogether. But here he diverged onto a track of his own. Whereas most ex-Trotskyist intellectuals of the thirties wound up in the fifties as enemies of the revolutionary ideal altogether, Mailer in giving up on revolutionary socialism proclaimed himself the leader of a new revolution: a cultural rather than a political revolution, a revolution that would "move backward toward being and the secrets of human energy" instead of forward toward the struggle for control over a more and more highly industrialized world. In his own eyes, in other words, he was still a radical—indeed more of one than ever before.

Lillian in her way, then, and Mailer in his, were living proof that the Communist party had lost its hold even over some who had formerly been its most devoted sympathizers and fellow travelers. And as I got to know both of them better, moreover, I began to believe that radicalism could survive perfectly well, and indeed even thrive, without the help of Marx or the Communist party or the Soviet Union.

In the past, I had always thought of radicalism in ideological terms, or at least as a point of view connected with and resting on ideas, analyses, predictions. Never much of a Marxist, I had nevertheless absorbed Marxism's own conception of itself as a doctrine based not on sentiment or visionary hopes for the future but rather on a scientific understanding of the laws of history, which were as inexorable as the laws of physics. This claim to the status of scientific truth was one of Marxism's greatest strengths. Certainly it was one of the main reasons it triumphed over all the other schools of radical thought with which it had to compete in the nineteenth century—schools Marx himself contemptuously dismissed as "utopian" and "infantile." On the other hand, the scientific pretensions of Marxism also turned out to be a great weakness. A scientific theory, after all, is always in danger of being refuted or superseded by the discovery of new evidence or by the failure of its predictions to come true. And that is exactly what happened to Marxism. Marx predicted that the plight of the working class under capitalism would get worse and worse; but it grew better and better. He predicted that the socialist revolution would break out in one of the advanced industrial countries, probably Germany; but it broke out in a backward country, Russia. He predicted that out of this revolution would come a society of true freedom and equality; but it created one of the most monstrous tyrannies in human history. For me all this meant that Marxism had to be rejected. And rejecting Marxism for all practical purposes meant rejecting radicalism in general.

Yet here was Norman Mailer, for whom this conclusion did not follow at all. Some of the things he was saying in those days made me very nervous. To speak, for instance, as he did, of the mysteries of instinct, energy, and blood was to come ominously close to the language of Nazism; and it was to come even closer to a romantic celebration of criminal violence. Mailer, in fact, did more than come close to such a celebration; he actually crossed over the line. For example, shortly before I first met him, he wrote an essay entitled "The White Negro," in which, among other things, he said that two young hoodlums who had recently beaten a storekeeper to death in the course of robbing him had murdered not only a man but the institution of private property.

Still, I was fascinated by Mailer. Even in college I had thought better of him as a novelist than had most of my friends or the critics we respected, to whom *The Naked and the Dead* was nothing more than a piece of old-fashioned naturalistic fiction; and the fact that it had scored a huge commercial success did nothing to enhance Mailer's reputation in the "highbrow" literary world. His next two novels, *Barbary Shore* and *The Deer Park,* were neither naturalistic nor especially successful, but neither did they win the acclaim of the best and most serious critics. I, on the other hand, was becoming more and more convinced of Mailer's importance, and I set out to demonstrate this in a long essay on him which *Partisan Review* agreed to publish (but with great reluctance on the part both of Philip Rahv and William Phillips). That essay—perhaps the first large-scale critical study of Mailer ever done—

had been near completion when I met him, and its appearance naturally gave a great boost to our already flourishing friendship. It also gave a great boost to Mailer's reputation in the literary world.

Bored with my own sensibly moderate liberal ideas, but with Marxism and all its variants closed off as an alternative, I saw in Mailer the possibility of a new kind of radicalism—a radicalism that did not depend on Marx and that had no illusions about the Soviet Union. Soon there would be others, but at that moment there was no one else in sight who held out the same tantalizing possibility. It was not the particular doctrines he preached that attracted me; on the contrary, I thought he was being simply foolish in constructing a theory of revolution with the psychopath playing the role Marx had assigned to the proletariat. But this very willingness to risk looking foolish in the pursuit of something very large and ambitious was exactly what I admired about Mailer. He was bold and he was daring; and he wanted to be great. "The sickness of our times," he once said in an interview, "has been just this damn thing that everything has been getting smaller and smaller and less and less important. . . . We're all getting so mean and small and petty and ridiculous. . . ." To refuse to settle for such a condition was itself a radical act at a time when the prevailing ideals ran to modest aspirations, modest expectations, modest achievements. In setting himself against those ideals, Mailer spoke directly to my own growing restlessness. He encouraged me in my discontents, even though the way out to which he pointed seemed no way out to me.

Yet another Norman came into my life around this time who also encouraged me in my discontents without, however, pointing to a way out that I could either take myself or accept as a collective hope. This was Norman O. Brown—Nobby, as he was called. Unlike Mailer he never became a close friend, but he did have an important effect on my thinking and I, in turn, had something to do with spreading that effect to the thinking of others.

In this I collaborated with Jason, who never shared my enthusiasm over Mailer but who did get excited about Brown's *Life
Against Death*. In fact, it was Jason who discovered that book in the
course of a visit to the offices of the small Wesleyan University
Press in Connecticut which had published it a year earlier with
hardly any response from anyone. The chances are that it would
have sunk without a trace if not for the accident of Jason's trip to
Connecticut. But leafing through it aroused his curiosity, and he
brought a copy back to New York which he then turned over to
me to see whether I thought it might be worth reprinting as a
quality paperback. *Worth* reprinting? By the time I had read the
first few chapters I was overwhelmed, and by the time I had
finished I was convinced that we had stumbled on a great book
by a major thinker. Not only did I urge Jason to publish it (not
that he needed much urging by then); I also went around trum-
peting its virtues to everyone in town. I even succeeded in getting
Lionel Trilling to read it and his subsequent endorsement en-
sured that attention would be paid to the new edition, which
indeed it was.

Life Against Death is, before it is anything else, a book about
Freud, and to understand why it struck me—and eventually so
many other people as well—with such force, one has to understand the role of Freud in shaping the larger sense of life of which
the new liberalism of the fifties was the political face. What Freud
did was to supply the most persuasive and authoritative theoretical foundation for believing that human possibilities were strictly
and insurmountably limited. Human nature was fixed and given
and not, as the "liberal imagination" would have it, infinitely
malleable and therefore infinitely perfectible. There was evil in it
as well as good. Evil was not imposed from without by institutions
or caused by unnecessary restraints: it came from within and it
had to be repressed, which meant—as the title of one of Freud's
most important philosophical works suggested—that there could
be no civilization without discontent.

Brown challenged all this. To be sure, others had done so

before, but never with the intellectual rigor and brilliance he brought to the enterprise. Earlier critics like Karen Horney and Erich Fromm had tried to undermine Freud by arguing that his theories had been valid only, or mainly, for the particular kind of society in which he himself had lived, but Brown disdained the cheap relativism of such tactics. He understood that the only way around a giant like Freud was through him, and he therefore set out to show that Freud's pessimistic sense of human potentiality did not necessarily follow from his fundamental analysis of human nature—an analysis Brown accepted as sound in all essential respects. The brilliance of *Life Against Death* lay in the amazingly convincing case Brown was able to make for the consistency of that analysis with his own vision of a life of "polymorphous perversity," a life of play and of complete instinctual freedom.

This vision no more appealed to me than Mailer's strikingly similar vision of a life devoted to the adventurous pursuit of immediate gratification. But just as the one Norman encouraged me to think that my own personal restlessness was worthy of respect and demanded to be acted upon, so the other Norman— the third member, as Trilling once dryly said, of "the Norman invasion"—provided me with grounds for believing that such action could, at least theoretically, be taken. Despite the absence of Marx and the presence of Freud, radicalism was still possible.

3

But if radicalism was still possible, there nevertheless remained a problem. Both Mailer and Brown spoke in the largest terms one could imagine: of Life and Death, of God and the Devil, of Good and Evil. Whole centuries marched through their pages and gigantic generalizations were made; nothing small was there. And yet in the end they were just as narrowly focused on the problems of the self as the culture they were criticizing. They were talking about individual psychology, not about society, and they were unable to establish a connection between the spiritual condition of the individual and the institutions by which that condition was shaped and formed. That was where Paul Goodman came in: it was he who in *Growing Up Absurd* found the missing link and who thereby gave the new radicalism a *political* potential it had previously lacked.

Goodman had for a long time been something of an outcast. In the thirties, as a young man, he had burst upon the avant-garde literary scene with a profusion and variety of writings: stories, poems, plays, critical studies, and treatises in philosophy and psychology. But even then he was out of tune and out of step. Politically he was neither a Stalinist nor a Trotskyist; in fact, he was not a Marxist of any kind but rather an anarchist. There are various schools of anarchism and I don't know which of them Goodman belonged to at that stage of his life, but the point is that being an anarchist at all would have put him at odds on fundamental questions with almost everyone else. For all other groups accepted an industrialized world and a powerful state as desirable and were split on the issue of who could or should control them, whereas the anarchists were hostile to technology and opposed to state power no matter who might be in charge. To make matters worse, Goodman was also a pacifist, a position not calculated to win him many friends in the intellectual world of the thirties, especially when it meant opposing American entry into the war against the Nazis. And finally he was a believer in and a preacher and practitioner of uninhibited sexuality of every kind at a time when this could only reinforce the impression of him as a slightly demented crank.

For these and other reasons he had by the fifties fallen out with the editors of most of the magazines for which he would normally have written—especially *Partisan Review* and *Commentary.* Nor were publishers interested in his books, which could not be expected to succeed either commercially or critically. Nevertheless, when I went to work at *Commentary* in 1955, Goodman was one of the writers I sought out and tried to publish. Later, during a brief stint as an editor in a major publishing house, I decided to put out his huge novel, *The Empire City,* which had never been published in a single volume and whose individual parts had only appeared previously in very obscure editions. I did not remain in the company long enough to bring this project to completion, but I was instrumental in persuading another publisher to do it instead.

The reason I did all this was not that I was such a great admirer of *The Empire City;* in fact, I had serious reservations about it as a work of art and about Goodman as a novelist. Nor was I fond of Goodman personally. Of the many literary megalomaniacs I have known, he was the most extreme. Once, in the early days of our acquaintance, he told me very casually that he was a genius —not a great genius but a genius, the difference being that a great genius was ahead of his own time by an entire generation, whereas he was only about five or possibly ten years ahead (which, by the way, and for what it may be worth, turned out to be a reasonably accurate estimate of how long it would take for him to become a celebrated and even a best-selling author).

Shortly thereafter, I invited him to lunch to meet a young poet and critic, my old college friend John Hollander, who had an encyclopedic knowledge of everything that had ever been published in the little magazines and who had probably read more Goodman than anyone except Goodman himself. John, very excited, instantly launched into an admiring and voluble disquisition on the virtues of Goodman's work. Although at the lowest point of his literary fortunes and scarcely able to get anything he wrote into print, let alone appreciated and praised, Goodman accepted this homage as though it were not only his due but an everyday occurrence. True to the crack I was later to make that Goodman was so self-centered that he wouldn't listen to you even if you were talking to him about himself, he seemed not to hear anything John was saying—until, that is, John interrupted the flow of praise by admitting that one of Goodman's essays had struck him as being somewhat less wonderful than the rest of his work. "Well," said Paul pleasantly, puffing on his pipe, "as you get older, you'll learn to read better."

He could be hard to take, then. Nevertheless, he did seem to me an interesting writer who deserved more of a hearing than he had been able to get in recent years, and so I had done my best to secure him such a hearing. *Growing Up Absurd,* on the other hand, struck me as much more than merely interesting or deserving of a hearing: I thought it was marvelous in itself and a major intellectual event. To a reader today, that response would probably seem puzzling. How could a book filled with so many familiar ideas strike anyone as a major event? But the very familiarity of those ideas is a measure of the tremendous influence *Growing Up Absurd* was to exert in the years ahead. Because not only were Goodman's ideas not familiar when I read the book in manuscript; they were as fresh and original as a newly created thing.

So fresh and original was *Growing Up Absurd,* indeed, that at first no one wanted to have anything to do with it. According to Goodman's count, nineteen publishers had seen and rejected the manuscript by the time he gave it to me in the winter of 1959 for possible excerpting in *Commentary* (to which I was just about to return as editor-in-chief after two years of working in book publishing and as a free-lance writer). For my part, I was so excited by it, and so certain of its importance, that I decided to serialize it in the first three issues of *Commentary* to appear under my editorship (February, March, and April of 1960). I also forced the manuscript on Jason Epstein, who was reluctant even to read it because he still looked upon Goodman as a has-been and a crank. Not for long, though. Not only did Jason become the publisher of *Growing Up Absurd,* he also eventually published many other books by Goodman, becoming in the process one of his most fervent disciples and promoters.

The reason *Growing Up Absurd* seemed so important was that it convincingly lifted the malaise that had overtaken me—and, as I believed, the entire culture—out of the realm of individual psychology and located it in the institutions of American society and the way those institutions were organized. It was, Goodman argued, hard to grow up properly under present conditions and almost impossible to live well even as an adult. For all the apparent freedom and prosperity of the society as presently constituted, it did not provide for the satisfaction of certain elementary needs of the human spirit—for useful and necessary work to do, for sex without shame or guilt, for a community to be loyal to, and so on. These demands, and others like them, Goodman said, were not in the least "outlandish," and yet they could not be met within the present system. The burden of this failure fell most heavily upon the young—those who were becoming "organization men" no less than those who were becoming delinquents or who (like the Beats) were dropping out altogether. But it fell on adults as well, which is why in spite of so much affluence there was so much instability, divorce, breakdown, and sheer unhappiness in all classes of society.

But if it was the system that was causing the trouble, then changing the system could presumably cure it. Goodman, who liked to think of himself as a practical man, was full of concrete proposals which he put forward rather airily, with a cavalier disregard of the difficulties that ordinarily would have been expected to block any attempt to implement them. But it was not the "practical" side of Goodman that excited me; it was his frank utopianism. He simply took it for granted, in the most relaxed way, that a good society, as measured by its capacity to allow for the full self-realization of every individual living within it, could be brought into being. And he also took it for granted that all the "realistic" arguments purporting to prove that no such society was humanly possible, and that we therefore had to settle for something less—something, in fact, rather like the society we were already living in here in America—derived not from a rational assessment of the nature of things but from lack of imagination, lack of will, and the protection of privilege.

Here, then, was the missing link between the malaise of the individual and the organization of society, and in finding it Goodman gave one something to *do*. This something did not consist of developing a conventional program of reform or pressing for a liberal legislative agenda. On the contrary, almost by definition no such reformist program or liberal agenda could succeed unless it were meaningless or merely cosmetic. But by making so convincing a case for the connection between the spiritual and the social, Goodman also made the entire enterprise of radical social criticism seem intellectually viable once again. There were criteria by which to judge: what people needed to enable them to achieve all the fullness of being of which they might be capable. And there were institutions to examine and analyze in the light of those criteria. The purpose was not to tinker (though Goodman sometimes implied that it was). It was to expose the failures of the American system and ultimately to rob it of moral legitimacy while at the same time, I told myself, keeping alive some vision of what a decent human life might look like.

For me, moving from liberalism to this new radical outlook was to be a gradual process, extending over a period of three or four years. At every stage there were new ideas to mull over, to discuss, to investigate further; and at every stage there were old ideas to reconsider, contradictions to be resolved, coherence to be struggled for and eventually achieved. It all took time, effort, reading, reflection, all of it accompanied by much pain, exhilaration, and other varieties of inner turmoil.

But there was also a great deal of external turmoil, most of it taking the form of arguments with friends who disapproved of the direction I was moving in. These arguments could be, and often were, very bitter indeed. Once, for example, Daniel Bell exploded at me in a rage over my sponsorship of Norman O. Brown, whom he considered dangerous and irresponsible. On another occasion, I got into a heated quarrel with Diana Trilling over my own piece on "The Young Generation," which in her view represented an unwarranted assault on Lionel. On still other occasions, I found myself embroiled in ill-tempered discussions with people like Philip Rahv, who thought my estimate of Norman Mailer ridiculously high. And a little later, after Paul Goodman had entered my life, I was constantly being challenged to explain why I had chosen to perpetrate him upon the world once again. One such challenge, from the Columbia philosophy professor Sidney Morgenbesser (who would in the late sixties move all the way over to the other side), became so nasty and insulting that, right in the middle of the meal, I stormed out of the restaurant where we had been having lunch.

The point is that to be a radical in the late fifties was to be in a small and somewhat disreputable minority within the intellectual community. On surveying the audience which had come to a drafty old union hall on Eighteenth Street to hear me discuss American foreign policy from the perspective of the new radicalism, my *Commentary* colleague Marion Magid once said: "Do you realize that every person in this room is a tragedy to some family or other?"

Beyond looking marginal and crippled, radicalism had not yet become an altogether respectable position, and one could easily be made to seem foolish by people who had been around the track once before and knew all the arguments on every side of every question that arose or was likely to arise. Thus in a symposium on the 1930s sponsored in 1959 by *Partisan Review* and held before a packed house in the same theater on the Columbia campus where the Wallace rally had been held a decade before (only this time with Lionel Trilling in the chair), Mary McCarthy and Arthur Schlesinger, Jr., both of whom denigrated the radicalism of the thirties—and, by clear implication, radicalism in general—had no trouble at all disposing of Norman Mailer and me, who were defending the opposite view.

True, Mailer practically threw the debate by appearing in a work shirt and blue jeans—which in those days could only have seemed a childishly provocative act to the kind of audience we were addressing and could only have encouraged them to believe that they were right in the first place in feeling that he was nothing more than a middlebrow novelist who did not deserve to be taken seriously. As for me, I was so nervous about participating in so high-powered an event that I spoke almost as bumblingly as Mailer, whose effectiveness as a speaker had not markedly improved since the Wallace rally despite ten years of practice. Yet even if both of us had been in better form, I think we still would have lost the debate. Like the idea of radicalism itself, we were too much on the defensive to stand up effectively against antiradical polemicists as formidable as Mary McCarthy and Arthur Schlesinger.

Much as she was later to do in her novel *The Group*, Mary McCarthy poked fun at the radicals of the thirties, whom she represented as unserious about their professed values as well as foolish in their criticisms of American society. She made a special point of attacking those radical intellectuals (like Paul Goodman and Clement Greenberg, though I don't remember whether she mentioned them by name) who had taken the position that World War II had nothing to do with them, and once again she described her exhilaration at waking up one morning to discover that she felt it was her war and that she wanted America to win.

Schlesinger's talk complemented this attack by arguing that the only important political activity of the thirties had taken place in Washington, within the Roosevelt administration, and that all the radical chatter going on at the time in New York—whether Stalinist, Trotskyist, Socialist, or some other sectarian variant—had amounted to just that: chatter, none of it of any influence or significance. It was liberalism that had counted then, said Schlesinger, not radicalism, and it was liberalism that still counted now. Liberalism had a practical program of improvement and reform; radicalism by contrast was visionary and—the most damning of all epithets—utopian. It had nothing to offer but unrealizable dreams.

Neither Mailer nor I could counter these arguments with anything substantial. We were certainly not prepared to defend the antiwar intellectuals of the thirties, and although I was angered by Schlesinger's lofty contempt for New York—a contempt somewhat contradictorily compounded of the social and academic snobbery for which Cambridge was famous and the philistine attitude toward ideas so characteristic of Washington—there was no denying that the New Deal owed little or nothing to the radical intellectuals of New York. Nor, even if we had wished to do so, could Mailer and I have claimed that the radical impulse we were trying to recommend came equipped with a clear program of political action of the kind Schlesinger could spell out without a moment's hesitation. I can't remember exactly what Mailer said that day in support of his general defense of the radical stance, but I do remember Schlesinger bringing the house down when he characterized Mailer's speech as a perfect example of the incapacity of the literary mind for political thought. He made no such devastating comment on my own speech, possibly because my fervent plea that we not allow the Stalinism of the thirties to discredit the idea of radicalism altogether scarcely seemed worthy of notice by a serious historian of the New Deal.

It did, however, seem all too worthy of notice to Kenneth Tynan, the leftist theater critic from London, who happened to be in the audience and who singled me out in a piece on the symposium as an example of how far out of touch with contemporary reality American intellectuals were. Here, he wrote, was a young radical (this was perhaps the first time anyone had called me that) who could in the year 1959 talk for a half-hour or more without once mentioning the danger of nuclear war and the need for nuclear disarmament.

Tynan was right. Whereas the H-bomb had become to the English Left what the Depression had been to the American Left of the 1930s, the new radicalism that was developing in the

United States in the late fifties was not primarily concerned with the problem of nuclear war. I for one was very skeptical about the self-dramatizing idea that all the troubles of the world—from juvenile delinquency to drug addiction to divorce—could be traced to the fact that we were living "in the shadow of the bomb." I simply could not believe that most people went around thinking about nuclear war or that the fear of it affected them in their day-to-day personal lives. Nor did I accept the subtler version of the same idea, according to which the effects were subliminal or unconscious. (I was to have a similar difficulty later in believing Susan Sontag's claim that her anguish over the Vietnam war had given her ulcers.) Admittedly Mailer, Brown, and Goodman, each in his own fashion, paid a certain obeisance to the shadow of the bomb, invoking it whenever it suited a polemical or a hectoring purpose. When, for instance, Mailer complained, "We're all getting so mean and small and petty and ridiculous," he added "and we all live under the threat of extermination." But the afterthought was clearly ritualistic and moreover supererogatory since he did not believe that this condition had been caused by the bomb or could be cured by its removal from the scene. And it was the condition that he, like the rest of us, really cared about.

On the other hand, there was at that time a growing preoccupation in certain circles in this country with the broader political context of which the issue of nuclear disarmament was only one element, and I myself shared in that preoccupation more and more with every passing day. This broader context was of course the cold war, and the question that now arose was whether that war was destined to last forever.

The United States had drawn a line against Soviet expansionism and for ten years the line had held. It had been held in Europe by deterrence and it been held in Asia by the American intervention into Korea. Despite all the blustering talk by the right wing of the Republican party, the United States under a Republican president (and with John Foster Dulles, the hardest of "hard" anti-Communists, as secretary of state) had refused to intervene when the Hungarians rose up in rebellion against the Soviet-backed regime in 1956. This meant that for all practical purposes there was to be no effort to move beyond containment to a policy of "rollback."

Nor could the Soviets be expected to push ahead. They had acted with great brutality in suppressing the Hungarian Revolution, but that after all involved holding on to what they already had, not expanding further into the non-Communist world. The Russians would go on probing for weak spots, they would go on encouraging subversion in the West and revolution in the "underdeveloped countries" (as the Third World was then called) by the local Communist parties under their control. But the fear of a major war with the United States would keep them from attempting anything more adventurous.

In short, after ten years the cold war had reached a point of stalemate, with neither side being able to look forward to a significant turning of the tide. Under these circumstances it began to seem possible that the cold war could be brought to an end, and a small movement made its appearance in the United States to encourage just such a development.

It was not a movement in the sense of being centrally organized; it consisted rather of a loose confederation of people who wanted to bring pressure on the American government to work actively toward a peaceful accommodation with the Russians. Most of these people were Quakers, pacifist in orientation, and politically neutral—or so they sincerely believed—as between the United States and the Soviet Union. They spoke, so they would have it understood, not for nations but in the interests of all of humanity. But there were also a fair number of "unreconstructed" Stalinists and fellow travelers in evidence for whom ending the cold war was a euphemism for getting the United States out of the business of holding the line against the Soviet advance. And finally there were people like Norman Thomas, the leader of the Socialist party, who leaned toward the Quakers but had a much more realistic sense of Soviet intentions than they did; and there were David Riesman and his friend, the psychoanalyst Erich Fromm, together with a whole galaxy of young disciples many of whom later became well known in their own right (Robert Jay Lifton, Kenneth Keniston, and Michael Maccoby, among others). Neither pacifist (at least not strictly speaking) nor pro-Soviet, the Riesman group tended to believe that the cold war had originated in an American misreading of Soviet intentions—an innocent misreading, but a misreading for all that —and could therefore be ended through unilateral action by the United States.

It was through the Riesman group that I first became involved in this movement. More specifically, it was through Nathan Glazer, who, as I have already mentioned, had collaborated with Riesman on *The Lonely Crowd* and whom I knew as a member of the editorial staff of *Commentary* during its first ten years of existence. Indeed, though he was not all that much older than I, Nathan Glazer had once played a key role in the kind of liberalism on which I had cut my intellectual teeth, as he was now coming to do in this aspect of my radicalization. By academic training he was a sociologist, but a sociologist of the old school who was interested in everything and took the view that nothing human was alien to his intelligence or beyond his intellectual grasp. To be an intellectual (or, as some would later say, a Jewish intellectual or a New York intellectual, though many were neither Jewish nor from New York) was to be, or at least was to attempt to be, a polymath. In this sense, then, Glazer was an intellectual rather than a sociologist—just as his colleague Clement Greenberg, the famous art critic, was an intellectual rather than a specialist in painting or his other colleague Robert Warshow, the film critic, was an intellectual rather than a specialist in film.

Nevertheless Glazer had drawn heavily on his training in sociology as an editor at *Commentary* between 1945 and 1955. He had known that the freshest and most exciting work being done in the social sciences in that first postwar decade was a product of the same impulse to move beyond the alienation and radicalism which had been overtaking the literary intellectuals; and he had set out to make use of it in a magazine aimed as *Commentary* was at a general audience. If once American social scientists had tended to concentrate on the strains and weaknesses of the American system, the questions that had come to seem most interesting in that period were why and how the system could work as well as it evidently did, and what the secrets were of its viability and of its resilient vitality.

The effort to answer such questions had not precluded social criticism; but what it had on the whole precluded was the old 1930s *radical* social criticism—criticism, that is, based on the idea that the American system was fundamentally unsound (as well as unjust) and therefore incapable (as well as unworthy) of surviving. It had also precluded—or perhaps eclipsed—radical social criticism in another way, by substituting different concepts and categories of analysis for such familiar old divisions as Left against Right, or progressive versus reactionary. However applicable such terms might be to other countries, the effort to apply them to the United States had led—so a new generation of social scientists had said— to distortion and misunderstanding. Thus, for example, populism, a movement which had generally been thought of as of the Left and progressive (because it represented a protest mounted in the name of the people against "Wall Street" and the "interests"), was, under the scrutiny of the new point of view, seen to have contained many elements, including strains of anti-Jewish and anti-black bigotry, usually associated with the "reactionaries" of the Right. Glazer himself, as a writer, had taken this approach in a piece he did for *Commentary* showing that McCarthyism, the epitome of right-wing reaction, had its roots in and derived much of its support from the populist tradition.

Glazer's preoccupation with McCarthyism had not, however, been limited to relatively academic questions concerning its origins and its sociological dynamics. He had also written several pieces on the major issues surrounding McCarthyism: whether the Communists really posed a threat to the internal security of the United States, and if so how serious a threat it was and what could and should legitimately be done about it. Like everyone else on the staff of Elliot Cohen's *Commentary,* and like most of its regular contributors, Glazer had taken the position that there was indeed a threat, and that Congress had both the right and the duty to investigate it. This did not mean that congressional committees had the right to harass and injure innocent people; nor did they have the right to violate the rules of due process. But neither did American citizens have the right to refuse their cooperation to a legitimately constituted inquiry into a matter of vital importance to the security of the country. Glazer believed that, all things considered, witnesses summoned before congressional committees should have testified instead of taking the Fifth Amendment, and that in testifying they should have told the truth.

Thus, there was no way that Nathan Glazer could have been considered "soft" on Communism or naïve about how the Communists operated, or less than fully committed to the defense of American society. Consequently, when in the late fifties he began manifesting an interest in the tiny and nascent "peace movement," this was almost enough by itself to convince me that, despite the presence among them of unreconstructed Stalinists and fellow travelers, the groups involved were not acting, either wittingly or as dupes, in the service of Soviet foreign policy. The last person in the world I would have expected to be mixed up in a Communist front was Nathan Glazer, and the last thing in the world I would have wanted for myself was to get mixed up in such a front. The whole point, indeed, was to find a path into radicalism without falling into the trap of lending aid and comfort to the Communists or their objectives. If there was to be a new radicalism, or a new Left, it was this unambiguous opposition to Communism that would above all else make it new.

But anti-Communism, although morally and politically necessary, was not intellectually sufficient. If the new radicalism, or the new Left, was to be truly new, it had to distinguish itself as sharply from Marxism on the level of theory as it did from Communism (or Stalinism, as many of us still called it, even though Stalin was dead and Khrushchev had denounced him) on the level of political practice. In other words, democratic socialism, despite a history of opposition to Communism as unambiguous as any anti-Communist could wish, was not and could not be the answer. Indeed, listening to Norman Thomas speak was to hear nothing one had not heard many times before, and to hear it spoken with all real passion spent. Nor did the situation look much better in the pages of *Dissent*, a magazine which had been founded in 1954 precisely in order to demonstrate that socialist thought still had something of crucial importance to contribute to the political debates of an age in which the socialist faith was being undermined within the intellectual community by doubt, defection, and apostasy.

Words like "faith" and "apostasy" seemed appropriate because Irving Howe, the founder and chief editor of *Dissent*, though best known as a literary critic, had an even deeper attachment to socialism—an attachment which I thought could only be understood in religious terms.

It was, of course, a cliché that socialism had served as a substitute for religion in the hearts of many of its adherents; like religion, it rewarded the faithful with a transcendent cause to which they could selflessly devote themselves and from which they could derive a sense of meaning and purpose in their lives. And since, like religion too, it depended ultimately upon faith rather than reason for its validation, it could survive the refutation of its claims by argument and evidence. The most extreme case was the Communists of the pre-Khrushchev period, who stubbornly continued to insist, against all reason and all the evidence, on the benign character of Stalin's regime. They were the secular equivalent of the early Christian theologian who declared that he believed in the Resurrection *because* it seemed absurd to the rational mind.

But most believers in socialism did not assume this defiantly paradoxical stance. Instead—like Victorian Christians responding to Darwin and other scientific assaults on the biblical account of Creation—they would retreat in the face of challenge to safer ground, making whatever concessions might be necessary to protect the core of the faith. Thus Stalin's crimes were interpreted not as direct expressions or inevitable consequences of the socialist revolution but as a betrayal of its ideals. In this way socialism as such was rescued from the discredit into which Stalin threatened to cast it, and hope for its realization was transferred from the Soviet Union to some other party or agency.

To those who blamed Stalin himself but retained their conviction that socialism could only be instituted by means of a revolution, it was Trotsky, Stalin's banished and eventually murdered rival, who became the repository of that hope. To those who blamed revolution or feared it for one reason or another, hope was now vested in the socialist parties, which were striving to bring about the millennium through peaceful democratic means. But Trotskyism suffered from its own weaknesses as a "scientific" theory. As for the socialist parties, the problem was that in competing seriously for power through the ballot box, they had to broaden their support and were therefore forced to become less and less distinctively socialist in their appeal. Worse still, when they did get into power, as in Sweden and England, they usually carried out programs which differed only slightly, if at all, from the kinds of programs identified with New Deal liberalism. Where they did go further—for example, by nationalizing certain large industries—the results were either anticlimactic from a socialist perspective, in the sense that they did not seem to bring about a significant change in the character of society, or they were damaging from an economic point of view, leading to decreased efficiency and production to the detriment of all and the benefit of none. If in the Soviet Union—and then in its satellites—socialism had brought totalitarianism, in Sweden and England it had brought the welfare state. Certainly this was infinitely preferable to totalitarianism, but in its drabness and blandness it still fell far short of the glorious promises of the socialist dream.

Irving Howe had personally traveled the route from Trotskyism to democratic socialism, giving up the necessary ground along the way. By the time he had founded *Dissent,* he was no longer even a Marxist except perhaps in the most general way, and he had even come to acknowledge (at least on certain occasions) that democratic socialism was for all practical purposes indistinguishable from welfare-state liberalism. Nevertheless he continued to call himself a socialist and to insist that socialism as a doctrine remained relevant, even urgent and vital. Yet in view of the fact that the socialism to which he was committed had no discernible content, I began to think that his stubborn loyalty to the word, as well as the idea, came out of the same primitive loyalty that made so many Jews go on calling themselves Jews long after they had ceased obeying the commandments of the Jewish religion, let alone believing in its theological doctrines.

It was in this sense that Howe's attachment to socialism was religious; and indeed—as became entirely clear many years later when he published his book on the history of the East European Jewish immigration to America, *World of Our Fathers*—he had a tendency to confuse Judaism itself with socialism and loyalty to the one with loyalty to the other. (A similar confusion between Judaism and liberalism was rampant among Reform Jews.)

My own guess was that Howe's confusion could be traced to the fact that he grew up in a secularist, Yiddishist world in which socialism was seen as the solution to all the problems afflicting the Jewish people as well as an alternative to the dishonorable course of complete assimilation. But whatever the source of this confusion in Howe's soul between Judaism and socialism, it was certainly there, and it certainly helped to explain his absolute determination to identify himself as a socialist. The less of a socialist he became, the more desperate he was to affirm his socialist faith.

And since there was so little of a positive nature left to affirm, what he mainly did was attack other intellectuals for deserting the true faith.

The most characteristic example of this tactic, and probably the most famous and influential, was a piece he wrote for *Partisan Review* in 1954 entitled "This Age of Conformity," in which he complained that a long list of prominent American intellectuals had now given up on socialism and were becoming liberals and even conservatives. In the cultural realm too, he charged, they had undergone a similar evolution. Having been partisans of the modernist movement in the arts, they were now questioning its value, and they were even becoming critical of the concept of "alienation" from bourgeois society.

Yet in his very call for a return to the true faith, Howe demonstrated why his point of view was incapable of satisfying the demand for a new radicalism. It suffered, by his own inadvertent account, from a double disqualification. First of all, it was in the most literal sense old rather than new. It harked back nostalgically to a former time, a kind of golden age in which "everyone" within the intellectual community had been a Marxist in politics, a modernist in culture, and a Bohemian in personal style. Even granting Howe's glowing account of that glorious past when the "critical consciousness and the political conscience" had come together in a perfectly harmonious alliance, conditions had changed so *radically* that at the least new ideas seemed necessary to describe them, to account for them, and most of all to respond to them. Yet here was Howe, who acknowledged how much conditions had changed, nevertheless recommending responses born out of a different age; and whatever the merits of these responses might once have been, they certainly seemed out of touch with the realities of the postwar period.

In addition to getting old and out of date, Howe's radicalism also suffered from not being especially radical. His very restatement of the old-time religion, indeed, showed how much ground it had already been forced to yield. Thus—with the need to distinguish the socialist idea from Stalinism on the one side and welfare-state liberalism on the other making it difficult to say what remained of that idea for anyone to stick with, let alone return to —he could not even bring himself to call for a revival of socialist commitment as such. Instead he had to rest content with asking for a generalized stance of "critical independence."

Similarly in cultural matters. Instead of calling for a return to the avant-garde militancy of the early days of the modernist movement, all he could demand now—when the modernist movement was itself becoming the "establishment"—was that "highbrow" standards be defended against an encroaching "middlebrow" culture. And instead of advocating that artists and intellectuals resume their alienation from bourgeois society by leaving the "suburbs, country homes, and college towns" in which they were all living in such corrupting physical comfort and move back to the "decent poverty" of cold-water flats in Greenwich Village, he asked only that they stop preaching what they practiced and at least return to the alienated attitude in the realm of ideas.

Howe said nothing about foreign affairs in "This Age of Conformity," and to judge by the bulk of the material he subsequently selected for publication in *Dissent,* neither he himself nor the democratic socialists as a group had a position on the U.S.-Soviet conflict that differed any more significantly from the standard liberal position of the day than their ideas about domestic reform differed significantly from those of New Deal liberalism. They were, after all, impeccably anti-Communist. At various points in the past, their own ideological ancestors and comrades had tried to cooperate with the Communists, only to be betrayed and, where circumstances permitted, imprisoned, tortured, and murdered. They therefore had every reason to support a strong stand by the United States to contain the expansionist thrust of Soviet power.

Even where they tried to be true to the title of their own magazine and dissented from American policy—by urging support for the democratic Left in other countries (the so-called "third force") instead of for the conservatives in Europe and the right wing in the underdeveloped world—they usually did so in the name of anti-Communism. Since, however, a large segment of the liberal community also believed that the democratic Left was a stronger bulwark against Communism than the Center or the Right, there was nothing particularly radical about this position either.

Howe did, to be sure, belong to the National Committee for a Sane Nuclear Policy (or SANE, as it was known), an organization founded in the late fifties to agitate for an end to nuclear testing and for other measures of nuclear disarmament as well. But when the organization split over the issue of whether Communists and fellow travelers should be permitted to belong, he sided—and not at all surprisingly—with those who favored driving out any elements which could not bring themselves to criticize totalitarian nations (principally the Soviet Union) with the same freedom and by the same standards they used in criticizing the United States and other non-Communist countries.

Knowing all this, I was not surprised by the paucity of representatives from the *Dissent* group in the peace movement when, toward the end of the fifties, I first began attending meetings. Norman Thomas was of course there and he was in effect the titular leader of the socialists in America, but I cannot recall ever seeing Howe or any of his colleagues on the editorial committee of the magazine at any of those meetings.

They were held, usually, in the offices of the Quaker-backed American Friends Service Committee. The Quakers were perhaps the wealthiest of all religio-ethnic groups in America, but they had a tradition of austerity which manifested itself in the dingy furnishings of their headquarters and even more in the way that meals were provided: peanut butter and jelly sandwiches would be sent for and a paper cup would be passed around into which each person present was expected to drop thirty-five cents for the sandwich, plus a nickel to tip the delivery boy.

All this, I had to admit, provided an appropriate context for the sparse attendance at those meetings and the grimness of the discussions that were held. A scientist from MIT or Harvard might be present to discourse on the horrible dangers of nuclear fallout. David Riesman, also down from Cambridge, might speak on the obstacles in the American character to an accommodation with the Russians. Norman Thomas, veteran of so many political defeats (he had run often for president as the Socialist party candidate), might deliver an assessment of the chances for progress in disarmament, and despite the natural buoyancy and optimism he exuded, he had no illusions about the prospects for success. Another ancient pillar of the American Left, A. J. Muste, was also a regular. Muste seemed a perfect foil for Thomas. He was small and Thomas was large; he was quiet and Thomas was hearty; he was humorous and Thomas was solemn. But whatever else Muste exuded, he looked and talked even less like a winner than Thomas.

Although more an activist than a theorist, Muste was on the editorial board of a magazine called *Liberation,* whose other editors in the late fifties and early sixties included Dave Dellinger, Staughton Lynd, and Bayard Rustin. They too would often show up at those meetings. All of them were pacifists, which of course meant that they were opposed in principle to war or even lesser forms of violence as a means of political struggle. But they were also all radicals who engaged actively in political struggle, and they had developed a strategy for doing so based mainly on the tactics of nonviolent resistance and civil disobedience which Gandhi had used so successfully in the fight to liberate India from British rule. Muste and his followers and colleagues had practiced nonviolent resistance in the form of sit-down strikes during the battle to unionize American industry, and to the struggle against nuclear arms they had now begun to adapt Gandhian tactics, in the form of such programs of civil disobedience as trying to enter military facilities and stage demonstrations there.

4

Around this time too such tactics were beginning to be imported by young Negro activists into the South—some of them in the Student Non-Violent Coordinating Committee (SNCC), and some of them in the Southern Christian Leadership Conference (SCLC), the group headed by Martin Luther King, Jr.—in their fight against segregated buses, restaurants, and other public facilities. Bayard Rustin, although a northern Negro, had been spending a good deal of time in the South helping to train King and others in the ways of nonviolent struggle, which he had learned at first hand during a stay in India working under the tutelage of Gandhi himself. In effect, then, Rustin in 1960 was the living link between the peace movement in the North and the civil-rights movement in the South.

Of the two, it was the civil-rights movement that seemed to me the less important by far. This was not because I had any reservations whatsoever about it. On the contrary, like everyone else I knew, I was enthralled by everything connected with the civil-rights movement in this period of its history—what Rustin was later to call, in more difficult and troubled times, the "heroic period." How could anyone but a segregationist true-believer fail to have been thrilled by the spectacle of young southern blacks rising up against a powerful system of oppression and toppling it bit by bit with nothing but the moral force of their cause and the clear nobility of their behavior? The issue in this struggle to do away with legally enforced segregation was as clear and simple as any political issue could ever be; and it was made even clearer by repeated confrontations between sheriffs and police dogs and cattle prods on the one side and, on the other, young black heroes enduring (in obedience to the dictates of nonviolent direct action) barbaric insults and assaults without resistance, without rancor, and often with a compassion in their eyes that amazed their friends and unsettled their enemies.

Thrilling as was word of the new and inevitably victorious struggle in the South, however, it seemed to have very little relevance to anything outside itself, including even the plight of Negroes outside the South. A few years later the "discovery" would be made that there was no essential difference between the situation of the Negroes in the South and their situation in the North. Not only would it be charged that the Negroes of the North were segregated almost as completely as those of the South; it would even be asserted that they had been put into that condition and were being kept in it by government policies designed for precisely this purpose. In other words, there was, according to this reasoning, no real distinction between the "de facto" segregation of the North—the kind that presumably had come about through the indirect operation of various social and economic factors—and the "de jure" segregation of the South, which had been explicitly instituted by law.

But in the late fifties and even into the early sixties, to compare the plight of the Negro in New York, where laws existed prohibiting discrimination on the basis of race or color, with that of the Negro in Mississippi, where laws existed requiring discrimination on the basis of color, would have seemed intellectually bizarre and morally offensive to most people. In any case, in the days of the heroic period itself no one was as yet making such comparisons, and this meant that the movement could still be considered relevant only to those few states in which legislation still existed requiring—in clear defiance of the Constitution—the separation of the black and white races in most areas of life.

Thus the civil-rights movement in the South, while certainly enthralling in its moral force, was, when looked at politically, only a mopping-up operation designed to bring a backward region into line with the rest of the country. To put the point still another way, there was nothing radical or even new about the objectives of the civil-rights movement in the heroic period. Indeed, that objective might more accurately have been described as conservative. After all, it was exactly the same objective the movement had always pursued: to do away with legally mandated segregation.

Moreover, in pursuing it, the movement had never in the past and was not now trying to overthrow the legally constituted system of the nation, but rather to enforce it in places where it was being violated. Despite the loose and lazy use of the word "revolution" in connection with the civil-rights movement of those days (the word was later to be applied just as promiscuously to many other movements as well), the only thing that was new about the heroic period was the employment of direct-action tactics in the pursuit of that objective. Previously the movement had resorted to litigation, winning its most spectacular victory in the 1954 Supreme Court decision declaring segregated school systems unconstitutional. Now instead of resorting to the juridical courts, the movement was appealing to another kind of court, the court of public opinion. The aim—the "conservative" aim—was to mobilize support throughout the country for federal intervention in the shape of a civil-rights bill that would bring the South into line once and for all, as well as a more energetic enforcement of laws and court rulings already in place (such as the 1954 desegregation decision, which was being resisted by various tricks and subterfuges).

Yet new as the tactics undoubtedly were, they seemed of doubtful applicability outside the South. Protest marches, sit-ins, and other demonstrations were all very well when the objective was something simple, concrete, and clear like doing away with legally enforced segregation. But what could they accomplish when the problem was a multifaceted one like poverty, for which no single agency of government could be held responsible and for which there was no simple solution? There would be those in the coming years who would argue that even the problem of poverty could be effectively attacked by such tactics. In 1960, however, that argument was not a visible presence in the world where such issues were seriously discussed and analyzed from the perspective of a new radicalism.

For that matter, neither was the problem of poverty itself a salient presence in that world. This may seem surprising, but there were reasons. As I have already indicated in another context, throughout the years following the Second World War, what struck almost everyone about the American economy was not its weaknesses or failures. It was the amazing power it had shown to convert from war to peace without the depression which had universally been prophesied, and then the astonishing growth which it had gone on to experience with a resulting level of material prosperity such as the world had never seen and such as many had never even dreamed possible. Not only was the sheer profusion and abundance of this economy the wonder and envy of the world. More incredible still was the fact that it was so widely shared, that so many people—ordinary people, working-class people—were beginning to live in a style that only the rich could afford in most other places. At a time, for example, when indoor plumbing or central heating was rare in many countries, and an automobile was the height of luxury even in most of Europe, let alone outside the Western world, plumbing and heating seemed to be taken for granted in America, and almost everyone seemed to own a car—and a house and a washing machine and a television set and a thousand other unheard-of conveniences.

In the face of all this, the usual lines of attack on the American system—or on capitalism in general—had been thrown into confusion. At first no one disputed the facts of the case by trying to show that American prosperity was more apparent than real, or that more Americans than met the eye were being left out of what John Kenneth Galbraith was to call the "affluent society" in the book he published under that title in 1958. Most of the critics accepted the evidence of their own eyes. However, some Marxists

who had predicted the onset of a postwar depression attempted
to rescue their theoretical credibility by maintaining that the
economy had never in fact met the test of conversion to peace-
time production. It was, they said, still being artificially propped
up by war (and an artificial one at that, since the cold war was
nothing but a deliberate ploy by the American capitalists to save
their own system by keeping it on a wartime footing when there
was no actual military threat to be guarded against). Others simply abandoned the economic argument as such and retreated
from questions of quantity and distribution to the more easily
contested ground of the "quality of life" under the new prosperity. Thus all throughout the fifties—a time when complacency is
supposed to have reigned supreme in the public prints in America
—there was a flood of books and articles on the dreariness and
emptiness of life in the affluent society.

According to this literature, jobs might have been plentiful and
well paid, but they were deadening to the soul. It went (as it had
always gone) without saying that this was the case in the factories,
where the worker, like Charlie Chaplin in *Modern Times,* was
scarcely more human than the machines he was forced to attend.
But if writers like Sloan Wilson, William H. Whyte, Vance Pac-
kard, John Keats, and dozens of others were to be believed, it had
even become true higher up on the scale, in the executive suite,
where Whyte's "organization man"—a creature almost as me-
chanical and as interchangeable and as little stimulated by his
work as the men on the assembly line—now reigned supreme.
The worker lived in a "ticky-tacky" house that looked like every
other house around it and spent his evenings drinking beer and
watching wrestling matches on television. The executive—easily
distinguishable from the worker by his gray-flannel suit and the
martinis he drank in place of beer—lived a bit farther out in a
much more expensive house that constantly demanded to be fed
with more and more furnishings and appliances, most of them of
inferior quality, but necessary to his anxious quest for "status."
To pay for all these things, he had to run harder and harder in

the "rat race," which made him more and more anxious, which in turn made it necessary for him to spend more and more time and money on psychoanalytic therapy, which, in a classic vicious circle, forced him to run still harder in the rat race until ulcers slowed him down or a coronary cut him off altogether in early middle age. (This line of attack would be adapted in the sixties by Betty Friedan to the particularities of his wife's situation and would give birth to the women's liberation movement.)

Whatever the merits of this indictment may have been, the point I want to make is that even the critics of American society in the fifties took its economic success as a given. That there were still "pockets" of unemployment and poverty, and that there was still a great spread in the distribution of income and wealth, everyone realized. But the significance of such familiar conditions paled by comparison with a situation that seemed to defy the rule that there could be nothing new under the sun: the apparent convergence of the entire population into a single class.

Rigid class distinctions in the European sense had never been thought to exist in democratic America, with its egalitarian culture and a history famously dotted with individuals and even whole groups who had moved "from rags to riches" within the span of a single generation. Yet not even in America had it ever been imagined that class distinctions might disappear altogether into a vast homogenized middle. Faced with the possibility that such a development might actually be occurring, very few even among the bitterest critics of the American system in those early postwar years could resist being dazzled or were able for a while to be persuasive about any contrary trends.

They were, of course, to recover soon enough. By 1959, Michael Harrington, a young socialist closely associated with the *Dissent* group, was taking powerful issue with the theory that American society was on its way to becoming entirely middle-class. There were, Harrington contended, fifty million poor people in America who, thanks in part to the influence of this very theory, were now "invisible."

Yet what was notable about Harrington's rediscovery of the poor is that it did not point the way toward a new radicalism. For one thing the figures themselves, as well as the definition of what constituted poverty, were open to serious question. I remember Irving Kristol scoffing at them shortly after the piece came out, and he was certainly not alone in his skepticism. But even for many like myself who accepted Harrington's analysis, the tendency was to view the persistence of poverty amid plenty not as in itself evidence of the need for radical change, but as a problem which could be solved—and inevitably would, now that attention was being called to it—by the inexorable growth of the American economy. In my judgment there was no question of the ability of the system to deal with such a problem; nor was there any question of how to do so. Like civil rights in the South, it represented a mopping-up operation, nothing more.

Of course Harrington himself thought that much more was called for: socialism, to be exact. But here, so far as I was concerned, we were back again to the difficulty of distinguishing between socialism as Harrington and his friends conceived it and the policies of the New Deal.

Those policies had once been attacked so viciously by the Republicans that many thought they would try to repeal them when they came to power under Eisenhower in 1952 for the first time in twenty years. Instead, except for a detail or two at the margin, the welfare measures of the New Deal were left intact by the Eisenhower administration, and the Republicans even accepted the idea that the federal government should intervene into the economy in order to maintain a high level of employment.

Being Republicans with an ideological heritage of opposition to government intervention, however, they were relatively inhibited in their management of the economy. This gave the Democrats a chance to blame any economic failures—such as the recession which occurred in the late fifties—on Eisenhower and to promise that all would be well when he was replaced in 1960 by a Democrat. It was in this political context that I looked upon the rediscovery of poverty: not as making a new case for radicalism in general or socialism in particular, but only as showing that the agenda of the New Deal still remained to be completed. That this needed to be done was self-evident, and I for one did not doubt that it would be done before very long. But neither did I doubt that it would accomplish little beyond itself. The plight of the poor—like that of the Negroes in the South—would certainly be improved, and that was justification enough. At the same time, nothing would be changed in the society at large. It would remain as it was, only more so, since the difficult spiritual problems afflicting it would now also be extended even to the two groups which had previously had simpler and more elementary things to worry about. Winning their civil rights and moving economically into the middle class would, in short, bring these laggard groups into line with everyone else not only politically, economically, and socially, but spiritually as well.

Neither the "Negro problem," then, as it used to be called, nor the problem of poverty (the two were not, and are not, the same, since more than two-thirds of all people living below the poverty line in America were then, and are now, white) seemed a potential source of the new radicalism that I and a number of other intellectuals were searching for. By 1960, that number was still very small and still represented a dissident minority within the intellectual community. On the other hand, it had by now grown large enough and—what is more important from the point of view of a battle of ideas, where what counts is argument and energy rather than numbers as such—it had also acquired enough weight to give me the feeling that it was destined to win, that it was indeed the fabled "wave of the future."

Looking back on this moment twenty years later, I can see that my exuberant optimism had a good deal to do with my own personal circumstances. In January 1960, two immensely important things happened to me: I celebrated my thirtieth birthday, an age at which I felt both very young and fully matured; and I took over the editorship of *Commentary,* already by then one of the most important intellectual magazines in the country. And the fact that these things were happening at the very beginning of a new decade was in itself a spiritually portentous fact to a person like me, the product of a literary education which had taught me to think of history as divided into decades, each with a distinctive character of its own. No wonder I was optimistic.

But there were also good objective and external reasons to feel optimistic, the best one being that my plans for *Commentary* were taking shape: the "new *Commentary,"* it was called from the moment the February 1960 issue, the first under my editorship, came out. And indeed it *was* new in almost every respect. It had a new cover design, a new format, several new features (including an introductory column written by me), a new and much greater emphasis on general articles than on pieces of special Jewish interest. But most important and most striking of all, of course, it had a new point of view; and to make certain that everyone would be in no doubt as to that particular aspect of the general novelty, I announced it explicitly in my first editorial statement.

I said that *Commentary* under my predecessor Elliot E. Cohen had been a major participant in the effort to demonstrate that Western civilization was not falling apart, as so many of its critics from the Marxist Left and the cultural Right had been proclaiming. This defense had seemed plausible for a while. But it had begun to wear thin in recent years, as more and more people had found themselves beginning to suspect that the prosperity of the Eisenhower age was a deceptive sign of vigor and health. "What is there about the life we lead," I went on to ask,

> and the conditions surrounding us that accounts for the rise in the consumption of narcotics (including legal drugs like tranquilizers and sleeping pills); the fantastic divorce rate; the phenomenal number of breakdowns; and the spread of senseless juvenile violence and crime even into the comfortable middle class?

In my judgment the best answer anyone had yet given was in Paul Goodman. Thus it seemed to me a happy convergence that I was launching the "new" *Commentary* with a major three-part serialization of a book that would later be published under the title *Growing Up Absurd.* As Goodman saw it, the pathologies of American life had developed out of the fact that we were the inheritors of a number of "incomplete revolutions" (economic, social, sexual) which had succeeded far enough to disrupt the traditional mores and yet not far enough to replace them with a coherent new pattern. What was needed, then, was to complete those revolutions.

The editorial program reflecting this view would involve criticizing existing institutions of every kind, to expose their shortcomings, their weaknesses, and their inadequacies as measured by the degree to which they were contributing or failing to contribute to our own future potentialities. What these potentialities consisted of, I had no doubt: to every individual his own fullness of being, and to the society as a whole vitality and a sense of common purpose. That such potentialities were real I also had no doubt, thanks to Norman O. Brown. And, thanks to Paul Goodman, neither did I doubt that there were practical measures which could be taken to achieve them. But first things first. Before the cure could be prescribed, the diagnosis had to be made. And that meant "an effort of will and consciousness that may, if we are lucky, preoccupy the best minds and talents of the coming decade."

If we are lucky: the "if" was disingenuous, because I was sure that we were going to be. In the course of the two or three months it had taken me to gather material for the inaugural issues of the new *Commentary,* I had encountered a much warmer response from the writers I spoke to than I had originally expected to get. Some of my old friends, especially Lionel Trilling, Irving Kristol, and Daniel Bell, were uneasy about the direction I was evidently heading in. Yet despite their misgivings they were willing to write for *Commentary,* and all of them appeared in the first few issues. So too did a long list of other intellectuals who in the recent past had shared to one degree or another in the postwar revulsion against radicalism: Nathan Glazer and David Riesman, of course, but also Alfred Kazin, F. W. Dupee, Arthur Koestler, Richard Chase, Robert Gorham Davis, Leslie Fiedler, William Barrett, Murray Kempton, Dwight Macdonald, Lionel Abel, Hans J. Morgenthau, David Bazelon, Hannah Arendt, Sidney Hook, Harold Rosenberg. Wary or enthusiastic, there they all were, and there they all wanted to be—where, it seemed clear, the action now was.

To make matters even more encouraging, new people were turning up all the time, who, like Paul Goodman himself, had been radicals all along and were eager to move from the margins of intellectual life closer to the center. There was, for example, Edgar Z. Friedenberg, an "educationist" who wrote out of a much broader intellectual background than was common among specialists in education. There was Staughton Lynd, a young historian, who had a good deal to say about the history of the cold war and about a wide range of domestic political issues. There was H. Stuart Hughes, also a historian, who had the great and unusual gift of being able to talk about the technical questions surrounding nuclear weapons in language easily intelligible to a general audience. And there were many others with less talent or energy who came and went but who also shared in the new radical spirit and helped to give it flesh.

Nor was it only writers who turned out to be more receptive to the spirit of the new *Commentary* than I had anticipated: readers did too. I had thought that changing the magazine as suddenly and dramatically as I had done would result at first in a loss of circulation, with old readers falling away in disapproval or even disgust before we had had a chance to replace them with new ones more in tune with the developing radical temper. Such defections did in fact occur, but not in the large numbers I had been expecting, and in most cases not even for political reasons. As for those of its older readers who were less than happy with the change in political direction—usually because they were veterans of the radical movements of the thirties, who, having once been burned and scarred, would remain suspicious of radicalism for the rest of their lives—they tended to stay on, disgruntled and defensive but attentive to every word.

But more significant than the numbers was the enthusiasm I could feel all around me, charging the air and mounting with each successive issue. The Goodman articles especially—but by no means those articles alone—aroused a degree of excitement, and even happiness, that suggested the presence of a hunger that some of us had known was there but which had turned out to be deeper than I or anyone else had suspected: a hunger for something new and something radical that would be free of the disabilities that had crippled radicalism in the past and had left it so discredited.

It was a hunger shared by writers and readers alike—in fact, as it turned out, by almost everyone in the intellectual community. In retrospect, after all that has happened since 1960, it seems obvious that this should have been so. But nothing could have been less obvious at the time. Some had been hoping for a resurgence of radicalism among the intellectuals, but no one had predicted it. And the reason no one had predicted it was that the conditions generally thought necessary for such a resurgence no longer existed and were unlikely to return in the foreseeable future: namely, widespread unemployment among the intellectuals and a correspondingly low social status. The assumption was that these conditions had accounted for the "alienation" of the intellectuals and their political radicalization in the past, most recently of course in the thirties, and that what explained the change in the forties and fifties was the new availability of jobs combined with the new respectability the intellectuals were achieving as well as the accompanying respect in which they were increasingly being held by society at large. But if that was the case —and there was, as I have already suggested, undoubtedly some truth in it—things were bound to get worse rather than better from the point of view of the hopes for a radical resurgence.

Since 1957, when the Russians launched Sputnik and thereby

demonstrated a higher degree of scientific and technological so-
phistication than they had been believed capable of, crash programs had begun to be instituted to expand and improve the
American educational system. The main target of these programs
was scientific and technological education—not a field in which
many intellectuals in our sense were to be found—but there was
a spillover into all other fields as well, including the liberal arts,
the natural habitat and breeding ground of the intellectual class.
The number of jobs was growing, the people who filled them
were better paid than ever before, and the market for serious
books and serious thought was expanding too.

Even though the purpose of all this was ultimately military—to
make sure that the United States would retain its competitive edge
over the Russians in nuclear weaponry—the new demand for
"excellence" inevitably affected areas remote from anything military or technological. "Brains" were now valued as perhaps never
before in America: they were as precious a national resource as
finance capital and as necessary to the national defense as ships
and planes. People who possessed them had to be sought out,
nurtured, encouraged, developed, protected. And so it was that
admission to the best colleges and universities and professional
schools, which had previously been governed by criteria having
less to do with intelligence and academic aptitude than with social,
religious, and ethnic background, had by the late fifties begun to
be based on a system of strictly competitive examinations designed to ensure the highest possible quality of intellectual performance. And so it was too that intellectuals were more and more
in demand to advise and consult with the publishing houses and
the foundations and, of course, the universities on how "excellence" could most efficiently be pursued in the world of ideas.

Even the politicians, it seemed, were cooperating in what might
almost have been taken by a paranoid radical as a deliberate effort
to "co-opt" the intellectuals. Franklin Roosevelt had summoned
a "brains trust" to Washington, mostly made up of professors of
economics, to help him develop programs for dealing with the

Depression and its effects, but the influence of intellectuals on the New Deal was on the whole negligible. As for Truman and Eisenhower, any intellectuals they may have had in their entourage were certainly kept well hidden. In general, next to the business world itself, the world of practical, electoral politics was perhaps more closed off to intellectuals than any other area of American life. It was closed off because politics in America at least since the Civil War had been more pragmatic than ideological and in the main controlled by professional politicians concerned with the distribution of patronage and the administration of the going system. These professionals had no need and even less use for big ideas or the kind of people who specialized in such irrelevant commodities. Their job was to get out the vote with favors and promises of future favor—appointments, sinecures, contracts, connections—and to make sure that those promises were kept when victory came. None of this activity required, or received, ideological justification. It was enough that it worked, allowing the country to get on with its real business, which was, to cite Coolidge's classic remark once again, business—and not only for his party, the Republicans, but, despite their recent propaganda to the contrary, for the Democrats as well.

Even Franklin Roosevelt—who as the scion of a rich patrician family was denounced as a traitor to his class for siding consistently with labor against capital in the struggle to unionize American industry—had pursued the objective of saving capitalism in a time of crisis, not destroying it; and it was in the name of that objective that most of the reforms of the New Deal were pushed through. Whether or not it was those reforms that saved capitalism in America remains a disputed question, but there can be no doubt of the intention behind them.

The point is that even in the thirties there was an ideological consensus between the two major parties, and under such circumstances the demand for intellectuals—that is to say, specialists in ideological conflict—was bound to remain minimal. And so it did, in the domestic sphere.

Of course, foreign affairs, as we have seen, was another matter. Nearly a decade before this post-Sputnik development, the cold war had created an entirely new demand for intellectuals, to serve in the launching of an ideological offensive against Communism and in support of democracy. As I have also mentioned before, we now know that a certain proportion of the talent used in this ideological offensive was secretly paid for by the CIA, which subsidized a worldwide network of magazines and other cultural activities. But we also know that scarcely anyone who benefited from those subsidies (and evidently most of those who did were, in the jargon of the intelligence trade, "unwitting") needed to tailor his views in order to qualify.

Nor had the financial support given by the CIA to certain types of intellectual activity been the only form the new demand for intellectual talent had taken in the cold war. There had also been the open subsidizing of research institutes and "think tanks" in the universities: some to provide studies of the more exotic regions of Asia and Africa into which the "struggle for hearts and minds" presumably had to be carried; others to do research on the Soviet Union, China, and the Communist world generally; and still others for research that was apparently remote from the ideological struggle, but that qualified for subsidies anyway—the most curious and ironic example being the help provided by the Defense Department to Noam Chomsky's highly technical work on linguistics, on the theory, apparently, that it could lead to a breakthrough in cryptanalysis. (Far from reciprocating the support he had received from the American government, Chomsky was later to issue a bitter denunciation of his fellow intellectuals for being pro-American, though unlike him, many he denounced had never received any government grants.)

In short, for anyone who believed that a radical resurgence depended upon a turn for the worse in the economic and social fortunes of the intellectuals, there was very little in 1960 to suggest that it or anything like it was destined to come.

But of course the theory that radicalism arises out of deteriorating circumstances is naïve. No doubt it sometimes does, but bad times are just as likely to frighten people and to make them timid and therefore acquiescent. Good times, on the other hand, inspire confidence and daring. There are "rising expectations" and the appetite grows by what it feeds on. What do intellectuals have an appetite for? Well, intellectuals are people and they are as greedy for all the good things in life as everyone else. But *as* intellectuals their appetite is not primarily for riches or political power or even fame; it is for attention and influence. Above all else, what they want is for the things they write to be read, to be understood, to be taken seriously.

There had been a time when most intellectuals in America had given up on any such ambition, when their assumption had been that the only audience they could expect would be composed of each other and, with luck, posterity. The fifties had challenged that assumption by making it seem possible that a broader audience could be reached without "selling out" or lowering and cheapening standards. Yet, as I have said, there got to be an increasing uneasiness in the fifties over the conditions under which this surprising new level of attention was being achieved. After all, intellectuals had always been critics of bourgeois society. There were even some who claimed that the intellectuals had come into existence as a self-conscious group precisely out of a revulsion against bourgeois society and all its works. Departing from this hallowed tradition of antagonism toward bourgeois society in the "American Celebration" of the fifties had been a large act, and it turned out to be a very difficult one to sustain. One's motives were open to question by the likes of Irving Howe, but also, and more troublesomely, by oneself.

And apart from motives, there was always the issue of how much, really, things had changed out there in bourgeois (or, to use the term that now came into currency as a replacement, middle-class) society. Had the old charges against it really been refuted? Certainly it was a better form of society than the totalitarianisms of Left and Right. But was it a good society? Had it really become significantly more humane and significantly more civilized than it had been in the old days of babbittry, philistinism, puritanism, bigotry, parochialism, commercialism, and all the other sins of a society dominated by the business class? Was there no other and more attractive alternative?

It was because they had never really ceased to be bothered by such questions as these that so many intellectuals responded so enthusiastically to the new *Commentary*. The magazine was providing them with an opportunity to assume the old and more familiar and much more comfortable role of critic once again—only this time without the corrupting connections of Stalinism to worry about. And what was even better, becoming critics of American society again, far from resulting in a diminution of their influence, gave every promise of increasing it. Celebrating American society may have gone hand in hand with jobs and status in the fifties, but criticizing it was evidently not going to mean losing these worldly goods in the nascent sixties. On the contrary, it was clearly going to bring rewards much greater than the minimal comforts which had seemed so luxurious to the rather niggardly imagination of a generation of intellectuals with the Depression of the thirties still vivid in their minds.

5

Did I—did they—did we—know that all this would happen? Did we know that we were one day to be rewarded with even greater influence in our new position? Not, I believe, at first. What I for one knew was that the intellectual community was moving back toward radicalism. But I did not realize, and neither did anyone else, not at first, how much of the country it would sweep along with it, and how fast the whole process would go. In the fifties Nelson Algren had once said: "It is better to be out than in. It is better to be on the lam than on the cover of *Time* magazine." Little did he dream that the day was fast approaching when being out would become one of the best ways to be in and being on the lam would become one of the quickest routes to the cover of *Time*. Yet Algren himself had better reason than some to sense the coming of this paradoxical climate. He was, after all, the author of a novel about being out, *The Man with the Golden Arm*, that had become a huge and much-praised best seller and that had put him not on the lam but into the bed of Simone de Beauvoir, which, thanks to a best-selling novel she then wrote about their affair, might in terms of the publicity it brought almost have been considered the functional equivalent of the cover of *Time* magazine.

I myself never appeared on the cover of *Time*, but they did print a picture of me only a few months after I had become the editor of *Commentary*. In those days *Time* was still being run by its founder, Henry Luce, and it was the very citadel of American nationalism—the mass-circulation counterpart of what *Commentary* had been in the early fifties. As such it had preached some of the same ideas but from a much less liberal point of view and in a highly simplified and vulgarized version lacking all nuance and qualification.

In this version, the United States had now taken over the role of world leadership previously played by a depleted and exhausted Great Britain. It was, said Luce, the American Century, and those of us living in it had a great mission to perform as the defenders and propagators of freedom against the challenge of totalitarian Communism. That the United States was equal to this mission was the main thing Luce tried to show in *Time* and his other magazines, *Life* and *Fortune*, and when he gave a hearing to any other point of view, it was unlikely in the extreme to be a sympathetic one. *Time* especially was famous for the many different tricks it had developed to undercut or ridicule ideas it disliked and the people who were spreading them.

One such was the unflattering photograph which could make the handsome look ugly, the serious look frivolous, and the honest look crooked. Therefore, when a *Time* photographer arrived to take my picture one day in connection with a story they were doing on how a representative group of American intellectuals viewed the state of the nation as a new decade was getting under way, I—having pushed *Commentary* off what *Time* would have regarded as the path of ideological virtue—expected the worst. Yet when I asked the photographer about the story, he said he knew nothing about it; they never told him what the story was when he was sent out to take someone's picture, all they ever told him was "good guy or bad guy." No kidding? Which one was I? "Good guy," he said pleasantly, and to my amazement it turned out to be the truth. A week later the story appeared, and there in a row of photographs of eminent intellectuals, some looking distinguished and others rather bedraggled, was one of a young man who resembled me but in so flattering a light that I was almost unrecognizable. The story is told that shortly after Saul Bellow's first novel was published he got a call from a Hollywood studio which he naturally assumed would be about buying his book for the movies, but what the caller wanted was to offer him a screen test on the basis of his photograph on the jacket. After that picture of me appeared in *Time*, I would not have been surprised to receive such a call myself.

That *Time* had taken me for a "good guy" was puzzling, and perhaps a case of mistaken identity. Or perhaps they had not yet caught up with the changes I had been making in the magazine and had simply assumed that the editor of *Commentary* would always be a person of the proper political persuasion. But since the editors of *Time* were careful readers of *Commentary*, and since no one was more sensitive to twists and turns in the ideological atmosphere than they, the more likely explanation was that they had misinterpreted the purpose of the new *Commentary*.

If so, it would not have been entirely without cause. For in my opening editorial statement I had said that one of the consequences of our failure to complete all the uncompleted revolutions of which Paul Goodman spoke was "our inability to keep up with the Russians in the arms race" (I was referring to Sputnik and the superiority in missiles which the Russians were supposedly achieving). This, I had argued, "shows lack of resolution even among those groups who might be expected to believe that a hydrogen war is preferable to a world dominated by the Communists." Now, those groups would have included the Luce magazines if they included anyone. But *Time* might well have overlooked this swipe for the sake of the novel confirmation it brought to one of Luce's favorite themes of the moment: the flagging of the national purpose. The president—Eisenhower, that is—had appointed a commission to investigate this problem, and Luce had run a series of articles on it in *Life* by the "great thinkers" of the day, who predictably enough responded, as of course the presidential commission did too, with banalities so empty that not even Eisenhower could have surpassed them.

Possibly, then, despite an inveterate tendency at *Time* to blame everything that was wrong with America on the heritage of the Enlightenment (whose great and in their eyes most villainous contemporary representative was John Dewey and especially the theory and practice of "progressive education" for which he was held responsible), they might have taken the concluding passage of my piece as an interesting new approach to the question of how our flagging national purpose might be restored and renewed:

> . . . since what the newspapers call "imaginative leadership" is simply the blessing heaven bestows on a people willing to pursue the destiny to which their history compels them as though it were a personal psychic need of every individual member, such a struggle [to complete Goodman's uncompleted revolutions] might also mean the discovery of alternatives to our present policy of depending exclusively on the "balance of terror" to ward off a hydrogen war.

If Luce himself or the people working under him at *Time* took this as a proposed new strategy for fighting the cold war, that in itself would have been enough to make me a "good guy"—just as, on the other side, certain references made by me to the "very real threat of the Soviet power" were enough to raise doubts about my point of view within the peace movement.

David Riesman, for example, told me that he liked almost everything I was doing with *Commentary,* but he objected to the vestiges of cold-war rhetoric in which I had couched the call for a revival of utopian social criticism. In his view, spelled out at length in a piece for one of the early issues of the new *Commentary* he wrote in collaboration with Michael Maccoby, ending the cold war was a precondition for the far-reaching political movement some of us were trying to create to cope with the radically new problems of a world in which—as we and almost everyone else believed in those days—abundance was replacing scarcity as the normal human condition. The United States was in the forefront of this process, which meant that we were in a position to become a kind of experimental laboratory in learning how to live with the revolutionary problems of abundance. In a disarmed world, the Russians too would begin to move toward the same condition, and since everything they did was done out of a desire to prove that they were as good as we were (Riesman went so far as to call the Soviet-American conflict a case of sibling rivalry, with the Russians as the younger brother), we could then "shift the emphasis of Soviet emulation" and provide them with a better goal for growth than we were now doing with our bombs and our toasters and our television sets.

Even in 1960, at the height of my radical exuberance, I had grave reservations about this conception, and others like it, of the Soviet-American conflict. I simply could not believe that the Russians were merely imitating us in everything they did. Thus it did not follow for me, as it did for many in the peace movement, that the cold war could be ended by American actions alone. Those who saw the matter in this way talked as though the only serious obstacles to a peaceful accommodation with the Russians were to be found in the American "military-industrial complex" and in the American character, with its anxieties over masculinity and its other neurotic fixations. The practical program was to work on those; and Riesman and Maccoby offered a few suggestions in their piece on how to arrange things so that defense contractors, for example, would no longer need to fear that disarmament would hurt them economically. But they had virtually nothing to say about the Russians: if we moved toward peace, the Russians would automatically follow suit.

My own view was much less sanguine. I still thought that the Soviet Union was out to conquer the world and that only American power stood in the way. I was also highly skeptical of the idea that a "peace party" existed in the Soviet Union "strong enough to prevail if the West should find a way of overcoming those forces within its own sphere who wish to keep the cold war alive." On the other hand, I did think that the fear of nuclear war was already working to moderate Soviet ambitions and that a negotiated settlement might now have become possible. It was possible not because Khrushchev had given up on the old dreams of a Communist world or because he was more a man of peace than Stalin had been, but because the risks of nuclear war had grown to the point where reducing the dangers of an outbreak overrode all other national interests and ideological ambitions. Even so, I was in the end willing to go along with Riesman and others to the extent of entertaining the idea that the United States might for various reasons be more reluctant than the Russians to negotiate such a settlement, and that it was up to us to take the initiative.

The approach I came to favor was the one being developed by a man named Charles E. Osgood, under the acronym GRID, which stood for "graduated reciprocal initiatives toward disarmament." Under this plan, we would take a unilateral step toward disarmament and if the Russians reciprocated, we would take another, and so on; if they failed to reciprocate—well, some people said we would have to take the next step anyway, to allay their understandable suspicions, though my position was that we would then at least know that the emulation theory had been wrong.

On one crucial point, however, I agreed entirely with Riesman: that so long as the cold war went on in its present form, no resurgence of radicalism was possible. Indeed, it was because I shared the view that ending the cold war was a precondition for such a resurgence that I looked upon the peace movement as so much more significant in the political long run than the civil-rights movement.

It is important to realize that, at this very early stage in the development of the new radicalism, almost no one had any hope of achieving a direct or immediate effect. Someone like Riesman, trying to shake the idea so prevalent among college students at the time that political action was pointless and futile, might talk of the difference a single irate letter to a congressman could make, but his real vision was of another kind of political activity: the development of ideas which were designed not with an eye toward what might be acceptable today, but that were uninhibited or unconstricted by the political realities of the moment. Equipped with such ideas, the movement could then look for effective ways to mobilize public opinion behind them, and this shift in public opinion would eventually cause a shift in Washington and all the other centers of power.

To be sure, working on Washington directly was not altogether precluded by this approach. Riesman himself participated in a project organized by several young congressional aides, including Marcus Raskin and Arthur Waskow (who together went on soon thereafter to found the Institute for Policy Studies, the main think tank of the new radicalism). The aim was to develop a new agenda that could be pushed by liberal congressmen of the stripe they themselves were working for, and to do so mainly by exposing them to the currents of radical thought stirring in such intellectual centers as the new *Commentary*.

I too became involved. On one of the very first occasions I ever visited Washington as anything other than a tourist, I spoke before a group of congressmen convened by Raskin and Waskow as part of a panel whose members were Paul Goodman, Harvey Swados (a novelist and journalist associated with *Dissent*), and Harold Taylor (the former president of Sarah Lawrence College and a figure who was to serve as a bridge between the world of "establishment" liberalism and the new radicalism). I can hardly remember what the subject of the evening was, but afterward there was a party at the Raskins' and I do recall getting into a heated argument with Waskow, who took the view that the notion of intellectual standards (which I had been defending) was nothing but an instrument of repression. Some years later Waskow was to undergo a curious metamorphosis which left him looking and sounding (or at any rate trying to look and sound) like a Hasidic *rebbe*, but in 1960 he was clean-shaven, buttoned-down, and gray-flanneled, and his way of angrily barking out statements made him sound like nothing so much as a drill sergeant in the marines. I should perhaps have known that my belief in standards, like my fear of Soviet military power and Soviet intentions, contained the seeds of future trouble with the radical movement. So too did my resistance to some of the things Raskin's wife Barbara was saying about the oppression of women (in the seventies she was to leave Raskin and write a confessional liberationist novel). But consensus on general principles seemed infinitely more important than these disagreements, and the arguments with Waskow and Barbara Raskin ended pleasantly enough.

For all their talk about a new legislative agenda and the like, I doubt that even Raskin and Waskow really thought they could make any headway within the going political system. But whatever they may have thought, neither I nor most of my closest collaborators at *Commentary* had any such expectation.

Thus in April of 1960, when no one yet knew who the candidates in the coming presidential election would be, Dwight Macdonald—who had been a Trotskyist in the thirties, a pacifist in the forties, nonpolitical in the fifties, and now announced himself as an anarchist for the sixties—wrote a piece for *Commentary* explaining why there was no point to voting in presidential elections at all. His main argument was that no significant differences existed any longer between the two major parties either on domestic issues or on issues of foreign policy, and that national elections had now become "elaborate techniques for avoiding, rather than resolving, political issues."

This argument was an updated version of an attitude most intellectuals—and of course all radicals, whether they were intellectuals or not—had been taking toward the American political system for a long time. Nothing could be expected of it: the choice between the two parties was a choice between "Tweedledum and Tweedledee" (or as a different version had it, reflecting the element of intellectual snobbery also contained in this attitude, "Tweedledumb and Tweedledumber").

George Lichtheim also wrote about the disappearance of issues from American (and indeed Western European) politics which, he said, had come to resemble the game of "ins" and "outs" that characterized eighteenth-century politics in England. Lichtheim, looking upon this phenomenon as a Marxist, albeit a highly unorthodox one, attributed it to the end of the class struggle (so unorthodox a Marxist was he), while Macdonald blamed it on the mediocrity of the current crop of politicians.

For me, the absence of issues seemed traceable to another cause. Issues may have derived from class and other interests, but they also derived from vision, and it was not the politicians to whom we ordinarily looked for vision but the intellectuals. It was the intellectuals who had failed us, I thought, by abdicating their traditional role as fanatical devotees of the dream of a good society. If intellectuals wanted to change the world, they would have to work on the consciousness of their age and let others fret about parties and movements and pushing bills through Congress or winning votes and elections.

The fact that no real issues were being raised within the going political system did not mean that no real issues existed. "It is an issue," I wrote

> that our society still lives by success, conceived in terms of status or money, and that the pursuit of success encourages the development of the worst human qualities and strangles the best. It is an issue that the curiosity of our children wastes away daily in the schools. It is an issue that work provides no satisfaction for the great majority of Americans, whether they sit at machines or behind desks. It is an issue that the air is filled with lies, that "public speech" has lost all connection with reality. It is an issue that everything we get *costs* too much—too much money, too much energy, too much spirit.

But the system was structurally incapable of accommodating such issues as these because they could not easily be translated into a legislative or executive program.

Yet even if they could have been translated into a program, who would have tried to put it before the electorate? Not, certainly, the Republicans. To me—and in this I was representative of the intellectual community—the Republicans were at once the party of stupidity and the party of resistance to change. There was no interest in ideas within the Republican party, not even ideas that served to confer legitimacy on the privileges of the business class which it existed to serve (". . . for many years," said Charles E. Wilson, Eisenhower's Secretary of Defense, in a statement which had become notorious, "I thought what was good for our country was good for General Motors, and vice versa"). How, then, could the Republicans be expected to care about or understand new ideas, especially when these ideas threatened to bring change, radical change, change of many different kinds? The best that could be said of the Republicans after eight years in office was that they had—albeit reluctantly and with ill grace—bowed to the necessity of allowing the basic reforms of the New Deal to stand, and that they had—again reluctantly and with ill grace—accepted the need to support the civil-rights movement in the South. Beyond such minimal steps they could not be expected to go in domestic affairs.

Nor, in foreign affairs, could they be expected to move very far in the direction of ending the cold war. To be sure, Eisenhower had presided over a "thaw" in the relations between the Soviet Union and the United States after the death of Stalin, and in general his actions as president had been far less bellicose than the violently anti-Communist rhetoric he and his secretary of state John Foster Dulles habitually used. Reversing Theodore Roosevelt's dictum, they had spoken loudly and carried a small stick. Thus Eisenhower's first major action upon becoming president in January 1953 had been to end the Korean war; nearly two years later he had refused to intervene to help the French in Vietnam; and two years after that, despite Republican campaign promises to replace the passive policy of containing Soviet power with a policy of "rollback" aimed at liberating the Eastern European satellites from Soviet control, he had also refused to intervene when the Hungarians (expecting American help) rose up in revolt against their Russian masters.

Nevertheless it was hard to believe that the Republicans, especially under so fanatical an anti-Communist as Richard Nixon, Eisenhower's vice-president and evident successor, would ever be capable of going beyond certain practical prudential steps to reduce the dangers of nuclear war. They lacked the necessary imagination no less than the necessary ideas.

As for the Democrats, they were hardly any better. In fact, the case could be made that in some ways they were an even weaker reed for radical hope to lean upon than the Republicans. The Democrats were promising—in the words of John F. Kennedy's main campaign slogan—to "get the country moving again" after a period of stagnation and drift under Eisenhower and the Republicans. To the extent that the motion they promised was motion in the direction of those mopping-up operations I was talking about earlier—that is, faster progress in civil rights and the elimination of all remaining "pockets" of poverty—they were of course to be preferred to the Republicans in domestic affairs. But the promise to get the country moving again quite clearly referred to foreign affairs as well, and here the complaint was that the Republicans had been too accommodating and too soft in dealing with the Russians, not that they had been too aggressive or hard. Senator John F. Kennedy in particular was making so great an issue out of the "missile gap" which the Republicans had allegedly allowed to develop between us and the Russians that Riesman and Maccoby could point to him as a contemporary representative of those American patricians "who since Theodore Roosevelt's day have seen war and preparation for war as the condition of national health." Such men, said Riesman, are preoccupied with the Communist threat only because they have "no goals for America in its own terms."

When Riesman wrote those words in the spring of 1960 Kennedy had not yet won the Democratic nomination, and Hubert Humphrey and Adlai Stevenson, both of whom were regarded as much more liberal, were still in the picture. Yet not even they, or the liberal wing of the Democratic party generally, looked like potential allies to most of us who were in the process of creating a new radicalism. If a mopping-up operation had seemed all that the country needed, Humphrey, the great fighter for civil rights, would probably have been the best man. But he did not strike anyone as the man to see beyond the problems of scarcity to the revolutionary new problems of abundance. Nor did he seem likely to push the country's foreign policy in a more conciliatory direction. It was Humphrey, after all, who had led the (unsuccessful) effort some years earlier to outlaw the Communist party.

In any event, Humphrey, to put it mildly, inspired no enthusiasm among intellectuals. He was looked upon as a midwestern "cornball" of no particular distinction. Stevenson, although also from the Midwest, was another matter entirely. In 1952, running against Eisenhower, he had aroused a degree of excitement among intellectuals such as had never been seen by anyone still alive. Even Dwight Macdonald, who had only voted once before in his entire life and then only out of "youthful inexperience," was swept along:

> He got me with his televised speeches on the night of the nomination: that moving, spontaneous, wonderfully *real* let-this-cup-pass-from-me talk on the lawn when he first got the news; and his formal acceptance speech a few hours later at the convention, which struck me as intellectually clear and morally serious, in short as noble. How hollow, fat-headed, and "official" his predecessors sounded that night, even Harry Truman!

As is abundantly evident from the terms in which Stevenson is praised in this passage, what excited the intellectuals was the air of cultivation he exuded. Stevenson was by no known definition an intellectual, but he spoke a language intellectuals could recognize and respect, and the fact that such a man could become the Democratic candidate for president seemed to put an official seal on the general notion that we had entered a whole new era in the history of America—an era less dominated by the values of the business class and more hospitable to those of the intellectuals.

This notion and the hopes it engendered were damaged by Stevenson's defeat in 1952, but they were by no means destroyed. They even survived his more humiliating defeat, again at the hands of Eisenhower, in 1956, and they formed the foundation of an insurgency within the Democratic party against Lyndon Johnson about ten years later. Stevenson himself, however, had emerged from the 1956 campaign with a much diminished reputation among the intellectuals. "By 1956," wrote Macdonald, "Stevenson was behaving like a politician or even, God help us, a statesman. He was avoiding 'the tough ones,' was generalizing as much as possible, and was severely repressing his alleged frivolity. So I didn't vote." Many other intellectuals did vote for Stevenson in 1956, but by 1960 not many had any intention of doing so, or even of actively supporting his slim chances of winning the Democratic nomination again. There were a few who remained loyal, among them several members of the peace movement who had persuaded themselves on the basis of very flimsy evidence that Stevenson was sympathetic to the cause of disarmament. I remember Harold Taylor assuring me of this: Stevenson had privately told him so, though of course he had to be careful about what he said in public. But very few intellectuals, even in the peace movement, shared Taylor's hopes.

It seemed, then, there was nowhere for a new radicalism to go except outside the conventional political channels; and so far as my friends and I could see, this impression was given official confirmation by the nomination of Nixon and Kennedy as the two presidential candidates. Both were mediocre and neither one held out the promise of any significant change in the direction of things. We were back, in short, to Tweedledum and Tweedledee —or so most intellectuals thought.

Most, but not all, for there was a group at Harvard, led by Arthur Schlesinger, Jr., and John Kenneth Galbraith, who had gone over during the primary campaign from Stevenson to Kennedy. In doing so, they had been charged with betraying not only Stevenson himself but their own liberal principles. Not only had Kennedy not compiled a notably liberal record in the Senate, he had been absent during a vote to censure Joe McCarthy, and what was even worse, his brother and close associate Robert had even worked for the McCarthy committee. But Schlesinger and Galbraith had argued that Stevenson was a sure loser and that Kennedy was becoming more and more liberal every day.

In the seventies, when formerly forbidden beliefs and practices of every kind were coming out of the closet, Galbraith would announce that he had long considered himself a socialist rather than a liberal (though the press persisted in calling him a liberal). Schlesinger, however, was then, and would continue through all the many shiftings and twistings of the period ahead, to call himself a liberal. What is more, he was an openly partisan Democrat, not only in his capacity as a citizen but even in his scholarly work as a historian. Like Macaulay and the other exponents of the

"Whig interpretation of history" for whom the history of liberty in England was the history of the Whig party, Schlesinger in his books represented the history of liberalism (in his lexicon a word synonymous with all political virtue) in America as the history of the Democratic party. To him, therefore, to be a liberal was to be a Democrat, and to work for the realization of liberal values was to work for the election of Democrats to office.

I think, though, that it would be naïve or disingenuous to interpret Schlesinger's commitment to the Democratic party as stemming entirely from his commitment to the ideals of liberalism. There was in my judgment an element of subtle self-interest there too. Schlesinger believed that, all things considered, the Democratic party provided a more likely vehicle than the Republicans did for the reentry into American political life of a certain class of person: "the best and the brightest," as they were soon destined to be known. There was a touch of irony in the fact that the Democratic party, of all political organizations, should have become the natural home of such people, since so many of their forebears—forebears either in the actual or the spiritual sense—had withdrawn from politics altogether in the so-called Gilded Age of the late nineteenth century because they were unable to stomach the growing power of the immigrant Irish bosses of New York's Tammany Hall and similar political machines in other cities who were then taking over the Democratic party. Of course, they were equally unable to stomach the new rich, who increasingly formed the power base of the Republican party. Many of the "men in the clubs of social pretension and the men of cultivated taste and easy life"—as Theodore Roosevelt described the old patrician class from which he himself came—gave up on politics and public service altogether. Henry Adams, the descendant of two presidents of the United States, was one great example; Edmund Wilson, Sr., the father of the great critic, was another. "Educated," wrote the younger Wilson in a passage from which I have already quoted, "at Exeter and Andover and at eighteenth-century Princeton" for a career in public life, his father, like many others of that generation, could not be "induced to take any active part in the kind of political life that he knew at the end of the century."

There was, however, a hardier and more vital strain in the old patriciate as well, represented by Theodore Roosevelt himself, who went into politics with the ultimate object of taking the country back from the big businessmen on the one side and the Tammany bosses on the other. But they lacked the power to do this on their own. In time, the progeny of this line, now led by the second Roosevelt, Teddy's younger cousin Franklin, having found Tammany to be the lesser of the two evils and perhaps the more manageable as an ally, wound up for the most part in the Democratic party. Thus the Democrats, traditionally—and still— the party of the "common" people, now also became the party of the "best" people.

As early as 1915 Van Wyck Brooks, in a prophetic book entitled *America's Coming-of-Age,* declared: "Tammany has quite as much to teach Good Government as Good Government has to teach Tammany," but not until Franklin Roosevelt was this advice truly taken to heart. Effecting a reconciliation between the "googoos" —as those upper-class ancestors of the reformers of a later day were generally called—and the ward politicans (later to be known as the "bosses" or the "regulars") was the first stage. The second came with John F. Kennedy.

Kennedy, a product by birth of the Boston equivalent of Tammany, had been processed into so perfect a replica of the WASP patriciate that he could have been taken as a living embodiment of the alliance between the two groups forged under Roosevelt. Now, under his auspices—and presumably at his initiative—an effort was mounted to implement the broader aspect of Brooks's program: to bring the "poet and the professor" (the "highbrow," in Brooks's own term) into the alliance as well. I do not mean to suggest that Kennedy was literally following Brooks, any more than Roosevelt had: it was the logic of an idea and of a social process working itself out in each case.

Be that as it may, in this effort to enlist the support of the "brightest" people for the Democratic party, Arthur Schlesinger, Jr., played a key role, perhaps *the* key role. And indeed why not? If Kennedy was the living product of the first stage in the formation of the new Democratic coalition, Schlesinger could well have been considered the incarnation of the stage ahead. The descendant of two eminent Harvard families, and an important Harvard professor in his own right, he was in himself the "best" and the "brightest" all rolled up into one.

Superbly equipped with these natural qualifications, Schlesinger proceeded to evangelize the intellectuals on behalf of Kennedy. Now, considering that Nixon was scarcely less despised by intellectuals in 1960 than in 1970, the very title of Schlesinger's tract, *Kennedy or Nixon: Does It Make Any Difference?*, indicated how hard a job he had undertaken in trying to sell Kennedy to the intellectuals. But hard or not, he knew exactly what strategy to adopt. Kennedy, he suggested, represented a new stage in the development of liberalism. The problem of material subsistence having for all practical purposes been solved (though "standards of living for the poorer families in the country" needed to be raised even higher than they had already gone), liberalism was now ready to deal with "the paradox of public squalor in the midst of private opulence" and to move beyond "a prevailing materialism which has debased our tradition and corrupted our morals." Behind this rhetoric lay the clear implication that Kennedy (who in contrast to Nixon had "taste") would concentrate less on the questions of quantity which had preoccupied liberalism in the past and more on what was getting to be called the "quality of life" in an affluent society.

This was so close to what those of us who were involved in the development of the new radicalism were saying that it could be interpreted—and no doubt was so intended by Schlesinger—as an effort at co-optation. He agreed, in other words, that the necessary next step was to concentrate on a whole new range of issues created by an age of abundance, and he differed from us only in arguing that the agency for doing this was not a new radical movement operating outside the two-party system, but a new liberalism operating inside the Democratic party.

Clever though Schlesinger's appeal was, however, it fell—to begin with, at least—on deaf ears.

———
6
———

John F. Kennedy has by now become so glamorous a figure in the general imagination—the epitome of high style, the glass of fashion and the mold of form—that it is hard to recall how unlikely a candidate he struck most of us for the role Schlesinger tried to cast him in. Virtually nothing about him in his prepresidential days suggested a concern for, or even any comprehension of, the spiritual or cultural dimension of political life. Despite his good looks and his elegant carriage, he did not emanate the air of cultivation Stevenson so markedly did; the language of his speeches was standard political fare, hard to distinguish from the usual stuff; and the famous wit he revealed as president was scarcely in public evidence in those days. Behind the Choate-Harvard veneer, he seemed entirely cut from the cloth of a tough Boston Irish politician, interested only in power and patronage, and not even much of a liberal of the older "quantitative" variety, let alone the potential leader of a new stage in the development of liberalism. When Riesman said of him that he belonged to a breed which had no vision of a better America, there seemed no reason to disagree. Of course he was not so lacking in vision as an old-style regular like Carmine de Sapio, the Tammany leader, of whom Daniel Patrick Moynihan, then an assistant professor at Syracuse, would say (in his first piece for *Commentary* in 1961) that the "extent of his *ideological* commitment may be measured by his pronouncement to the Holy Name Society Communion Breakfast of the New York Sanitation Department that 'there is no Mother's Day behind the Iron Curtain.' " But neither on the showing of his career was Kennedy a man who cared about government as distinguished from politics: about the uses of power for the sake of noble ends in contrast to the winning of power for the sake of personal ambition.

I had never met Kennedy, but I was acquainted with many people who had, including a few who had known him and his wife, Jacqueline, for many years. These people were members of the *Paris Review* circle, which more or less automatically meant that they were highborn, rich, and literary either in the sense of being writers themselves or of wishing to associate with writers. It also meant that they had grown up in the same social world as Kennedy and his wife—the same schools, the same summer resorts, the same parties. There was, for example, George Plimpton, a very old friend of Jackie's, who played a social role analogous to Schlesinger's political one in forging an alliance between the "best" and the "brightest" and the Kennedy White House. Plimpton had founded *The Paris Review* in, obviously, Paris a few years earlier, but he had come back to New York in the late fifties and had set up social shop in an elegantly shabby apartment on a very good street in the East Seventies where, it seemed, the partying never stopped, and where society girls with cold steel behind their starry eyes mingled with hirsute Beat poets, black activists, Jewish intellectuals, visiting Englishmen (usually titled), old school chums now on Wall Street dropping in to see the Bohemian fun, famous writers and artists of the older generation, publishers, hangers-on, drunks, junkies and incipient junkies, theater people with pretensions ("Broadway intellectuals," in Lillian Hellman's brilliant term), and an occasional stray off the streets. Into just such a party one night in the year 1961 walked the newly anointed First Lady of the Land, Jacqueline Kennedy herself, returning what were by now rumored to be frequent visits by Plimpton and others in that room to intimate little gatherings in her house, the White House.

In addition to those small gatherings there were large state dinners at the Kennedy White House. Nothing unusual about that, except that one suddenly found the guest lists being published in the papers and discussed in the circles one traveled in oneself. Possibly Eisenhower's and Truman's state dinners had also been publicized in this way, but if so I for one had never noticed, and if I had, the chances are that professional New York intellectuals like me would have had as little personal connection with the names on the lists as with the two presidents themselves. Now, however, writers and intellectuals, as well as other people I knew, were receiving invitations to dinner at the White House. Those who received such invitations were of course flattered and delighted, and those who did not were dejected and upset, but except for socialites like Plimpton, everyone was disconcerted. What did it mean? Would accepting an invitation to the White House compromise one's freedom to criticize—and in the case of some, to despise—the Kennedy administration? I actually listened to, and to some extent participated in, discussions of exactly these questions, callow and unworldly though they strike me today. But the novelty of the situation was great, and while intelligence, learning, wide knowledge, and even wisdom were in abundant supply within the intellectual community of New York, worldliness was not one of its salient qualities.

The curious thing was that being the sort of person who could be expected to be critical of the Kennedy administration was a very good way for an intellectual to secure an invitation to dinner, or some other form of attention from the White House (phone calls from staff members, requests for advice, and the like). For the Kennedy White House cared, and cared passionately, about its reputation among intellectuals. As the president himself showed he well knew, when he appointed Schlesinger (talent of an order that can never be bought by money) to a position that in a monarchy would have been recognized quite straightforwardly as official court historian, it was the intellectuals who would tell posterity what to think about his administration; and he naturally wanted them to say the right things. But given the drift toward radicalism among the intellectuals, which was growing stronger every day, this inevitably made the Kennedy administration a prisoner of the need to prove that its ultimate objectives were at least consonant with those of the new radicalism. This was what Schlesinger had implied in his campaign pamphlet, and why he said a little later that the main difference between Paul Goodman and people like himself and his colleagues in the Kennedy administration was not one of goals but lay in the fact that Goodman represented the utopian stream in American thought as against the pragmatic tradition for which the Kennedy people spoke.

Now there could be no doubt that Paul Goodman was a utopian, and while less kindly epithets than "pragmatic" could easily have been applied to the Kennedy administration, that one was at least arguably accurate. But to me it seemed absurd to claim that Kennedy was pursuing the goals, or even a rough approximation of them, that Goodman and those of us who were more or less in agreement with him hoped some day to achieve. As president, in fact, Kennedy had not yet even allayed the suspicions which had bothered so many liberals during the campaign, suspicions about his commitment to the older kind of "quantitative" liberalism, much less done anything to move beyond it into a new and more radical phase.

One of these "quantitative" liberals, the economist Oscar Gass, wrote two devastating critiques for *Commentary* of Kennedy's performance in his first year in office, demonstrating in what seemed to me irrefutable terms that the "New Frontier" of Kennedy resembled not the New Deal of Roosevelt but rather the "Great Crusade" of Eisenhower. The New Frontier and the Great Crusade, said Gass, shared a "conservatism of fundamental social outlook." The exponents of the "high doctrine" of the New Frontier liked to speak of providing for "education, medical care, housing, slum clearance, urban and suburban planning, social security, . . . the sick and the aging, roads, recreation, water, assistance to distressed classes and areas, resources and energy development" (the list was taken from an article by none other than Schlesinger himself, by then a presidential assistant) and they were very fond of invoking the rhetoric of sacrifice. But as Gass went on to show, in dealing with unemployment, with minimum wages, with retirement benefits under social security, with health insurance, with education, the New Frontier had either done nothing or had duplicated action already taken by the Great Crusade.

In summing it all up, Gass was not kind, but he was not particularly unfair either:

> . . . Always and running through everything, there is the characteristic New Frontier polarity of portentous general language and modest specifics. Only let a speech begin, "The trumpet summons us again," and we can be sure we are being called to wash our hands. The White House does not escape the tone of café society, yet it strives for the demeanor of Churchill during the Battle of Britain. How Churchill is envied his "toil and tears, sweat and blood"! The Washington leadership of the New Frontier has an appetite for sacrifice—in comfort. St. Anthony wishes to suffer temptation—on the cobbled, shaded streets of Georgetown.

But to me a much more glaring and egregious proof of the weakness of Schlesinger's claim was the evident inability or unwillingness of the new administration to take forceful action against the resistance in the South to desegregation and the persistence in the North of various forms of racial discrimination. Kennedy had promised during the campaign that he would eliminate discrimination in housing with "the stroke of a pen"—that is, by issuing an executive order against it—but the order was very long in coming. To make matters worse, with the president's own brother Robert as attorney general, federal judges of segregationist bent were appointed in the South, presumably in order to

reward the southern Democrats on whom Kennedy had depended for his narrow victory over Nixon, and to keep them in
line for the future. (In other words, Kennedy was doing exactly
what Nixon himself as president would later be excoriated by
Kennedy's own people for doing: he was pursuing a "southern
strategy.")

In consonance with this strategy, the Justice Department was
so mild in enforcing desegregation in the South that a group of
young Negro activists arranged to meet with Robert Kennedy in
an effort to persuade him that the situation was desperate and
that if the federal government did not put its full power behind
the civil-rights movement in the South, a whole generation of
Negroes would lose their faith in the country altogether, with
consequences no one could foresee. According to James Baldwin,
who had helped set up the meeting and from whom I heard the
story, it went very badly from the point of view of the young black
activists. When a young man who had been jailed many times, and
who literally bore the scars of repeated beatings he had received
at the hands of southern police for the crime of nonviolent
demonstrations in support of his constitutional rights, said that
he and his friends would probably be unwilling to fight for this
country in a war, Kennedy's response was one of incredulity
compounded with outrage.

I must admit that I feel a wistful sympathy today for Robert
Kennedy's obdurate inability to understand how anyone could
think himself justified in refusing to fight for his country, no
matter what. But I certainly felt no such sympathy, wistful or
otherwise, then. To me Baldwin's story was yet another indication that the Kennedy administration could hardly be trusted
even to fulfill the aims of the old liberal agenda, not to mention
the new radical one.

The situation was even worse in the area of foreign affairs. Not
only had Kennedy conducted a belligerent campaign against
Nixon and the Republicans, accusing them in effect of being too
easy on the Russians; and not only had he begun his presidency

with a bellicose inaugural address (promising that the United States would spare no effort in its worldwide struggle with the Soviet Union); but he had then allowed a plan to go forward for the invasion of Cuba through the Bay of Pigs by an American-backed force of exiles seeking to topple the Castro regime. There were, to be sure, gestures of accommodation as well: an occasional speech on the need for disarmament and, most important, the signing of a treaty with the Soviets banning all atmospheric testing of nuclear weapons. But on balance the Kennedy administration in its first year or two in office gave no sign of wanting to move any further toward disarmament or beyond the cold war in its relations with the Soviet Union and the rest of the Communist world. If anything, the contrary seemed to be the case.

I did not, then, see the Kennedy administration as an ally or as an instrument in the development of a new radicalism. In fact, I began to think of it more and more as an obstacle to any such development, and even perhaps as an enemy. And it was not only the Kennedy administration in itself that I began to see in this way; it was the entire liberal "establishment" of which the government in power represented the strictly or narrowly political arm. I agreed with Oscar Gass that the Kennedy administration was not especially liberal by the standards of the New Deal, but it was after all a Democratic administration founded on a heritage of liberal ideas and much given to the uses of liberal rhetoric. Gass might, and justifiably, sneer at the discrepancy between that rhetoric and the actual policies being pursued. Yet the rhetoric mattered, as rhetoric in politics always does, because it sets the terms and defines the goals by which actions and policies are judged. For example, when Kennedy's people defended themselves in public against criticism from the liberal community for moving too slowly or not at all in civil rights or on measures of social welfare, the usual tack was not to question or repudiate the criteria by which they were being criticized; not at all. What they usually did—a good example was a little book called *Decision-*

Making in the White House by Theodore Sorensen, one of
Kennedy's closest assistants—was to complain of the limits on
presidential power and to blame Congress or the bureaucracy for
preventing the White House from doing whatever it was the
liberals wanted it to do.

That Kennedy himself during his campaign had dismissed such
talk of limits as an excuse for presidential inaction did not seem
to bother his apologists, but it certainly bothered me. In fact, it
more than bothered me; I was disgusted by it. Here were people
who had preened themselves on their youthful "vigor" and energy and boldness, and now suddenly, when it suited their convenience, they were taking refuge in what seemed to me the same
weary middle-aged philosophy which had worked so effectively in
the recent past to inhibit the emergence of a larger vision of social
and political possibility.

Feeling as I did about this, I took a mildly vindictive pleasure
in commissioning articles like those by Gass attacking the administration from what might be called the established liberal
perspective. Yet at the same time, I was becoming more and more
dubious about the established liberal perspective itself. I had in
a relatively casual spirit been operating on the idea that liberalism
was a gentler or more moderate or more cautious form of radicalism, but I now found myself beginning to wonder whether the
two might not really be mutually antagonistic. In the late thirties,
in the days of the Popular Front, the Communists (as I mentioned
earlier) had called themselves "liberals in a hurry," but they were
not liberals at all, and they were not taken in by their own propaganda, even if many liberals were. But what about the new radicalism of which I myself was a part? Were we liberals in a hurry, or
were we (in an entirely different sense from the Communists, of
course) antagonists of liberalism? Conversely, was the fulfillment
of liberal aims good for our movement or bad for it? Was liberalism a stage on the road to the new radicalism or a diversionary
path leading further and further away from it?

A substantial number of the pieces I published in *Commentary* during the first year or two of my editorship implicitly answered those questions by taking a frankly antiliberal stance, and I myself was very strongly inclined toward the same position. It was an iconoclastic position in the quite literal sense that it smashed into ideas so well entrenched as to seem no less untouchable than graven images of the saints.

No doctrine, for example, was more sacred or more venerated among liberals in those days than the need for and the desirability of increasing the power of the federal government as against the states and the cities and—within the federal government—of increasing the power of the presidency against the Congress and (although this was in the process of changing) the Supreme Court. Liberals believed, and with good historical reason, that the federal government was likely to be more liberal than state and local governments; and they also believed, again with good reason, that the White House was a better instrument of liberal reform than the Congress or the courts. Therefore the more power that was concentrated in Washington, the more liberal American society would become; and the stronger the president became, the more liberal still would the country have a chance to be.

However conservative its programs and policies might be, in its devotion to this conception, the Kennedy administration was as liberal as any liberal could have wished. Indeed, it was widely reported that the president's "bible" was a book by a political scientist named Richard Neustadt, who was one of the leading advocates of the strongest possible presidency. And Theodore Sorensen and others implicitly argued that increasing the power of the White House in its struggle against the Congress was the only way to increase the pace and extent of liberal reform.

Nothing, then, could have been more antagonistic to the liberal faith than an attack on the whole idea of centralized power. Coming from Republicans or self-styled conservatives, such an attack would have been as easy to discount as it had been in the past, when it was always discredited as the special pleading of interested elements like big business trying to avoid regulation, or southern segregationists trying to persist in their unconstitutional ways. But coming from a magazine of the Left like *Commentary* and from a writer like Paul Goodman, who was independent almost to a fault, the attack on centralization was impossible to dismiss as an ideological cover for retrograde or selfish interests. When Goodman said that large concentrations of power of every kind were inimical to freedom, he was clearly talking about the freedom of every individual, not about the freedom of corporations (themselves a large concentration of power that he wanted to see broken up). He was talking too about the need for small "human-scale" communities in which the individual counted for something, in which he could participate, to a degree that mattered, in the decisions that affected his life. Communities like those were impossible in a world of concentrated political power—the very world that liberalism had done so much to create and whose perfection in liberal eyes lay in the direction of a greater and greater degree of concentration at the center.

Another liberal dogma—related psychologically if not by strict logical necessity to the belief in centralized power—was the belief in economic growth. The economy had to keep expanding, producing more goods and more jobs and the profits and wages by which the making and the selling and the buying of those goods became possible, and so on around the track again, and again, and again. Conservatives also believed in growth, but to a lesser extent than liberals, since conservatives tended to worry more about unbalanced budgets and inflation and were quietly willing to slow the economy down when it threatened to become "overheated." Here too the Kennedy administration, both in its rhetoric and in its policies, was as liberal as anyone could have wished. In promising in his campaign to "get the country moving again," Kennedy had meant, among other things, that he would stimulate an economy which had grown stagnant toward the end of the

Eisenhower administration; and after an initial hesitation, he eventually made good on this promise in 1963 by instituting a massive tax cut which did indeed have the desired effect.

This liberal devotion to growth was not born out of any great love for material goods or material satisfactions. If anything, it had to contend with a bias against a way of life based on the accumulation of such goods and satisfactions. Because of this bias, many liberals, most prominently John Kenneth Galbraith, opposed the Kennedy tax cut. In 1958, in *The Affluent Society,* Galbraith had argued that American prosperity was dependent on the production and consumption of goods that no one really needed or wanted and that people only coveted because they had been seduced by the wiles of advertising. It was to be expected, then, that Galbraith would be against a policy like the tax cut which was calculated precisely to encourage the making and buying of still more "useless" and "unnecessary" things. But this did not mean that he was against economic growth. On the contrary, what he wanted was growth through government spending—on schools, hospitals, and roads (astonishing as this last item may seem today, when liberalism of the Galbraithian variety is practically synonymous with veneration of mass transit and hatred of the automobile—not merely the tail fins Galbraith despised, but the automobile as a whole).

Commentary published several pieces critical of the authoritarianism implicit in Galbraith's ideas, especially his cavalier assumption that he knew what other people needed and wanted better than they did themselves. In the most extensive of these pieces, the social critic Ernest van den Haag said that Galbraith's proposals, which van den Haag summarized as "produce less, spend less; let the government spend more," amounted to a dangerous "and perhaps in principle immoral" abandonment of "the individualism which is the raison d'être of liberalism in favor of increased government domination." But van den Haag did not challenge the idea that growth was desirable or for that matter inevitable: we are, he said, "already rich beyond the dreams of avarice and our technology promises untold further wealth to all of us."

Oscar Gass, on the other hand, ridiculed the idea that economic growth was possible without the production and consumption of what Arthur Schlesinger, echoing Galbraith, called "gadgets and gimmicks." If we wanted the one, we had to accept the other. But Gass was among the few economists of the day who entertained any doubts about growth. Almost everyone else had fastened onto the ever-expanding "pie" as the answer to the problem of how the poor could be lifted out of poverty without dispossessing the rich and therefore without violent class conflict and bloody revolution. With growth there was enough, and more than enough, to go around for all. Everyone benefited, everyone developed a stake in the system, no one was enriched at the expense of anyone else. Galbraith, Schlesinger, and other liberals might argue that a greater share of the wealth generated by growth could and should be devoted to "public need" as against "private indulgence." But they did not doubt that the contradictions which Marx had said would lead to the destruction of capitalism had been resolved by the laws of economic growth.

Obviously, then, to question the desirability of economic growth was perhaps even more threatening to the liberal faith of the day than challenging the idea of centralized political power. Yet that is precisely what I and some of my political friends began to do. I encouraged several contributors, again including Goodman, to open the issue for discussion, and I even published what may have been the first piece ever to appear in America by a British economist named E. F. Schumacher, who ten or fifteen years later was to become perhaps the most influential critic of growth in the English-speaking world and the most famous exponent of the view that "small is beautiful." Schumacher argued that technology and industrialism were a prime cause of poverty in the underdeveloped world and not the cure they were supposed by all liberals to be. His main polemical target was another close adviser to Kennedy,

W. W. Rostow, whose book *The Stages of Economic Development* represented the most important statement of the universally accepted belief among liberals that the best nonmilitary way to compete with Communism was to help the poorer nations turn themselves into modern industrial societies on the model of the United States. In challenging this view Schumacher was still only talking about the underdeveloped world. But the hostility to industrial civilization which animated his analysis could—and would, with certain minor adjustments—spill over into a critique of the American and Western model itself.

Unlike Goodman's criticisms of centralization, this attitude toward modern industrial civilization was easy to dismiss as retrograde and reactionary in the literal sense of implying a return to an earlier premodern system of economic and social organization. Schumacher was aware of this and actually brought up the charge himself, not so much to deny it as to suggest that it was beside the point. What mattered, he insisted, was not whether this perspective was reactionary but whether the proposals flowing from it would do more good and less harm than the standard liberal approach.

But reactionary or not, the anti-industrial perspective had a great resonance for me, as it was bound to have for anyone of my generation who had been brought up culturally on the suspicion and outright hostility of the Anglo-American literary tradition toward industrialism and all its works. Machines and factories—those "dark Satanic mills," which as William Blake had said as far back as the late eighteenth century were ruining "England's green and pleasant land"—had so consistently been the object of fear and loathing among poets and novelists and critics that the English writer C. P. Snow could characterize the literary tradition of the past two centuries as "Luddite" (after the movement of nineteenth-century craftsmen who responded to the onset of industrialism by trying to smash the machines which were making their own skills obsolete).

As it happened, F. R. Leavis, with whom I had studied for three years at Cambridge and who had influenced my own thinking about literature more than anyone else, launched the most savage attack imaginable on the lectures in which Snow had made this charge and on Snow himself as a novelist. Leavis asked me to publish this attack, and he was furious when I refused on the ground that it had already appeared in England; then Snow, at that time a fairly close friend, grew bitter at the fact that instead of leaping to his defense, I had persuaded Lionel Trilling to write an article on the controversy; and both Leavis and Snow were furious with me, and with Trilling, for the characteristically even-handed account he ultimately produced.

By then the Leavis-Snow controversy had grown into the subject of a worldwide discussion involving several different issues, on some of which Trilling sided with Leavis and on others with Snow. So far as the main point went, Trilling endorsed Leavis's position that the literary tradition was much more complex than an epithet like "Luddite" could suggest. No doubt that was so, and yet however many qualifications a greater rigor might have required, I thought "Luddite" a fair enough generalization and I remained unpersuaded by the Leavis-Trilling counterattack. Certainly, as a student of literature at major universities both in America and England, I had emerged after seven years of intensive reading, largely under the guidance of those very two men, with an idea about the literary tradition very close to Snow's. After all, what else were most of the canonized writers saying— from Blake to Dickens to D. H. Lawrence, from Cooper to Mark Twain to William Faulkner, from Carlyle to Ruskin to Eliot and Leavis himself—if not that industrial civilization was a plague and a curse? (Leavis might seethe at Snow's "simplistic" allegation, and yet I remembered seeing him wince in ostentatious distaste whenever the sound of an airplane or an automobile penetrated into his garden at Cambridge; an American friend and I used to amuse each other by trying to imitate the blissful smile we imagined would cross his face at the equally intrusive lowing of a bull.)

But despite my reservations even as a relatively credulous student about this "Luddite" attitude, it had penetrated my thinking at least to the point where I could never wholeheartedly accept the automatic liberal identification of progress with growth and technological development. On the other hand, I had never taken it seriously as a practical attitude. Though it obviously had a great deal to do with how one felt about life, it seemed altogether irrelevant to the ways of the world, much less to any workable political program. Industrialism and technology were here to stay, and it was simply foolish to think that they could be wished away. It was also foolish to think that they could be governed by any laws other than the laws of growth—growth that was inevitable, inexorable, and without any imaginable limit (and this quite apart from the probable desirability of growth as the only peaceful road to a more prosperous life for everyone on earth). But what intrigued me about Schumacher was the suggestion he offered that a skeptical attitude toward industrialism, technology, and growth might indeed be politically relevant, even today—and not only in the underdeveloped countries, but here in America too.

Like all my political friends, I devoted a good deal of energy in those days to thinking and talking about how to "humanize" industrial society, by which we meant how to keep creating and distributing wealth without at the same time producing and consuming so many of those "gadgets and gimmicks" that, according to Oscar Gass, were the inescapable consequence of economic growth. Did the answer perhaps, then, lie not in the Galbraithian prescription of more government spending on "public needs," but in a slowdown of growth and in a resistance to the liberal idea that any and all technological advances were to be welcomed? Even to entertain so heretical a thought was an act of dissociation from the liberal orthodoxy of the day.

7

A third major issue on which I found myself more and more sharply in conflict with the orthodox liberal view was the issue of race. Here the liberal idea was that the "solution" to the "Negro problem" was an "integrated" society in which whites and blacks would live and work together and mingle freely in every other way, just as whites now did. The only obstacle to the emergence of such a society, it was then thought, lay in discrimination against Negroes. From this it followed that the job of public policy was to do away with such discrimination in every area or institution it touched—schools, employment, housing, and so on. Once the barriers of discrimination were down, an integrated society would naturally emerge.

To me this entire conception of how things stood in America seemed ignorant and naïve. I had no quarrel with the ideal of integration as such, but I strongly doubted that it could ever be realized in the United States. In the South, resistance to desegregation remained fierce, and the cautious policies of the Kennedy administration held out little promise of breaking it down in the foreseeable future. In fact, to judge by Jimmy Baldwin's account of the meeting between Robert Kennedy and the young black activists from the South, the administration was even unable to understand the need for a more vigorous enforcement of court orders to desegregate. Under these circumstances Baldwin and many other Negro intellectuals—including some who had been intimately identified with the ideology and tactics of nonviolent struggle—were beginning to talk about the possibility of taking up arms and continuing this fight by violent means.

One of the earliest intimations of this possibility was the case of Robert F. Williams, who as president of a small chapter of the NAACP in North Carolina had announced that he and his people were arming themselves and would henceforth follow a policy of "self-defense" against the harassments of the Ku Klux Klan. For advocating this policy Williams was expelled from his position by the national office of the NAACP, whose opposition to armed struggle was both principled—that is, they *believed* in peaceful political action—and tactical—that is, they judged that violence could not possibly accomplish anything but the shedding of Negro blood in a situation in which Negroes were a small and relatively powerless minority.

Ultimately, after a complicated series of events culminating in criminal charges against Williams, he fled to Cuba where he made broadcasts denouncing the United States and urging armed insurrection by blacks. Still later, he grew disillusioned with Castro and made his way to Peking and then in the late sixties back to this country. But in 1961, while he was still in North Carolina, I ran a sympathetic piece about him by a young black writer named Julian Mayfield, who used the case as an occasion for an assault on the traditional leadership of the American Negro community —a leadership which had been largely middle-class in origin. This leadership, said Mayfield, "including the newer type like Martin Luther King," was "losing its claim to speak for the masses of Negroes" and might well be replaced in the near future by young men and women like Robert Williams "who have concluded that the only way to win a revolution is to be a revolutionary."

Not surprisingly, the publication of this piece enraged the NAACP, both because of what it said and because a presumably liberal magazine like *Commentary* should have been so far "led astray" as to have given sympathetic attention to the likes of Robert Williams. Roy Wilkins, the president of the NAACP and as such the single most important spokesman for the liberal point of view within the Negro community, denounced Mayfield for resurrecting the attack on the NAACP (which the Communists had launched in the thirties and forties) as merely "reformist" and middle-class; Mayfield responded by accusing Wilkins of "red-baiting," while denying that Robert Williams had any connection with Communism or any "foreign power."

But whether Williams already had a connection with Cuba or only developed one later, it was not on that account that he had caught my interest. If anything I would have been put off by the knowledge of a Communist connection, since I agreed with Wilkins when he said that the Communists had no real interest in "Negro advancement" but were only exploiting the race issue in the hope of inciting "an eruption against the American system." Unquestionably, this had been true of the Communists in the past. Having only recently read through the works of Edmund Wilson, I could still vividly remember his account of how in the thirties, as a young writer sympathetic to the Communists, he had been horrified to discover while covering the so-called Scottsboro Trial that their objective was not to save the young Negroes accused of rape in that case from the electric chair—as the NAACP was trying to do—but on the contrary to make martyrs of them in order to prove that "bourgeois justice" could never work.

Nor did I agree with Mayfield that armed struggle was the answer for blacks. But I did think that Williams and Mayfield might represent the beginnings of a new mood within the Negro community. For they were not the only people talking about violence as a necessary step in what in certain circles was increasingly being called the "Negro revolution," as opposed to the "civil-rights movement." There were also the Black Muslims, who, in addition to advocating armed struggle (or perhaps only prophesying it—it was never clear), preached hatred of the whites and repudiated the whole idea of integration. Not much was known in those days about the Muslims, or about the traditions of black nationalism and separatism which had always competed with integrationism among Negroes and of which the Muslims were at the moment the most visible expression. But there was

a good deal of curiosity about them in the air, thanks largely to
the efforts of their leading spokesman, Malcolm X, who was such
a powerful and interesting personality and so effective a rhetori-
cian that he became irresistible to the television producers and
began participating, as it seemed, in every discussion show ever
broadcast on civil rights or issues of race in general.

One day, while having a drink with Baldwin (many of whose
best early essays, the ones brought together in his first collection,
Notes of a Native Son, had been published in *Commentary* during the
fifties, before I became its editor), I discovered that he too had
grown interested in the Muslims and especially in Malcolm X. Of
course he did not take their program seriously; it was silly to think
that a separate nation could be founded on territory ceded to the
blacks as back pay for all the labor which had been extorted from
their ancestors under slavery. Nor did their theology—a weird
semiliterate version of Islamic doctrine—appeal to him. And certainly, as an open and active homosexual with a taste for the
dissolute life, he was not attracted to their stringently puritanical
moral code which forbade promiscuity, drinking, and smoking,
and insisted on discipline, hard work, thrift, and all the other
"middle-class" virtues that he himself was always excoriating in
his work. Nevertheless he was intrigued by the Muslims, and
when I proposed that he write an article about them for *Commentary,* he jumped enthusiastically at the idea. Then, as if to prove
that his sympathetic interest in the Muslims did not extend to
their moral code, or that his contempt for the business world did
not include its tendency to sharp commercial practice, he violated
his understanding with me by selling the article he eventually
wrote to *The New Yorker* for a good deal more money than I could
have paid him. It was called "The Fire Next Time," and it created
a huge sensation first as an article and then as a book.

Using the Muslims as an occasion, Baldwin evoked a sense of
the rage, the bitterness, the hostility simmering below the surface
in the Negro community and warned of the apocalyptic consequences these feelings might soon bring to American life. In the

years to come, and especially after the riots of the mid-sixties, the notion of "black rage" was to become so common that one could be taken aback by the sight of a smile on a Negro face. Snarling almost became *de rigueur* in the manners of blacks toward whites —a new form of proper etiquette. And it also became a useful political tactic'(Tom Wolfe would call it "mau-mauing") in dealing with politicians, foundation executives, and white liberals in general. But in the early sixties, when "The Fire Next Time" was first published, most white liberals were startled by the idea that Negroes were angry and might well erupt into violence if "something" were not done soon.

One reason they were startled was that they knew very little about Negroes. For all their ideological fervor over integration, very few had ever lived among Negroes, and they tended toward benign stereotypes in their conception of what the black community was like. Such stereotypes formed the basis of much well-intentioned propaganda aimed at reassuring whites who were worried about what might happen to their children in integrated schools or to their neighborhoods when Negroes began moving in. Consequently what was always being stressed was how *nice* Negroes were if you really got to know them. Now suddenly the Negro, victimized and virtuous, was being succeeded by the menacing black, both in nomenclature and in style, and it was Baldwin who as much as anyone else introduced the new type to the white liberal consciousness.

Baldwin still spoke in "The Fire Next Time" as a believer in integration—he even defined the ideal world as one in which all consciousness of color would entirely disappear—and he held out the hope that white America, and indeed the West as a whole, might still repent in time to avoid the destruction it so richly deserved for centuries of oppressing the blacks. In this sense, while "The Fire Next Time" in its sympathetic portrayal of the Muslims could be read as a portent of a revolt against integrationism within the black community, it could also be taken as a reaffirmation of the integrationist faith and a call for a rededicated effort to realize the integrationist dream.

A great many people did in fact take it that way, but I was not one of them. It was clear to me then and it soon became clear even to Baldwin and his admirers, who were at first reluctant to face the fact, that for all his talk about transcending color through the power of love, integration had ceased to be the answer for him and that black nationalism or separatism now appeared to be the only imaginable alternative.

That this should have happened to James Baldwin of all people was astonishing in itself and a very ominous portent indeed. For as a writer, Baldwin, more than any other Negro intellectual with the possible exception of Ralph Ellison, represented the living embodiment of the integrationist ideal. The subject matter of almost everything he wrote was Negro life, and he treated it from the inside, with intimacy, authority, and authenticity. But his prose style and his sensibility in general owed more to Henry James than to any indigenously black influence. Nor was it only in the rhythms and cadences of his work that Baldwin was a Jamesian writer. Henry James once told his brother: "I have not the least hesitation in saying that I aspire to write in such a way that it would be impossible to an outsider to say whether I am at a given moment an American writing about England or an Englishman writing about America. . . ."

Something analogous to this was the case with Baldwin when he was writing about Negroes and whites—so much so that when his early essays began to appear in *Partisan Review* and *Commentary* in the late forties, my friends and I at Columbia fell to wondering whether or not he was a Negro. Surely only a Negro could know that much, but surely no Negro could write with that degree of detachment. Yet it was this very combination of qualities that accounted for the enthusiasm over Baldwin in the offices of *Partisan Review* and *Commentary*: he was a Negro intellectual in almost exactly the same sense as most of them were Jewish intellectuals. As they had grown up in Brooklyn or the Bronx, so he had grown up in Harlem; as their experience of an immigrant Jewish milieu had shaped their sense of life and supplied them with material to write about, so had his; and—this was the crucial connection—as they had moved out of that milieu into the broader world of Western culture, he had too, taking his bearings as a writer not from ancestral ethnic sources but from the traditions of the literary mainstream.

That so thoroughly integrated a Negro writer should be drawn to black nationalism or should begin flirting with black separatism was simply amazing, and doubly so to anyone who knew from personal acquaintance how meager Baldwin's contacts with the Negro community had become and what a small proportion of Negroes he numbered among his many friends.

Yet I admired him for this display of loyalty to his origins and to his people. I thought it honorable and, given my awareness of how much it went against his grain, a courageous stand for him to take. I did not, however, have much sympathy for black nationalism, and *spiritually* courageous though Baldwin seemed to me to be, I thought "The Fire Next Time" lacked a commensurate intellectual courage in failing to follow the logic of its own vision to the very end. To the extent that I shared in that vision, this is what I set out to do in a piece for *Commentary* entitled "My Negro Problem—and Ours."

As I had given Baldwin the idea for "The Fire Next Time," he repaid me with the idea for "My Negro Problem—and Ours." In the course of an angry conversation with him over his having sold to another magazine a piece which I had suggested and commissioned, I talked a bit about my own experience as a boy growing up in a racially mixed neighborhood in Brooklyn. He listened with great intentness, and then urged me very forcefully to write it all down, even though the stories I had to tell did not reflect particularly well on the Negroes I had known in school and on the streets, and even though the conclusion to which I was drawn pointed in a very different direction from the one he himself was heading in.

Nothing I did either as an editor or as a writer in the early sixties was as radical as the act of putting those stories and that conclusion down on paper and then publishing it all in *Commentary*. And they were radical in a way that could by no stretch of the imagination be thought consistent with prevailing liberal opinion. They were not, that is, an example of "liberalism in a hurry" or of a more militant commitment to common goals. On the contrary: they were an outrage to liberal ideas and liberal pieties alike. Liberals thought of Negroes as persecuted and oppressed, but the stories I told were all stories of how I and other white children had been persecuted and oppressed by the Negro children among whom we lived and with whom we went to school: how we had been repeatedly beaten up, robbed, and in general hated, terrorized, and humiliated. Liberals thought that if whites and Negroes could only be brought to live together, they would soon develop mutual understanding and sympathy, but I said that my own experience had convinced me that living together only exacerbated the hatred that existed—and existed not because of ignorance and bigotry alone but for good historical and psychological reasons—on both sides of the racial divide. Liberals thought that integration was inevitable, but I said that the combination of white resistance (including the resistance from liberals themselves that was becoming manifest now that the civil-rights movement had shifted its focus from desegregating the South to integrating the schools and neighborhoods of the North) and black impatience signified that blood might well run in the streets before integration ever came, if indeed it ever would.

Thus far my account was on the whole consistent with Baldwin's. I was even able to draw on him for corroboration when I argued that the hatred of whites I had encountered in Negroes, and suffered from as a child at their hands, was neither peculiar to my neighborhood nor an accidental condition. "We have it on the authority of James Baldwin," I wrote, "that all Negroes hate whites." In itself this idea was not a serious affront to liberal opinion. To be sure, liberal opinion in those days tended to be

wary of generalizations of any kind about Negroes or any other
minority group. ("Generalizing" usually meant "blaming" the
entire group for an unlovely trait—like the love of money in Jews
or laziness in Negroes—that only a few allegedly possessed.) But
stated in a certain way, to mean that people suffering from persecution will understandably respond by hating their oppressors,
the proposition that all Negroes hated whites would have been
acceptable—a bit uneasily but acceptable still—to liberal opinion.
That is not, however, the way I stated it. Naturally I acknowledged that the experience of oppression was a prime source of
Negro hatred; again drawing on Baldwin I spoke of "the sense of
entrapment that poisons the soul of the Negro with hatred for the
white man whom he knows to be his jailer." But drawing on my
own experience, I also raised the question of how the Negroes
among whom I had grown up during the Depression could have
regarded the whites across the street and around the corner—all
of whom were "downtrodden people themselves breaking their
own necks to eke out a living"—as jailers. Had I and the other
white children been seen as jailers to our Negro classmates in
school? If so, it could not have been because we were locking
them up or keeping them down; if anything, it was the other way
around:

> *We* went home every day for a lunch of spinach and potatoes; *they*
> roamed around during lunch hour, munching on candy bars. In
> winter *we* had to wear itchy woolen hats and mittens and cumber-
> some galoshes; *they* were bareheaded and loose as they pleased.
> *We* rarely played hooky, or got into serious trouble in school, for
> all our street-corner bravado; *they* were defiant, forever staying
> out (to do what delicious things?), forever making disturbances
> in class and in the halls, forever being sent to the principal and
> returning uncowed. But most important of all, they were *tough;*
> beautifully, enviably tough, not giving a damn for anyone or any-
> thing. To hell with the teacher, the truant officer, the cop; to hell
> with the whole of the adult world that held *us* in its grip and that
> we never had the courage to rebel against except sporadically
> and in petty ways.

What I went on to suggest, on the basis of this experience, was that Negroes hated whites not only—or perhaps not even primarily—for social and political reasons, but also for psychological and spiritual ones. It was not only oppression but repression—the repression, that is, of their anarchic impulses—for which they blamed and hated the whites.

In this version, the idea that all Negroes hated whites was bound to affront liberal opinion. For one thing, it shifted the emphasis away from politics and economics, which was where most liberals wanted the discussion of race to remain. Worse still, it came uncomfortably close to saying that Negroes were by nature more primitive and more instinctual than whites—a notion traditionally associated with racist myths and once used to justify both slavery and Jim Crow. No matter that I clearly disavowed any such implication, or that many Negroes, including Baldwin, were (in a process that would soon become bewilderingly familiar) beginning to resurrect this and other traditionally racist allegations and claiming them as virtues and even as marks of black superiority. Thus, for example, the idea that Negroes "had rhythm"—once derided as racist because it seemed to suggest that Negroes were less civilized than whites—had only recently been turned on its head by Baldwin in his novel *Another Country*. There, in a memorable passage, he had sympathetically described the feelings of a white character watching a group of Negroes on the dance floor and wishing that he could be on "the kind of terms with his own body" that came so naturally to all of them; alas, however, being white, he never would. But as a (white Jewish) correspondent sternly declared in a letter to *Commentary*, the fact that a "brilliant writer, Negro," was saying such things "should not constitute an invitation to a less talented writer, liberal and Jewish [namely me], to answer with a reminiscence of his own." A reminiscence, added the Negro playwright Lorraine Hansberry—who in *A Raisin in the Sun* had successfully exploited all the conventionally pious integrationist ideas about Negroes—that amounted to a "recitation of perfectly old-fashioned racist motifs."

If it was an affront to liberal opinion to say in the way that I did that all Negroes hated whites, the parallel assertion I made that all whites were "twisted and sick" in their feelings about Negroes was not so much an affront as a threat. But here the response was more complicated. Obviously, to anyone who believed, as most liberals passionately did, in integration, the observation (taken by them as an accusation) that whites were fundamentally and universally antagonistic toward blacks would not only seem personally insulting and call for indignant denials on that ground alone; if true, it would also constitute a virtually insuperable obstacle to the achievement of integration and would therefore have to be denied on that ground as well. And so indeed it was by a substantial portion of the hundreds of people who wrote to *Commentary* or discussed "My Negro Problem—and Ours" in other papers and magazines. (A variant of denying the truth of the idea was to call it irrelevant and to castigate me for bringing it up: whatever the feelings of whites might be, according to this line of defense, the Constitution demanded integration and would have to be obeyed.)

But there were other liberal integrationists, most of them Negroes, who, unlike Lorraine Hansberry, saw in this particular section of the article a valuable polemical tool. The most prominent of these people was the psychologist Kenneth Clark, whose commitment to integrationism was lifelong and who had even performed a series of experiments which the Supreme Court cited in its 1954 desegregation decision as scientific proof that segregated schools resulted in damage to the black children attending them.

These experiments, incidentally, were later widely and persuasively criticized by other psychologists as faulty and there was also much unhappiness among constitutional scholars over the use of such data, faulty or not, to buttress a constitutional argument. Suppose, they asked, it could be shown by other and sounder experiments that segregation had no bad effects on the children or even that it really had good ones; would that make segregation constitutional?

But all that is another story. The point I want to make here about Kenneth Clark is that he was happy to see a white liberal confessing to feelings about Negroes that had previously been thought confined to racists and bigots. Not only could this serve as an instrument for playing on liberal guilt—something Kenneth Clark clearly relished doing—but even more importantly it worked to buttress the argument I alluded to earlier in another context that the racial situation in the North was essentially no different from the one in the South. Negroes were segregated in the North just as they were in the South, and according to this argument it was racism in both cases that accounted for this phenomenon. In the South, racism operated openly through law (*de jure*) but the *de facto* segregation in the North was no less real and not even—as was often imagined—the product of a multiplicity of social and economic factors coming together to produce an unintended result. If one looked closely, one found that the distinction between *de jure* and *de facto* segregation began to disappear. School boards, for example, gerrymandered district lines to make sure that some schools would be all white and others all black; was this not a case of legally created segregation and therefore requiring to be dealt with in exactly the same way and by exactly the same measures as were needed in the South?

When anyone tried to counter this analysis by refusing to acknowledge that a body like the New York City board of education, composed of people with impeccable liberal credentials who had moreover always been in the forefront of the fight for civil rights, could have been guilty of segregationist intent, Clark could say that they were indeed guilty and doubly so: guilty of the intent as shown by the results of their policies, and guilty of cowardice and dishonesty in refusing to face up to the fact.

In 1964, about a year after "My Negro Problem" appeared, I brought a group together under the auspices of *Commentary* to discuss the subject of "Liberalism and the Negro." By then the tendencies which had only just made an inchoate appearance in the earlier discussion were hardening, and Clark now went so far as to call liberalism an "affliction" to the Negro, an "insidious adversary" which because of its "hypocrisy" was much more difficult to deal with than the "out-and-out bigotry" of the racists of the South.

This particular attack on liberalism was not an attack on liberal ideals; liberal opinion in the first half of the decade remained committed, as did Clark himself, to the goal of an integrated society. It was liberal individuals and institutions—in his contribution to "Liberalism and the Negro" he specifically mentioned college administrators, school teachers, social workers, and labor unions—who were the target; and what Clark was accusing them of was a failure to live up to their own stated (or as he unfortunately put it, "verbalized") ideals. The accusation was meant as a goad, and it was also meant to justify a new strategy involving new measures of coercion to bring about integration, specifically preferential treatment and "benign quotas."

That I was by then more than willing to go along with policies like preferential treatment, and that they seemed promising to me, was a measure of the change in the direction of my own thinking about radical measures to overcome the Negro's inherited disability since I had written "My Negro Problem—and Ours." (In another ten years, as I will eventually have occasion to describe, I would find myself switching sides on such policies with the liberals who had at first been so appalled by them.) For in that earlier essay I had concluded that neither integration nor black separatism could lead us out of the "nightmare" of racial hatred in the United States, and that the only way out was by a literal application of Baldwin's idea of transcending color through love; and that, I said, "means not integration, it means assimilation, it means—let the brutal word come out—miscegenation . . .". I did not argue that "the wholesale merger of the two races" could be pursued programmatically or that it was an immediately feasible solution. But I did say that it was the only way that color could ever become irrelevant as a political factor in America.

Neither Kenneth Clark, nor almost anyone else for that matter, including most of the people who were enthusiastic about "My Negro Problem" for one reason or another, could go along with this conclusion. For some it was repugnant because it seemed to confirm that standard racist charge, made by black racists like the Muslims as well as white ones, and always heatedly denied as a smear, that the secret goal of the integrationist movement was precisely a "mongrelization" of the races. This did not bother the critic Hilton Kramer, who wrote, "In this matter the most reactionary southerners have often been more honest . . . than enlightened liberal opinion that tacitly preserves the separate-but-equal ideal when it comes to sexual mingling of the races while promoting integration in schools, buses, and other social facilities." But on this point Kramer was a lone exception. For others the idea of miscegenation was "utopian" and therefore a distraction from the real political business at hand, and for still others it was unacceptable because it involved the judgment that there was no reason why Negroes should wish to survive as a distinct group.

Even if I had said nothing on this point, that judgment would still have been logically entailed by my characterization of the "wholesale merger of the two races" as "the most desirable alternative for everyone concerned." But true to my grim determination not to shrink from any implication of the analysis, however distasteful or offensive it might be, I raised the issue explicitly. And to exacerbate an already delicate situation, I did so in a way that was bound to offend Jews as well as Negroes. "In thinking about the Jews," I wrote:

> I have often wondered whether their survival as a distinct group was worth one hair on the head of a single infant. Did the Jews have to survive so that six million innocent people should one day be burned in the ovens of Auschwitz? It is a terrible question and no one, not God himself, could ever answer it to my satisfaction. And

when I think about the Negroes in America and about the image of integration as a state in which the Negroes would take their rightful place as another of the protected minorities in a pluralistic society, I wonder whether they really believe in their hearts that such a state can actually be attained, and if so *why* they should wish to survive as a distinct group. I think I know why the Jews once wished to survive (though I am less certain as to why we still do): they not only believed that God had given them no choice, but they were tied to a memory of past glory and a dream of imminent redemption. What does the American Negro have that might correspond to this? His past is a stigma, his color is a stigma, and his vision of the future is the hope of erasing the stigma by making color irrelevant, by making it disappear as a fact of consciousness.

I wrote these words early in 1963, when there was very little of a positive nature being said by anyone about the culture and history of the Negro people. Integrationist enthusiasm was still at its height and the emphasis of integrationism in that phase of its development was on the horrors of Negro life in the past and of life in the ghettos of the present. A lonely Negro voice like Ralph Ellison's or a white one like that of Ellison's friend the critic Stanley Edgar Hyman might be raised to protest against this reduction of an entire people to the status of pitiable victim and the concomitant dismissal of their complex response to oppression in their art, in their religion, in their special forms of social organization, as though all this amounted to nothing. "Watch out there, Jack," wrote Ellison in answer to a 1963 piece by Irving Howe which had been guilty of doing just that, "there're people living under here." Ellison never attacked "My Negro Problem" in public, but I used to run into him fairly often at parties in those days, and one time he laced into me for my attitude toward black culture while making fun of the idea that wholesale miscegenation, assuming it were even to occur, could lead to the disappearance of color. All it would do, he said, would be to increase the number of "colored" children (a point, I had to admit, which had never occurred to me before).

As a great admirer of Ellison's novel *Invisible Man,* I would perhaps have taken his criticisms of "My Negro Problem" more to heart if not for the fact that he had always been cold toward me personally. That this should have been so was a tribute to the depth of his hostile feelings, since very few writers are able to resist liking anyone who admires their work as much as I admired *Invisible Man*. For my part I found Ellison the man stuffy and pompous; he was in truth amazingly like one of the characters he himself had satirized for those very qualities in *Invisible Man*. He also struck me as a Negro equivalent of certain prissy German Jews I knew (*yeckes,* in the derogatory Yiddish term for the type) who were forever preening themselves on their superior refinement, education, and culture. Once I even heard him declare in a statement that could easily have issued from the lips of a typical *yecke* but was, as with so much about Ellison's personality, very hard to square with the author of *Invisible Man* : "As for me, I have values."

Today, looking back at this entire period, I am inclined to think that Ellison's position—which combined a truly stubborn insistence on the richness of Negro life, past and present, with an equally stubborn refusal to take this as a reason for opposing integration or supporting black separatism—was much sounder and indeed more honorable than Baldwin's. And one of the things that was most honorable about it was that it spoke, as he said, out of "an American Negro tradition . . . which abhors as obscene any trading on one's own anguish for gain or sympathy." At the time, I took Ellison's invocation of this tradition as a sly attack on Baldwin, and I must confess that I suspected him of envying Baldwin, who was the only other Negro writer in America in his class and who was rising to a higher point of public esteem while he himself was bogged down in a battle to complete his second novel—a battle he had already been fighting for a decade (and which he would go on fighting unsuccessfully for another decade or two to come). Possibly there was an element of this in Ellison's reserve—to use the mildest of the various terms which might apply—toward *The Fire Next Time* and Baldwin's position in general. But as I see the matter now, it strikes me that envy, if it was present at all, was probably the least important element in Ellison's attitude, which must have been one of frustrated anguish over the spreading of ideas about the issue of race that he rightly believed dangerous and damaging to Negroes and whites alike and to the future relations between them.

8

Still, so far as the general attitude toward black culture was concerned, a point of view much closer to Ellison's was just then beginning to come into vogue. On some issues, proponents of this point of view soon went much further than he would have wished—as when they began calling the English language "white" and demanding that the slang of the ghetto streets be taught as "black English" in the schools to Negro children instead. But they also went beyond aesthetics—that is, the affirmation that Negroes had produced valuable works of art, and even entire modes of expression like jazz and blues—into culture in the broadest sense; and here Ellison seemed to approve.

For example, he was to join in attacking a report on the Negro family written in 1965 by Daniel Patrick Moynihan, then a young assistant secretary of labor in the Johnson administration. The Moynihan Report, basing itself on an analysis of census data, said that an increasing number of Negro children were being raised in fatherless families, either because they were illegitimate or because their fathers had deserted them, and it went on to suggest various measures the government might take to deal with this problem. Moynihan, a liberal who understandably thought that he had made a contribution to the civil-rights movement by establishing a case for government action more intensive than the mere enforcement of formal legal equality and integration, was flabbergasted to discover himself becoming the target of vituperative abuse from the Negro community. He was charged (in a phrase later used by William Ryan, a radical white sociologist, as the title of a book) with "blaming the victim" by attributing the "pathologies" of Negro life—the high rates of poverty, male unemployment, crime, functional illiteracy, welfare—to the deficiencies of the Negro family. To be sure, he had explicitly disavowed any such interpretation of the report. He had also emphatically placed the "blame" for the condition of the Negro family on the heritage of slavery and discrimination and on a poorly designed system of welfare which in effect encouraged Negro fathers to desert their families. This was why the main proposal he offered was the adoption of a family allowance that would benefit not only fatherless children but also children with fathers living at home.

Yet neither this proposal, nor anything else in the Moynihan Report, could protect it from the furies of the new climate of opinion among Negroes (and soon enough, among their white liberal supporters). It was a climate shaped by the spirit of "black pride" and it involved an aggressive assertion of the worth and even the superior value of everything black people—for it was now, and in association with this new spirit, that the name "Negro" began to be replaced by the mandatory epithet "black" —had ever done. Under the dictates of the new spirit, discussion was required to interpret the family, or any other institution or pattern of behavior among blacks, as a creative response to external conditions of oppression. Looked at in this way, the "fatherless" family became a family with surrogate fathers, or a family whose children, far from being neglected (as the "white" perspective seemed to imply), were lovingly and responsibly tended by mothers, grandmothers, aunts, sisters, siblings.

That Moynihan should have been so surprised by the storm

over his report came as something of a surprise to me. After all, only two years earlier, in 1963, he had collaborated with Nathan Glazer on a book entitled *Beyond the Melting Pot,* which was one of the earliest challenges to the idea that ethnic differences were disappearing in America and were destined to disappear altogether as the various immigrant groups were assimilated more and more thoroughly into the general American culture.

Using New York City as a case study, Glazer and Moynihan tried to demonstrate that the Jews, the Irish, the Italians, the Negroes, and the Puerto Ricans, although "Americanized" to various degrees, were at the same time stubbornly maintaining a good many of their distinctive ethnic characteristics. *Beyond the Melting Pot* was written as a piece of neutral (or "value-free," as this style used to be known) social science, neither approving nor disapproving the persistence of ethnic identification, except to the extent of pointing out how this or that ethnic characteristic helped or hindered a particular group in bettering its economic and social position. From this perspective, the "matriarchal" Negro family certainly seemed to be a hindrance. But Moynihan, more than most liberals in those days when ethnicity was generally regarded as a mark of primitivism and backwardness, understood that getting ahead economically and socially—becoming, that is, "middle-class"—was not the only objective, or even the most important one, for an ethnic group. There was also a spiritual objective which took the form of a demand that the distinctive culture of the group be accorded an equality of respect to match the equality of opportunity demanded in the realm of material conditions. This spiritual objective was now coming to the fore so powerfully among blacks that it threatened to override the material goals of the community.

Anyone unable to understand the force of spiritual factors—a category of person which included most American intellectuals who, though preoccupied professionally with spiritual matters, all seemed to be materialists in the sense of taking it for granted that economic considerations always played the decisive role in social and political affairs—would naturally think it perverse to the point of madness for a group to allow such spiritual factors to prevail over its economic interests. But Moynihan was not a materialist in this sense and he was fully capable of appreciating the power of ethnic assertion once it was unleashed. The trouble was that he had failed to anticipate that it would be unleashed in this particular case at him and at his expense.

By the time the storm broke over his head, he and I were close friends, having met shortly after I became the editor of *Commentary*. Irving Kristol, during a brief stint in the late fifties as editor of *The Reporter*, had run a piece by Moynihan and had recommended him to me as a writer I might be able to use. On the lookout for new talent, I telephoned him. But before I even had a chance to discuss possible contributions, he announced that he had been a great admirer of mine ever since reading in an interview that I had insisted as a condition of getting married that my wife-to-be provide me with a study furnished and decorated all in brown. "I appreciate the sentiment," I said, "but we've had a baby since then and we couldn't spare the room, so I don't have that study anymore." To which he replied in a tone of high indignation befitting the great deceit by which he had been victimized: "You don't? Well, to hell with you then!"

How could I resist this? I couldn't and I didn't, and I found that I liked him even more the first time we actually met a few weeks later over a drink at Le Moal in New York. In a pattern with which I was to become so familiar over the next fifteen years and more that by now I could almost choreograph it, he asked me whether I thought he ought to take a job he had just been offered by Arthur Goldberg, then Kennedy's secretary of labor. I had the distinct impression that in consulting me, as he was no doubt consulting many others, he was not trying to figure out what to do but was rather looking for reassurance over a decision he had already reached; but at the same time I also had the impression that he was himself not entirely aware that this was what he was up to. Be that as it may, if he was looking for reassurance, he had come to the right place. As I was so often to do in the future (in contrast to so many of his other friends), I enthusiastically advised him to take the job. Why not? He had already worked in government, in the office of Averell Harriman during Harriman's term as governor of New York, and though he clearly possessed a rich intellectual gift, he just as clearly had a feel for politics and government that was very rare among intellectuals in America.

Intellectuals who were political in this practical way were a familiar phenomenon in England. There were, for example, R. H. S. Crossman, C. A. R. Crosland, and Denis Healey—all future cabinet ministers and all talented intellectuals by any definition of that term (they were all, by the way, past or future contributors to *Commentary* as well). But for all the journalistic talk that went on then and would go on even more after the assassination of Kennedy, the only members of the Kennedy administration of comparable intellectual caliber were Schlesinger, who was serving as a White House aide (but not, one gathered, with much say in the framing of policy), and Galbraith, who was ambassador to India, an important assignment in those days but (according to an unkind quip just then making the rounds) far enough away from Washington to keep him from exerting any influence.

To be sure, Schlesinger and Galbraith were not the only academics in the Kennedy administration, but the others tended to be technocrats or specialists. There were also many other people in the administration with quick minds and sharp perception, but they were not intellectuals in the sense of combining a great facility in the handling of ideas with the learning and the ability to see those ideas critically within a broad cultural and historical context.

In the dearth of intellectuals within its councils, the Kennedy administration was no different from previous administrations, but the explanation I offered a while back in discussing this matter—that American politics has generally been so pragmatic that it has rarely needed the services of specialists in ideological conflict—was only one-sided. The other side was the endemic indifference of most intellectuals to the kind of nonideological, practical, pragmatic political life going on in America. Because it was a kind of politics which intellectuals found dull or at most a ritual charade involving nothing more elevated than the division of spoils, they did not as a group ever develop a feel for it, a sense of its rules, its complexities, its nuances, a sense of how the game was played and how the system worked. As a historian whose passion was the New Deal, Schlesinger did have such a feel and so, to a lesser extent, did Galbraith. But as I now knew from the piece Moynihan had just written for *Commentary,* in this respect neither of them could remotely compare with him.

From the point of view of a magazine for intellectuals, the subject of Moynihan's piece could not have been less promising: the condition of the Democratic party in New York State. For if national politics could scarcely engage the interest of intellectuals, local politics was considered almost entirely beneath notice and beneath contempt, a mixture of corruption, venality, and mediocrity with no redeeming value whatever. Yet not only did Moynihan not share in this attitude; he exposed it (but with good humor) as an expression of ethnic bias, a weapon variously used by WASPs and Jews in a war to overthrow and replace the Irish and Italian Catholics who had at a certain moment seized control of New York politics and who wielded their power in a manner easily subject to ridicule and moral attack by their social and intellectual "betters." Only an intellectual would have been capable of this analysis, but no intellectual I had ever met would have known enough, or cared enough, about practical politics to be capable of writing it.

But Moynihan was Irish and Catholic, and Tammany seemed to be in his bones. He knew what the inside of a clubhouse was like, he loved and was amused in an altogether unpatronizing way by the types who spent their lives there, he understood how mayors and aldermen and district chiefs went about the business

of getting elected and governing huge heterogeneous cities. He
knew what their achievements were (they could keep the ethnic
peace and they could get a subway system built); and he knew
what their limitations were (to quote the wonderful crack again:
"The extent of [DeSapio's] *ideological* commitment may be measured by his pronouncement to the Holy Name Society Communion Breakfast of the New York Sanitation Department that 'there
is no Mother's Day behind the Iron Curtain' ").

But in addition to being Irish and Catholic, Moynihan was also
a college professor and an intellectual who could move as easily
and naturally among the "reformers" as among the "bosses."
Equipped with this extraordinary doubleness of vision, and this
singular mix of experience and talent, he could write about
American political life in a way no practical politician was able to
do, and at the same time he could act effectively within the world
of politics and government to a degree that no other intellectual
of his generation could begin to match. He owed it to himself,
then, to enter that world whenever the right opportunity came
along, and the job offer from Arthur Goldberg at the Labor
Department was clearly such an opportunity.

It was precisely against this background that I was later surprised to find him so bewildered by the angry reaction to his 1965
report on the Negro family. If it had happened to anyone else, he
would no doubt have understood it immediately as a sign that, for
better or for worse, a new stage had been reached in the development of ethnic consciousness and ethnic politicking among
blacks. Indeed I told him all this, and he was very happy to hear
it. But so wounded was he by the attacks—how could anyone
think such things of him, let alone say them?—that no sooner
would he manage to detach himself long enough to get a solid
conceptual grip on the whole business than he would forget and
fall to brooding again. (Many times over the years he would turn
to me and ask: "Would you mind explaining once more what all
that nastiness was about?")

Naturally when something similar had happened to me two years earlier as a result of writing "My Negro Problem," I did not behave any more coolly and analytically than Moynihan would in his own turn, though my response had differed from his in taking the form of anger rather than anguish. I was infuriated by the vituperative letters I received, all of which seemed to me products of stupidity or incomprehension or straightforward ill will. But the most serious charge came not in a letter or even by way of a direct comment on the article. It was in a speech given by a young black activist named Stokely Carmichael in Philadelphia where, according to a report in one of the New York papers, he had called me a "racist."

By now, of course, the word racist is used so promiscuously that it no longer carries any meaning or even any sting. But in the early sixties it was understood to have a precise meaning and it possessed an enormous force, second only to the word "Nazi." A racist was a person who believed that some races were genetically inferior to others. To accuse someone of harboring this belief was not only to accuse him of accepting a discredited theory —that was the least of it—but to go for the moral jugular, to try to wipe him out.

I have never done any research into the question, but my impression is that I may have been the first white liberal to have the term "racist" flung at him in the public prints by a "responsible" Negro spokesman. Calling Stokely Carmichael "responsible" may seem odd, given the subsequent course he was to follow as a floating revolutionist and agitator who seemed to turn up whenever violence threatened or erupted in almost any black ghetto in the country. But in 1963, at the time he called me a racist, he was still mainly associated with SNCC, whose rhetorical style had always been as gentle as its tactics had been nonviolent. (In the late fifties one of the trademarks of the SNCC "kids," and of their white counterparts in the earliest days of the New Left as well, was a soft voice and an exaggeratedly sweet manner.)

If I had been capable of the kind of detachment I was later to urge on Moynihan in his own time of travail, I would have realized that the resort to rhetorical violence by a young Negro of Stokely Carmichael's political background was a portent of things to come; and indeed SNCC as an organization was on the point of turning from nonviolence to militant nationalism (though for some reason it never changed its name, and even after it began preaching revolutionary violence in the late sixties it went on incongruously being known by an acronym that stood for "Student Non-Violent Coordinating Committee"). But I was not detached; I was angry; and I decided to sue Carmichael for libel.

I had, I thought, a good case, and a good cause too. The charge of racism was self-evidently false: literally the last thing any racist would advocate was a wholesale merger of the two races. Since Carmichael had to have known this, he was clearly giving voice to a lie. And since my reputation and even my livelihood were at stake here, I stood to be damaged professionally.

That was my case. As for the cause I wanted to further, it was to establish a minimum standard of civility in the public discussion of difficult and sensitive issues. Why should such reckless and damaging and wounding language be permitted to foul and corrupt the intellectual and political air? If the most vicious smears could be hurled with impunity at anyone who tried to speak his mind with candor on a matter of such overriding importance as the relations between the races, there would soon be no candor at all, and all serious discussion might well be interdicted.

I realized that as a writer and an editor I had an interest in weakening the libel laws, not in invoking them. And I also knew that suing a prominent young Negro with a record of heroic action in the South would not exactly make me popular. On the contrary, going after Carmichael would run afoul of the taboo which was subtly being established against saying anything critical of Negroes, and the insidious practice of judging them by different—that is, lower—standards than were ordinarily applied to whites.

Given this taboo, I had to expect to run into trouble if I went ahead with my decision to bring action against Carmichael. Nevertheless I was determined to do so, and to make sure that no one misunderstood my intention, I hit upon the idea of asking only for a dollar in damages.

It was, I still think, a good idea—not just the dollar in damages but the suit itself—and for all I know, it would have had a civilizing effect on public discussion in the turbulent years ahead. But I never had the chance to find out because the lawyers I consulted talked me out of it. They all thought I had a good case, but they explained that libel suits always go on for years, taking up enormous amounts of time and energy, that money is generally the only reward one can expect for winning, and—since I was determined not to ask for damages—that I had nothing to gain in exchange for everything I stood to lose. So far as the issue of public principle was concerned, all the lawyers I talked to were unimpressed and a few were amused at my unworldliness in imagining that any principle could be established by such a case.

The phenomenon of the double standard, to which the poet and critic Kenneth Rexroth had given the name "crow-Jimism," and which much later came to be known as "liberal racism" (that was the term my wife Midge Decter was to use in an article about the looting that took place in New York during the great power failure of 1977), had been much on my mind while working on "My Negro Problem." In fact, I brought it up explicitly and pointed to it as the other side of the coin of white liberal retreat and another indication of the "sick feelings" which, I was arguing, all whites harbored toward Negroes. As examples of such "crow-Jimism," I cited the "broken-down white boys . . . who go to Harlem in search of sex or simply to brush up against something that looks like primitive vitality, and who are so often punished by the Negroes they meet for crimes that they would have been the last ever to commit and of which they themselves have been as sorry victims as any of the Negroes who take it out on them." I also spoke of "the writers and intellectuals and artists who romanticize Negroes and pander to them, assuming a guilt that is not properly theirs." And finally there were "all the white liberals who permit Negroes to blackmail them into adopting a double standard of moral judgment, and who lend themselves—again assuming the responsibility for crimes they never committed—to cunning and contemptuous exploitation by Negroes they employ or try to befriend."

In its implicit assumption that Negroes were not the equals of whites any more than children were the equals of adults, this complex of attitudes *did* merit the epithet "racist"; the idea that Negroes were more primitive or, alternatively, more childlike than whites, and therefore not to be held fully responsible for their actions, was indeed one of the more benign forms that racism had traditionally taken in the South. Now, just when it was finally being driven out of the culture of the South, it seemed to have migrated to the North, and to be finding a new home there in the most unlikely place: the hearts and minds of white liberals who, paradoxically, were keeping it alive under the sincere impression that they were wiping it out.

9

This northward migration of the racial culture of the South was perhaps an inevitable accompaniment of the actual physical migration of so many Negroes from South to North. But it was also helped along by another actual physical migration, very tiny by comparison and yet very significant in its own special way: the convergence of southern writers and intellectuals from all over the South into New York and specifically into positions of power and influence in the journalistic world.

Hardly anyone noticed this development. Even after it had matured in the mid-sixties, the regnant cliché was that the literary world and the publishing and communications industries were being run by the "Jewish establishment." Truman Capote, himself a southerner by origin, once went so far as to claim that the "Jewish establishment" not only controlled all the magazines but exercised this control in the "Jewish" interest, pushing and puffing and promoting only Jewish writers and preventing anyone else from coming to public attention. He did not explain how he had become such a famous novelist himself under these adverse conditions, though Gore Vidal—a southerner by ancestry if not by birth—who made a similar charge accounted for his own case as an exception: the "Jewish establishment," he said, always permitted an "O.K. Goy" or two to flourish.

Yet neither Vidal nor Capote took note of the fact that the harshest critical treatment of the Jewish novelists was always to be found in magazines like *Commentary* and *Partisan Review,* in sharp contrast to the practice of the southern writers, who were always praising each other in magazines *they* controlled, like *The Kenyon Review* and *The Sewanee Review.* They also praised and encouraged each other in private, whereas in the world of the "Jewish establishment" it was almost considered bad form, or a mark of low intelligence, to say anything kind in conversation about any other member of the group. Philip Rahv, as editor of *Partisan Review,* carried this practice so far that (alone of all editors I have ever known) he even denigrated pieces he himself had published in his own magazine.

Vidal and Capote did not invent these ideas about the Jewish conspiracy in the literary world; for years they had been whispered with varying degrees of intensity and conviction in English departments all over the country. But only whispered, partly because they were not entirely believed, but also because of an uneasy feeling that they contained traces of anti-Semitism. It was one thing to observe that many Jews were writing and editing and publishing and being acclaimed and even, for the first time, finding a place in the "establishment." I had run a piece by Benjamin DeMott saying exactly that, and I frequently lectured on the subject myself. But it was something else again to say that all this was illegitimate and that it was probably the result of a conspiracy, a manipulation of the culture in the interest of Jewish power.

It was at that point that a true sociological observation turned into an anti-Semitic calumny—and, indeed, Capote's entire analysis bore an uncanny resemblance to ideas which had been spread about the role of Jews in the cultural life of Berlin and Vienna in the 1920s and which played a part in creating the climate of opinion that Hitler could later appeal to. Not that Capote realized this. So effective had the taboo been on any open expression of hostility or even unfriendliness toward Jews since the fall of Hitler that Capote, like almost everyone else in America of a certain age, was entirely unfamiliar with the traditional ideologies of anti-Semitism; and it was this very ignorance that emboldened him to say things that he would have been ashamed or frightened to say if he had known their history and pedigree.

To compound the many ironies involved here, at the very moment Capote and Vidal and others were beginning to give voice to this traditionally anti-Semitic theory, even the slender basis of truth on which it rested had begun to disappear. By the mid-sixties, that is, so few of the major publications in New York were being run by Jews, and so many by southerners, that a much more plausible case could have been made for the existence of a conspiratorial southern mafia than for a Jewish one. The managing editor of *The New York Times,* for example, was then a man from Mississippi, Turner Catledge, and another southerner, Tom Wicker, was one of its major columnists, while *Harper's, Esquire,* and *The Saturday Evening Post* all had editors born in the South and raised there.

For now, nearly a full century after the Civil War, the South was very definitely on the move. The process of recovery had begun with the so-called Southern Renaissance which culminated artistically in the work of Faulkner and chronologically in the 1940s and 1950s when southern novelists were all the rage; the list runs from Faulkner himself through such lesser talents as Robert Penn Warren, Eudora Welty, Carson McCullers, Flannery O'Connor, Truman Capote, and William Styron. At the same time, the New Critics, so many of whom were southerners (John Crowe Ransom, Allen Tate, Cleanth Brooks), became the dominant force in the universities and in the literary quarterlies.

As it happens, very few of these writers were liberals of any kind on the issue of race, or for that matter on any other issue either. As I indicated earlier, most of them were forthright conservatives ("an ex-agrarian ontological aesthete," is how Ransom, the senior member of the group and the editor of the magazine with which it was most closely associated, *The Kenyon Review*, once described himself). A few were even self-styled reactionaries: Tate actually gave the title *Reactionary Essays on Poetry and Ideas* to one of his books. No doubt there was an element of perversity and bravado in this. (Tate was, after all, the man who in 1949 literally challenged the philosopher William Barrett to a duel in the pages of *Partisan Review* after Barrett had criticized a literary jury of which Tate had been a member for awarding a prize to Ezra Pound despite the fact that Pound was a vicious anti-Semite, and had committed treason in World War II by broadcasting propaganda on behalf of the Axis powers.) But perverse or not, in calling himself a reactionary Tate was also being serious: he did in fact believe that the social and political order in the pre–Civil War South was better than life in the postbellum world.

Given the acquiescence in slavery implicit in such a position, one would hardly expect Tate to be a liberal on the issue of race; and he was not. Nor were most of the other prominent southern writers of the forties and fifties. Though no one else went quite so far as the cantankerously defiant Tate, they all tended to be defensive on the issue, and about the South generally. They *loved* the South and they wanted to celebrate its virtues, especially against self-righteous northern liberals who thought of the entire region as one vast sinkhole of oppression. They all *knew*, though they could never quite permit themselves to say, that whatever crimes and sins the South had to answer for in its treatment of the Negro, the concrete situation there was not the unrelieved horror it had been made out to be by outsiders—those "intruders in the dust," as Faulkner called them in the title of one of his novels. At the very least, the realities were more complex, and among these complexities was a bond between black and white stronger and more intimate than anything that existed in the relations between the two races anywhere else. There was guilt —no one could deny it—but there was also love; and if the South could only be left alone, it would find its own way out of the tragic heritage that was at once its glory and its curse.

By the late 1960s, the generation of novelists and poets and critics who on the whole felt this way about the race issue had been succeeded by a new generation which was much more liberal in its racial attitudes and ideas. Many members of the younger generation began by writing or trying to write novels, but the real creative energies of the South seemed to have gone out of fiction by then. Those who continued to devote themselves to the novel were generally pale replicas of their elders. Where the new generation of southern writers was to make its mark was not in fiction but in journalism.

The typical pattern was a job on a local paper or magazine in the South, at first as a way of earning a living while working on a novel; then a growing interest in and zest for journalism in its own right or as a second-best resort when the novel (or series of novels) failed to get written or if written, failed to get published, or if published, failed to be acclaimed. Considering the superior literary talent of so many of these young southerners—they could, even the least of them, write, and write better than the vast majority of American newspapermen—it was no wonder that their work attracted attention in editorial offices all over New York.

But they had another quality which also helped: they were unashamedly ambitious at a time when ambitiousness itself, together with all the ideas about life that had traditionally made ambition into a virtue, were on the decline everywhere else in America. The sociologists Peter and Brigitte Berger would observe, in speaking of the large number of dropouts from the elite colleges in the late sixties when the influence of the counterculture was at its height, that this development represented a "sociological windfall" for the children of the working class who were still eager to get ahead and to whom the society would now be forced to turn to fill the jobs which would otherwise have gone to their sociological betters. But something similar to this "bluing of America" had already taken place in the world of journalism, except that the beneficiaries in that case had been graduates not of Fordham in the Bronx and St. John's in Brooklyn but rather of the University of North Carolina in Chapel Hill and the University of Texas in Austin.

These young southern WASPs had the kind of drive that had not been seen among their northern counterparts since the days of Horatio Alger, or among American Jews (their closest rivals and competitors) since the days of Sammy Glick. At the same time they were shrewd enough to know that being too openly ambitious, in the manner of these older prototypes, could no longer further the ends of ambition and might very well even frustrate them. It was not so much that ambitiousness itself—by which I mean actually being ambitious, as distinguished from talking favorably about it—had fallen into ill repute. Certainly this did happen among college students and many other people, including a substantial number well over the age of thirty, who came under the influence of the "youth culture" in the latter part of the sixties. But a great many others managed to get away with being ambitious by pretending to despise ambition and everything associated with it (competitiveness, money, status) as bourgeois or "middle-class" values.

Such hypocrisy was not exactly new in America, where the rich and the powerful had always manifested an unlovely tendency toward pious denigration of the worldly goods they possessed and had not the slightest intention of relinquishing if they could possibly help it. But I doubt that this kind of hypocrisy had ever before reached the brazen and comical heights it did in the sixties when a whole new breed of hustlers (rock stars, publishing tycoons, drug dealers, and other enterprising entrepreneurs) amassed huge fortunes by preaching against "the rat race," "materialism," "consumerism," and "middle-class values" in general, while providing entertainment and other services to a new mass market defined precisely by its repudiation of such values but still prosperous enough, thanks to parental allowances and grandparental trust funds, to enrich those catering to its particular tastes.

This was the extreme instance of the new hypocrisy about ambition. But there was also a more moderate expression of the same phenomenon, which simply took the form of what, in a more spiritually literate culture, would have been recognized instantly as bragging or more solemnly as the sin of pride, but which—with a bland consistency that never failed to astonish me and astonishes me still, to this day—seemed to be almost universally accepted as a mark of virtue. Thus people (and again, not only young people) went around with straight faces saying of themselves that they were superior to most of their fellow countrymen, that they, as opposed to most others around them, cared only for higher things and nobler values. Unlike everyone else, they believed in peace and justice as the proper ends of politics; unlike everyone else, they believed in love and cooperation instead of hatred and competition; and unlike everyone else they believed in art as against commerce. In short, unlike everyone else, they were good people, decent people, people of conscience and compassion and "concern." Yet instead of being laughed off the stage or shunned in embarrassment for talking this way about themselves, they were taken entirely at their own self-gratulatory valuation and greeted with applause, especially if they were young, in which case they were (literally and in all seriousness) celebrated as the best and most "idealistic" generation the world had ever seen. And even if they were not so young, all they had to do was pay obeisance to the regnant pieties in order to set off similar rounds of applause. Having signed the spiritual loyalty oath and testified to their acceptance of the true faith, they were free to pursue their ambitions without fear of incurring disapproval.

The new breed of southern writers was very good at this particular game. In putting it that way, I am perhaps imputing a greater degree of consciousness to them than may actually have been present. But then again, even if they were not fully conscious of what they were doing, they were undoubtedly operating on a sound instinct. Still, conscious of what they were doing or not, they did it: they signed the loyalty oath against ambition and they then pursued their careers with a single-minded ferocity that made even a more than ordinarily ambitious young man like me feel laggard, lazy, and unfocused.

There was, for example, my friend Willie Morris, who had risen like a multistage rocket from his hometown of Yazoo City, Mississippi, to the University of Texas in Austin, where he soon made a great splash as editor of the college newspaper; then came a Rhodes scholarship and a spell at Oxford, followed by a return to Austin, where he made another great splash as editor of the crusading *Texas Observer*, a small magazine that specialized in local muckraking and that had attracted a great deal of attention because of young talents like Morris; then came a job in New York at *Harper's* and finally, without missing a beat, he became at thirty-two the youngest editor in the hundred-year history of that magazine, where he also proceeded to make a great splash by publishing writers like Norman Mailer who had formerly been too difficult or too risqué for what had traditionally been a bastion of middlebrow gentility.

I got to know Willie almost from the moment he arrived in New York and even before he had ascended to the top position at *Harper's*. He wrote a few pieces for *Commentary* and he came to dinner at our house and to several of the large parties we used to throw at fairly regular intervals in the early sixties. They were

big parties, sometimes running to 150 guests or more and including many people of an older generation who had not seen or
spoken to one another since the political wars of the thirties and
forties, and many who would soon break off relations because of
the political wars of the late sixties and seventies. (Once at the
height of those later wars, my wife and I and our daughter Ruth
visited the Moynihans, who were then living in Cambridge and
who invited some people over to see us. Ruth, then about nine
years old, looked around the room and said wistfully to Maura
Moynihan, also about nine, "We used to have parties like this in
our house too, but that was before pol'tics.")

But our parties had generally been much larger and more
heterogeneous than the one at the Moynihans' that night, and
they also lasted a lot longer, rarely breaking up much before
sunrise. Willie Morris, and not he alone, had a habit of passing
out peacefully sometime in the early morning hours and then
being awakened and taken home by his wife or a friend as the last
guests were leaving. Early one Sunday afternoon, though, as my
wife and I were sitting and gossiping over coffee in the kitchen
after a few hours of sleep following the previous night's festivities, there was a sound from one of the little maid's rooms in the
back hall, and to our utter astonishment, Willie suddenly appeared, even more rumpled than usual from having slept in his
clothes, and rubbing his eyes with bewilderment at finding himself there instead of in his own home. "What time is it?" he asked
politely but without the slightest trace of embarrassment. "Is the
party over already?"

He was like that. This air of fecklessness, combined with a deep
southern accent that neither Oxford nor New York had mode-
rated in the slightest degree and a "shit-kicking" country-boy
manner to go with it, all concealed the booster-rocket engine of
ambition within which had carried him from Yazoo City to the
"red-hot center" of the New York literary world in record time
and without as much as a minute deviation from the plotted
course.

Some years later, when he was forced to resign from *Harper's* in a budgetary dispute with the owners, and when he then went off to live and write in Bridgehampton at the eastern end of Long Island—not exactly an obscure small town and in the summer socially indistinguishable from fashionable Manhattan, but still . . .—I had to admit that the appearance of fecklessness and the complaints he had always made about life in the "Big Cave" (as he called New York) were more genuine than I had ever believed. But that part of him at least was given its due in the way he talked about himself, whereas the ambitious part, which, up to the point when he was running *Harper's* by day and holding court at Elaine's by night, had been the determining force in his life, was never even acknowledged—not in his conversation and not in his autobiography, *North Toward Home.* Very far from it: to hear Willie talk, or to read him, one would think he had no interest in and no use for ambition, career, success; his mind was on higher and sometimes lower things but never on things in the middle.

With all their hunger, their talent, their energy, and their unin-hibited drive, it was no wonder that so many southerners should have made it to positions of power and influence in the shaping of the national consciousness. According to my wife, who worked on the editorial staff of *Harper's* under Willie Morris and got to know not only Willie himself very well, but dozens of "good ol' boys" who came around in search of assignments, they would have been altogether unstoppable if not for the fact that "they always needed a beer." Of course almost everyone, including me in those days, drank too much: for literary people it went with the territory. A writer was expected to drink and suspected if he didn't; and far from being frowned upon, drinking heavily was admired as a sign of manliness, and of that refusal of respectabil-ity that seemed necessary to creative work. Southerners were especially given to the mystique of drink, partly because of the legendary alcoholic habits of Faulkner—the writer they all wor-shiped above all others and therefore wanted to emulate—and also partly because so many of them came from "dry" counties where getting a drink had acquired from its illegality something of the same charge it had possessed everywhere else during Prohibition and that smoking pot was now beginning to have for people of a younger age.

Drinking has often proved compatible with a productive literary life, but alcohol has also destroyed many writers, and it has done even greater damage to people in other walks of life. With this in mind, my wife was able to foresee the election of Jimmy Carter to the presidency long before she or anyone else had even heard of him. "The first one of these 'good ol' boys' who comes along and can manage without a beer," she said one evening after a day at the office in the company of a troupe of good ol' boys who couldn't, "is liable to end up running the country."

As I have said, politically these younger southern writers and journalists were much more liberal than the preceding generation, especially on the issue of race, but not on race alone. Yet from the perspective of almost any northerner there was something quaint and old-fashioned about their liberalism. Back home it could seem very daring to uphold certain positions, and one could even fancy oneself a moral hero for assuming them. But these same positions had for so long been taken so completely for granted in the New York circles in which these transplanted young southerners tended to move that the way they preened themselves on their political daring could strike one as faintly comical. To hear the group around *The Texas Observer* congratulate one another on their bravery in fighting the "oil and gas lobby" in Austin, for example, was to be struck by how far back they must have started ideologically in their progress toward liberalism. No one in literary New York would possibly have considered himself courageous for attacking a big corporation; indeed, it would have taken courage to defend the oil and gas lobby, or its local equivalent, in New York.

To be fair to the southerners, their northern friends were to fall into the same faintly comical moral confusion during the Vietnam war. Opponents of the war, a group which by the late 1960s included at least ninety-nine percent of literary New York, liked to think that they were "dissenters," and they were not above ascribing a certain heroism to themselves on that account. Yet while they were of course dissenters from official government policy, they ran no risk of getting into trouble of any kind whatsoever—not with the government, not with their employers, and not with their friends—or even of getting into an argument. Where they all lived and worked, opposition to the war was universal and dogmatic, and the only arguments were over degrees of zealotry or about tactics for getting out. Nevertheless they spoke in self-gratulatory tones of their dissent with the clear implication that the courage to dissent was as admirable and as important in itself as the issue one was dissenting about.

These self-gratulatory tones were even more pronounced than usual at a ceremony of the National Book Awards being held in Lincoln Center one day in 1967 when Vice-President Hubert Humphrey was scheduled to speak and a move got started to walk out on him in protest against the war. Before the festivities began, I was standing around in the lobby of Philharmonic Hall with a group which was debating the wisdom and propriety of the demonstration, with some announcing that they meant to join in and others defensively explaining why, despite their passionate agreement with the antiwar sentiments of the protesters, they considered this particular expression of it a bad idea. The argument grew heated until someone turned to the one stranger who happened to be standing there, the pianist Eugene Istomin, and asked what he meant to do. "Oh," he said calmly, "I'm not going to walk out. I'm all in favor of American policy in Vietnam." From the amazement which greeted this announcement I realized that not a single person of the ten or so in that group had ever actually met a supporter of the war; and from the way they all glared at him in horrified disbelief, I could see how this community of "dissenters" felt about anyone who dissented from *them*. On the issue of the war, I was on their side, but I think I was the only person present who admired Istomin's courage in speaking his mind and in standing his ground in a group that he might have been forgiven for comparing to a moral lynch mob.

Nor was this all. To cap the day off, after the ceremony—when some walked out on Humphrey and many others did not—an elegant reception was held at the 21 Club, during which a nasty quarrel erupted between two writers, neither of whom had joined in the demonstration, because one of them had just gone too far and shaken Humphrey's hand.

For the southerners, of course, neither the oil and gas lobby nor the Vietnam war could compare in importance with the problem of race. Race was the issue they cared about the most, morally no less than politically. As they had learned from Faulkner (though they might have known it without him, from their own experience), the sin of racism was the curse of the South, and all the troubles and miseries of the region were a punishment for that sin. But they tended to differ from Faulkner in their attitude toward external coercion. He opposed federal intervention as a futile weapon in a struggle whose essence was moral and spiritual rather than legal and political and which would therefore require a very long time to work itself out; they supported federal intervention, though often reluctantly and with an uneasy sense of betraying their own.

Yet this very uneasiness was a measure of how profoundly right Faulkner's diagnosis had been in stressing the spiritual roots of the problem (profoundly wrong though he also turned out to be in underestimating the effectiveness of legal coercion and in overestimating the length of time it would take to change the hearts and minds of the South). For the fact was that these young men had in the course of growing up in the South been so thoroughly imbued with a sense of the inferiority of the Negro that something close to a heroic inner struggle was needed to overcome it.

One could, then, understand why they would feel so pleased with themselves at the successful conclusion of so difficult a spiritual contention (even, I fear, when it was not quite as successful as they thought). But if for some reason one had a mind to be less than fully sympathetic to them, one could also say—as I sometimes did, cruelly but not altogether unfairly—that a southern liberal was a person who, having struggled his way to the realization that Negroes were human beings, would never have to do anything else in his life in order to feel virtuous. (At the age of nineteen, Tom Wicker wrote of himself, "he had made the great discovery that blacks were as human and individual as anyone. It was not much to learn, yet it was more than some people learn in a lifetime.")

The irony was that this very quality—like their hypocrisy about ambition, and like their liberalism in general—turned out not to be the weakness I thought it was but an additional advantage in the establishment of their influence. I thought they were backward—political hicks, to be blunt—but the joke was on me because in their backwardness they were also perfectly in tune with the liberalism of the immediate future. By this I mean that "fighting the oil and gas lobby," and all its many corporate equivalents or analogues in all other areas of the economy, was soon to become more fashionable among liberals than it had been since the turn of the century, when the muckrakers and the trust-busters were riding high.

And if the southerners were in this sense as much avant-garde in their political attitudes as they were laggard, they were even more in tune with the future direction of liberalism on the issue of race. One way of describing the new direction, indeed, would be to call it "southerly" in its conception of the racial problem. That is, it increasingly took the view I have alluded to several times before that the North was in all essential respects no different from the South in its feelings about Negroes and in its treatment of them.

In the development of this view, transplanted southerners

played a major role. I think one can say today, now that the count is more or less in, that the spread of the ideas associated with it did a great deal of damage. Those ideas helped to poison relations between the races just when relations might have begun to improve, and they also led to a squandering of political energies on trying to solve the wrong problem. For in the South racism—that is, the belief that blacks are an inferior race—really was the main problem; therefore fighting it really was a precondition for any further progress. And since racism had borne concrete political fruits in the form of laws mandating segregation, there was a concrete political way to fight it. This was where Faulkner and those who shared his "spiritual" conception of the situation went wrong. If racism in the South had been merely a matter of feeling, or of ideas and attitudes, then federal courts, and federal laws, and federal marshals could have done nothing about it and could only have made things worse by their intrusive meddling. But racism in the South went beyond feelings or theories. It was enshrined in law no less than in the hearts and minds of the white people of the region; and while those hearts and minds might ultimately, as Faulkner believed, have been beyond the reach of the Supreme Court, the institutional structure of Jim Crow most emphatically did fall within the power of law and political action to affect.

In the North, however, the situation was radically different. To the southern eye, it looked as though the Negroes of the North were segregated, that they were being penned up in ghettos and kept out of the neighborhoods and schools of the whites. But that was a distorted view, based on a faulty understanding of the realities. Negroes were not *segregated* in the North. They did live together in certain neighborhoods, but so did Italians and Jews and Slavs and other ethnic groups, all of whom clustered together for a great variety of reasons, of which discrimination (from which they all suffered themselves) was only one and not necessarily the most important. They might, for example, feel more comfortable living among "their own kind," surrounded by stores catering to their tastes and with churches and synagogues conveniently at hand.

In this, Negroes in New York and other great northern cities differed hardly at all from other ethnic groups. To the southern eye, accustomed to a homogeneous society where almost everyone not black was of Anglo-Saxon Protestant ancestry, these groups were an undifferentiated mass of whites. But in a city like New York, even the category *white* was misleading. I remember being on a television panel once in the early sixties with two southerners, one black (Julian Bond, then of SNCC and later to become a member of the Georgia state legislature) and one white (Charles Morgan, a civil-rights attorney associated with the American Civil Liberties Union) and trying to explain that dividing the world into white and black made it impossible to understand the realities of life in New York or to act intelligently in the forging of political alliances on behalf of civil rights. But neither Bond nor Morgan would accept this, and they both looked at me with eyes at once suspicious and patronizing for having said it. Even assuming that such subdivisions still mattered and were not merely being rediscovered as a new weapon to be used against the blacks—which was how many blacks later came to view what the social critic Michael Novak would call "the rise of the unmeltable ethnics"—what difference did the subdivisions among white people make so far as black people were concerned? From the point of view of the Negro, the ethnics were white, and many of them were at least as racist in their attitudes as the whites of Anglo-Saxon background with whom the southerners were almost exclusively familiar.

Since at that moment the ethnic resurgence was only in its infancy, the more complex analysis it involved of the realities of group life and racial conflict in the North had no chance against the ascendant southerly analysis of those realities with its simplistic diagnosis of racism as the prime cause of all the black man's woes.

Simplicity, however, was not the only attraction of the southerly analysis. In retrospect, at least, it seems clear that it owed its success to the fact that there was something in it for almost everyone. To begin with the transplanted white southerners who did so much to promote this analysis: to them it offered a new way of exonerating the South without having to justify its racial sins. The love they all continued to feel for the South and their loyalty to it—which I regarded then and still regard as a virtue—exerted an unremitting internal pressure on them to defend it against the self-righteous and superior sneers of the liberal North. But the guilt of the South, and their own participation as individuals in that guilt, had always disarmed them and tied their tongues. Now suddenly, in the idea that racism was as prevalent in the North as in the South, they had a weapon with which to fight back. Thus they could present themselves—and the South as a whole—as specialists, experts, in the spiritual contention with racism. Having grown up with it, having lived with it, and having learned how to root it out, they provided a pioneering model for northern liberals, who were only just now beginning to realize how pervasively infected they themselves and the surrounding culture were with the same disease.

What these young southerners were doing here was analogous to what the older generation of southern writers had done with the economic and social backwardness of the region of which, down deep, they also felt ashamed. By connecting this backwardness with the defeat of the South in the Civil War, and by asserting that the experience of defeat and its punishing consequences had given southerners a "tragic sense of life" profounder in its understanding of the nature of things than the facile liberal optimism that allegedly prevailed everywhere else in America, the generation of Faulkner had been able to turn a sense of inferiority into a claim of superiority, a humiliation into a source of cultural pride. In similar fashion, Willie Morris, in a little book he wrote in the late sixties about a visit to his hometown, could say that the South was showing the rest of the nation the way to racial integration and harmony.

10

To be fair to the southerners, they were not alone in performing such unconscious maneuvers of the mind and the spirit as I have just described. Different as the two cases may at first seem, the southerners had an interesting counterpart in certain German-Jewish intellectuals in New York who, despite everything, could never get over their love of Germany or their compulsion to regard America as somehow inferior to the country of their birth. One of the products of this complex of feelings, I have always thought, was the theory of Nazism developed by Hannah Arendt and several other German Jews.

According to this theory, Nazism was not a specifically German phenomenon; it was a species of that revolutionary new form of tyranny called totalitarianism and as such a product of forces common to the modern world in general rather than (as other theories held) peculiar to Germany in particular. In this way Germany itself could be exonerated of the blame for Nazism. More than that: from a certain point of view, Nazism could even be seen as a mark of Germany's advanced cultural development.

Of course no one, least of all Hannah Arendt, ever put it in those terms or would ever have consciously entertained such an idea. But it was there, lurking below the theory, as I was to discover all too vividly in the course of a public debate with her at the University of Maryland in 1965. The subject of the debate was her book about Adolf Eichmann, the Nazi officer who had been responsible for rounding up the Jews of Europe and deporting them to the death camps, who had escaped to Argentina after the war, and who had then been found and kidnapped by the

Israelis and put on trial in Jerusalem. She had covered the trial and written a notorious book, *Eichmann in Jerusalem,* which had enraged many people because it accused the Jews of complicity in their own destruction, and also because it seemed to downplay the evil of Nazism by speaking of Eichmann's "banality."

As an admirer of Hannah Arendt (I considered her earlier book *The Origins of Totalitarianism* a great work) and as her friend, I was reluctant to join in the campaign that was being waged against her by certain Jewish organizations and also by a group in the intellectual community led by Irving Howe and Lionel Abel who, not content with writing critical reviews, took the extraordinary step of organizing a kind of protest meeting against the book. Nevertheless I had my own very serious criticisms to make of *Eichmann in Jerusalem,* and despite my fear that it might mean the end of our friendship, I decided to write a piece about the book for *Commentary.*

In the event, nothing so drastic as a breaking-off of relations occurred, though there certainly was a considerable cooling in the warmth she had previously felt toward me. "Let me ask you a question before you go," she said to me late one afternoon after an argument, one that had gone on for hours as her apartment grew darker and darker and as I wondered whether she would ever switch on a light, "why did you do it?"

There was something vaguely insulting in the question—an insinuation that perhaps I had been put up to my piece by others —but I let it pass: she was, after all, entitled to feel that I had let her down and she was behaving much better under the circumstances than most writers would. She even let it be known that I was the only one of her critics with whom she would consent to debate in public—which was how we happened to be together in Maryland in the spring of 1965 (along with Dwight Macdonald, her great friend and defender).

So deep were the passions aroused by *Eichmann in Jerusalem* that the huge gymnasium in which our debate was staged was packed to capacity, with people literally hanging from the rafters; and even though we spent most of our time on arcane philosophical questions, from the cheers each of us elicited after every remark, one would have thought it was a political rally. I, for example, was cheered when I said at one point that Miss Arendt exaggerated the extent to which the Nazi concentration camps had succeeded in creating a fully realized totalitarian reality, and she was cheered when she responded by saying that my remark could only have been made by a person who had never been in a concentration camp or even "in the neighborhood of a concentration camp." Though I repressed the impulse to say so at the time, it was in this response that one could detect the implication that German culture—despite Nazism, to be sure, but also conversely in a certain sense because of it— was more profound than the superficial liberal culture of democratic America which failed to provide anyone growing up in it with the spiritual and intellectual advantages to be derived from living in the midst of so great an evil.

Now, the idea about race in America that I have found in some way analogous to this, the idea that there was no real difference between the North and the South, in addition to offering the white southern liberal a way of turning the shame of his native region into a kind of glory, also had something in it for the white liberal of the North.

Whole forests have been decimated to provide enough paper for all the stories and articles and books written over the past twenty years on the subject of liberal guilt on the issue of race. Innumerable white liberals have spoken of their guilty feelings and innumerable others have tried to explain any number of phenomena by pointing to those feelings as the source. Yet while I have met many white liberals who sincerely thought they felt guilty over the plight of the Negro, I have rarely met a single one who really did experience a sense of guilt over this issue. And since very few ever did anything to Negroes but contribute money to the NAACP and political support to the civil-rights movement, it is no wonder that these guilty feelings to which so many of them were apparently eager to lay claim so often emitted a smell of inauthenticity.

In some cases, no doubt, it was a titillating experience to think of oneself as a racist (and the lengths to which people will go in order to make life more interesting for themselves should never be underestimated). But in other cases, in my judgment much more numerous, when liberals said "we" in speaking of the way Negroes were treated, they were not really including themselves at all; the word "we" was a polite euphemism for "they." (This habit of saying "we" and meaning "they" became a clue to much of the rhetoric of the sixties—as, for example, during the Vietnam war, when people whose only connection with the war was their opposition to it, took to talking about "our" crimes against the Vietnamese.)

The they behind the "we" of Vietnam were mainly the people in power—the government—but the they behind the "we" of integrationism were the masses of white people in general. To say that these people were racists of the same stripe as the racists of the South, and to say further that their racism was the root cause of segregation in the North no less than in the South, was to provide a perfect justification for relying on coercion to override any resistance they might mount to the integrationist program. If, for instance, the residents of a neighborhood in Queens said they were against busing children out of their own local schools or busing Negro children in because they feared for the safety of the children or for the quality of the schools, this was contemptuously dismissed as a cover for racism. As such, it was entitled to no more consideration than the same resistance which had been offered to integrating the schools of the South. And just as an appeal to the federal courts had been necessary to deal with recalcitrance in the South, so the courts were called in now to do the same thing in the North.

Similarly with housing integration. If people said they were against it because they wanted to maintain the ethnic homogeneity of the neighborhood; or if they said they were against it because they were worried about the potential it contained for violence and crime; or if they said they were concerned over the effect it would have on the resale value of their homes—all this too was dismissed as a cover for racism. Yet every one of these reasons was honestly meant and, what is more, had a solid grounding in experience.

The Italians who had been living for generations in the Arthur Avenue neighborhood in the Bronx, for example, *did* want to live among other Italians, and while they certainly had no love for Negroes, they would have been almost as unhappy over the prospect of Jews or even other groups of fellow Catholics like the Irish or the Poles moving in and diluting the character of the place. As for crime, the fear was genuine and not in the least illusory, since most muggings and other violent urban crimes were in truth committed by Negroes (mostly against other Negroes, but integrated residential patterns soon led to an integration of victims as well); and real-estate values did go down when Negroes moved into a given area. But to the integrationist liberals, none of this mattered or could be accorded any more respect than the rationalizations which had always been offered in the South. Segregation, whatever its cause or whatever the sentiments sustaining it, was against the law; and if people would not obey the law voluntarily, they would have to be forced to do so.

As it happened, a great many of the liberals who demanded such measures of coercion were personally beyond the reach of those very measures. *Their* children were mostly in private schools, and *their* neighborhoods were walled off from Negroes by barriers of money; nor did anyone seem eager to locate public-housing projects on the affluent streets where they lived. That there was hypocrisy in their position, then, was obvious—at any rate to everyone but themselves. But hypocrisy was the most trivial part of what amounted at bottom to an aggression by a new and rapidly growing group of prosperous and well-educated people calling themselves liberals against a less prosperous and less well educated combination of groups, mostly in the working and lower middle classes. The purpose of the aggression was to assert moral superiority not only to these groups themselves but to the old-style political leadership of the Democratic party which represented them. It was, in other words, a further stage in the struggle by the "reformers" of Moynihan's analysis against the "regulars" for control of the Democratic party. In this struggle the southernization of the race issue provided the reformers (or the "New Class," as they were more generally coming to be known) with an invaluable weapon.

And finally, the idea that there was no real difference between the North and the South also had something to offer the civil-rights movement. A movement, any movement, needs an agenda, a program, concrete objectives, and the trouble with the civil-rights movement in the North was that it had long since achieved the principal objectives it had been created to pursue.

Thanks in large part to the efforts of Negro organizations like the NAACP and the Urban League—working together with such groups as the American Jewish Committee and the Anti-Defamation League whose primary purpose was to fight discrimination against Jews but who, on the theory that "bigotry is indivisible," joined in political battles of which Negroes rather than Jews would be the main beneficiaries—by 1960 laws were on the books in New York and many other northern states outlawing discrimination in almost every area of life. Within a decade after World War II, there were fair-housing laws that made it illegal for anyone to be denied housing because of "race, creed, or color"; there were fair-employment agencies set up to enforce the same standards in the world of jobs; and there were even voluntary programs designed to overcome the effects of *de facto* school segregation.

In the South, of course, there were no such laws designed to protect the civil rights of Negroes; on the contrary, the laws that existed were designed for exactly the opposite purpose. Nor was there any chance of changing them locally through the political process, for among the rights which Negroes had not yet fully won in the South was the right to vote. The lion's share of the work to be done by the civil-rights movement, then, was in the South—bypassing the local political obstacles through litigation in the federal courts and through agitation in Washington.

Much of this work was done by northern Negroes (and whites) but it seemed to be of no direct relevance to their own situation. Thus their greatest victory in the courts—the 1954 school-desegregation decision—applied (or so everyone thought at first) only to the legally segregated school systems of the South. So too with the great legislative victories of the next decade—the Civil Rights Act of 1964 and the Voting Rights Act of 1965. These were federal laws to override local southern ordinances, but they went no further than (and in some respects not even as far as) comparable legislation already on the books in northern states like New York, Illinois, and California. In that sense, nothing that had been accomplished by the civil-rights movement in a long time had any significant bearing on the problems of Negroes in the North.

Nor did the civil-rights movement have a strategy for dealing with those problems. Why indeed should it have had? The assumption had always been that once the Negroes had won their civil rights—or to put it another way, once the barriers of racial discrimination had been torn down and every Negro was being treated on his own merits as an individual rather than as a part of a special group defined by the color of its skin—everything else would take care of itself.

But now experience in the North was evidently exposing that assumption as false. Civil rights, it seemed, were not enough. After years of formal legal equality, Negroes were still unequal in condition. Too many Negro children were still doing poorly in school, too many Negro women were still on welfare, too many Negro men were still unemployed or employed in inferior jobs. These were the problems in the North, not segregation or denial of the right to vote. To deal with those problems it was necessary to go beyond formal legal equality to—what? The civil-rights movement by its nature could have no answer to this question and even to accept it as a valid question was tantamount to saying that it had put itself out of business and should now give way to other movements focusing on other problems and organized around other assumptions.

Of such movements, each with its own answer to the question of what the next step after civil rights should be, there was no lack in the 1960s. They ranged from groups advocating a turn inward —a redirection of energies toward developing the cultural and spiritual resources of the black community—to groups advocating new and broader alliances with various white constituencies on behalf of common economic objectives like full employment and urban reconstruction. And there were subdivisions within each of these competing schools of thought—each feverishly trying to establish itself as the legitimate successor to the civil-rights movement.

The civil-rights movement, however, was not quite ready to fade from the scene, challenge or no challenge, and what saved it was precisely the idea that the North had much more in common with the South than anyone had previously suspected—that, in other words, there was no difference between *de facto* and *de jure* segregation. Thanks to this discovery, the civil-rights movement could now return an answer of its own to the question of what the next step should be after formal legal equality had been achieved: since civil rights as such had not led naturally and on their own to the integration of the races, the job ahead was to find other ways of promoting this goal.

Thus once again, and for the first time in years, the civil-rights movement had something to do on its own home territory: it could fight to integrate the North. This opened up a whole new field of action. There would be endless cases to make, proving the presence of segregationist intent in the apparently random operation of social forces leading to separation of the races; there would be polemics; there would be demonstrations; and there would be lawsuits to bring.

In the early sixties, all this integrationist activity seemed to flow organically from the traditional struggle for civil rights and against discrimination. But it would soon lead to policies which departed radically from the traditional principles of the civil-rights movement. The aim of the civil-rights movement had always been to eradicate all consciousness of color from the law—to make it "color-blind"—whereas the integrationist movement into which it was now transformed began, as the sixties wore on, to press paradoxically for a degree of color-consciousness in the law greater than anything that had ever been seen before in American life.

In pressing for those policies the new integrationists made a great effort to show that they were entirely consistent with the old campaign to do away with racial discrimination and the old ideal of treating everyone as an individual without regard to "race, creed, color, or country of national origin." And no wonder: in the not so distant past, that formula had virtually had the status of a religious dogma among liberals, and to offend against it must have left a great many of the new integrationists feeling very uneasy indeed. After all, some of the same people who only a short time before had considered it a great victory when colleges were forbidden to ask for photographs of applicants (since these had once mainly been used to identify Negroes) now found themselves demanding that colleges—and all other institutions as well—be forced to inquire into the race of applicants. Of course in the past the purpose of singling out Negroes had been to discriminate against them, and now the purpose was to discriminate in their favor. Nevertheless, benign discrimination still was a form of discrimination—of, that is, special treatment—and not even its generous intent could altogether conceal the inexorable implication it carried that on the whole and as a group Negroes were inferior to whites.

Here, then, was yet another example of how racism, in the true meaning of that promiscuously used word, had migrated from the South to the North and found a home in the hearts and minds of people (both black and white) who wanted nothing more than to fight against it and who imagined that this was what they were doing.

11

My differences with the established liberal opinion of the early sixties on the issue of race were thus even deeper and wider than the gap between the new radicalism of which I was part and the standard liberal position on the issues of centralized state power and economic growth. But I was also growing more and more disaffected by the liberal consensus of that period on international affairs.

Nowadays the people called liberals tend to have a relaxed attitude toward the Soviet Union and Communism in general; they tend to favor a reduction in defense spending; and they tend to oppose American military action of any and every kind. In the early sixties, however, the only liberals who held such attitudes were the fellow-traveling liberals, and they had long since lost out to the anti-Communist or "cold-war" liberals in the struggle for possession of that valuable title.

For me, turning against anti-Communist liberalism was much more difficult intellectually and much more painful emotionally than opposing centralization or economic growth or even integrationism. In speaking earlier of the Leavis-Snow controversy, I said that the Anglo-American literary tradition was suspicious of and even hostile to industrialism and technology, and that this gave a special resonance to the attacks on centralization and growth mounted by writers like Goodman and Schumacher. But the hostility of the literary tradition was not confined to industrialism alone. One could say—as Trilling in fact later would—that the literary tradition of the past two hundred years stood in an "adversary" relation to the entire civilization that had grown out of the industrial revolution. Whether that civilization was characterized as bourgeois, in terms of the social class that dominated it; or as capitalist, after the economic system that fueled it; or as secularist, after the spiritual predisposition it fostered; or as liberal, after the political philosophy around which it was organized —no matter the angle of approach, the literary tradition tended to see more evil than good in modern civilization, if indeed it saw any good at all.

True as this was of the literary tradition since the eighteenth century, it was truer still of the "modernist" writers (Pound, Eliot, Yeats, Lawrence, Joyce, and the rest) who had dominated the culture since the early days of the twentieth. One could find an enormous variety of broadly political ideas or sentiments in the works of these writers, including support for fascism, but the one thing it was almost impossible to find was a good word for the liberal civilization they seemed to be at one in despising. Thus in opposing the liberal consensus on issues like centralization and economic growth, I was acting in harmony with ideas and attitudes I had absorbed in the course of a long and intensive literary education.

Even my criticisms of integration were true to the spirit of that education, if not so much in the substantive position I took, then in the confessional style in which I had first chosen to discuss my relations with and feelings about Negroes. Authenticity in the expression of feeling and honesty in the exploration of ideas were among the most prized of all virtues in the literary world of my youth, and in aiming for those qualities when I wrote "My Negro Problem" I was acting in obedient conformity to its standards even as I was offending in the content of the essay against the values of polite liberal society. (Later, I would discover that there were severe limits to the literary world's own commitment to those standards, but in "My Negro Problem," at least, I came nowhere near to crossing them.)

In short, in turning against the liberal consensus on domestic issues, I was finding my way toward a political position that was in some essential respects more consistent with everything I had been educated to believe as a student of literature. But in turning against cold-war liberalism, I found myself coming into very sharp conflict with everything I had been educated to believe as a young intellectual. As I have already indicated, by the time I became the editor of *Commentary* in 1960, I had for some years been growing less and less comfortable with the "hard" anti-Communist position that most of the older intellectuals I respected were identified with and that I myself had once found entirely convincing. This growing discomfort had led me into an association with the peace movement and a new belief in the possibility of doing something to reduce the danger of nuclear war in particular and of ending the cold war in general. It was not that I thought the hard anti-Communist position had been proven wrong; on the contrary, never for a single moment did I doubt the soundness of its ideas about the character of Stalin's regime inside the Soviet Union, or about his aggressive designs on the rest of the world, or about the need for a determined American resistance to those designs. What I did begin to question was whether these ideas were still applicable to the Soviet Union under Khrushchev. A good case could be made either way. On the one hand Khrushchev had denounced Stalin and had agreed to a "thaw" in his relations with the United States; on the other hand, he had brutally suppressed the Hungarian Revolution and had made menacing gestures in other parts of the world.

It was impossible to be sure, and my own uncertainty was reflected in *Commentary* during my first year or two as editor. The hard anti-Communist line was represented in the magazine by writers like Richard Lowenthal (arguing that Khrushchev's Russia was still a totalitarian state) and Theodore Draper (arguing that it still, in 1961, and indeed more than ever, entertained "unlimited aims"). But for *Commentary* this was nothing new. What was new was the appearance of writers like Staughton Lynd maintaining that the United States had been at least as much to blame for starting the cold war as the Russians, and of H. Stuart Hughes in an article called "The Strategy of Deterrence" providing an elegant justification for a view that was just then being propagated more crudely under the slogan "Better Red Than Dead."

That *Commentary* of all magazines should have gone so far as to make room for such articles as those, and that its editor should be in such evident sympathy with their general drift, struck a great many people, including the Trillings and several other close friends, as an outrageous betrayal. They were right to be worried and they were right to feel betrayed. What worried them was that my own apostasy might be a straw in the wind, the portent of a general change of climate in the world of ideas—and beyond it, in the world where political decisions were made. To the naked eye it might look as though Lynd's interpretation of how the cold war had begun or Hughes's nuclear pacifism were (as the subtitle of the Hughes piece itself proclaimed) "dissenting views" shared by only a tiny minority within the intellectual community and an even tinier minority among the populace at large. But my anti-Communist elders knew better. They knew, that is, how fragile the liberal anti-Communist consensus really was and conversely how deceptive was the apparent weakness of fellow-traveling liberalism, especially among intellectuals. Intimidated by McCarthyism and discredited by Stalinism, the fellow-traveling liberals had temporarily lost their nerve, but they had by no means been converted or given up. They were still there, waiting for just such a shift in the wind as the new *Commentary* at once represented and was helping to bring about. That I should be involved in this process could only have seemed an act of political betrayal.

But the betrayal was also personal—or so I think they must have felt. Here was I, Lionel Trilling's student and protégé and friend. Had he taken the trouble to teach me so much in the classroom and out, had he encouraged and helped me along in so many different ways, that I should wind up sponsoring the resurgence of ideas and attitudes he had spent most of his adult life battling against? It was one thing for a friend of Trilling's like David Riesman to be engaged in this way. Riesman was a contemporary and had a history of his own. But I was a disciple and, moreover, the successor as editor of *Commentary* to Lionel's own mentor, Elliot Cohen.

It was Cohen who, as a precocious young editor working in the 1920s on a Jewish magazine called *The Menorah Journal,* had first printed Lionel's work. Cohen had also influenced Lionel's political development. In the early thirties he had led the way first into Stalinism and then shortly thereafter into anti-Communism; and he had in addition done a great deal in the ensuing period to encourage Lionel in the direction of a more sympathetic and even loving attitude toward American culture and American society. "Indeed," Lionel was to say of him at his death in 1959, "he taught the younger men around him that nothing in human life need be alien to their thought, and nothing in American life, whether it be baseball, or vaudeville, or college tradition, or elementary education, or fashions in speech, or food, or dress, or manners." This combination of attitudes inevitably became the guiding spirit of *Commentary* upon its founding in 1945; and so it remained until I took over after Cohen's death: Lionel's student succeeding Lionel's teacher.

But instead of ensuring the continuity of the tradition, as might have been expected, my appointment was turning into a disruption, a breaking of the chain. I was declaring that a great many things in American life were and should be "alien" to our thought. And now what was even worse, much worse, I was raising doubts about the continuing relevance of liberal anti-Communism—doubts which extended all the way back to its belief that the cause of the cold war was Soviet expansionism, and all the way forward to its conviction that Soviet domination of the world was the greatest of all possible evils.

And so heated arguments erupted at private dinner parties and eventually also into a number of public debates. There was one sponsored by the American Committee for Cultural Freedom at which Diana Trilling and I were among the speakers and at which I even found myself being pushed into defending the proposition that surrender to the Soviet Union would be preferable to a nuclear war if it ever came to such a choice. Of course very few even of the hardest of hard anti-Communists ever advocated the actual use of nuclear weapons (though Bertrand Russell, who later became the world's leading nuclear pacifist, had once urged the United States to threaten the Russians with nuclear annihilation if they refused to submit their own, then much smaller, arsenal to international control, and if necessary to make good on the threat). Nor on the other side did many people join H. Stuart Hughes in advocating unilateral disarmament on the part of the United States. Certainly I was not that radical in my own thinking. My response to Hughes's article was a bit like the response of certain readers to "My Negro Problem": the criticisms of accepted policy (integration in my case, deterrence in his) seemed sound and even unanswerable, but the radical conclusion to which they led (miscegenation for me, unilateral disarmament for him) remained unacceptable. Nevertheless, just as many people who shrank from the radicalism of my solution to the Negro problem were still willing to defend the article for the light it shed on the problem, so I was willing to defend Hughes's piece in the same way.

There was also another, subtler, element involved in all this: the element of tone and literary grace. Such things are not supposed to count in political debate or for that matter in intellectual analysis generally. What is supposed to count there is the logical soundness of the argument, its coherence, and the extent to which it fits the available evidence. But try as I may, I have never succeeded in disciplining myself to overlook or remain unaffected by the tone in which an argument is presented or the language in which it is embodied. "Not everything is a poem," Sidney

Morgenbesser once shouted at me in exasperation when I responded to his criticisms of Paul Goodman's ideas by bringing up the colloquial vigor and directness of Goodman's style.

I used to think that I owed this habit of mind to my literary education, and certainly that was a factor. But I was now accumulating new evidence every day that most literary people were as resolutely indifferent to the "aesthetic" qualities of a political argument as any philistine positivist. Philip Rahv, an editor of the most distinguished literary magazine of our time and himself one of the leading literary critics of the day, said to me that good writing had as little to do with the truth of what was being said as a pretty face had to do with the character of the woman behind it. Strictly speaking this was so, but I couldn't help feeling that there was something missing in it, and that it came strangely from a man to whom literary values were presumably of great importance.

I felt the same way about the response of some of my friends to Stuart Hughes. All they seemed to see in "The Strategy of Deterrence" was a series of propositions. Yet there was much more to the article than that. There was, for one thing, the way he talked about the theorists of nuclear strategy in opposition to whom he was writing: Henry Kissinger, Thomas Schelling, and above all Herman Kahn. Around the same time Hughes was doing his piece, an eminent scientist with political views very similar to Hughes's wrote that he was ashamed to be living on the same planet with the author of a book like Herman Kahn's *On Thermonuclear War* which by "thinking about the unthinkable" could—so this scientist said—only serve to make a nuclear war more likely. But Hughes, equally opposed to Kahn's belief in the strategy of deterrence, could write of that book: "I think one can say without qualification that Kahn has written one of the great works of our time." It was a great work, he went on to explain, because it did for nuclear war what Clausewitz, the greatest military strategist of the past, had done for "conventional" war: it looked "thermonuclear war in the eye" and treated it "as a reality rather than a bad dream." As to the moral assault on Kahn, and the other analysts of nuclear strategy, Hughes had this to say:

> In terms of intellectual rigor, the only fault I find in them is a tendency to slant their interpretations in favor of the United States. In terms of moral choices, I need say no more than that they have made the opposite choice from mine. But this does not mean that I think them immoral—far from it. Faced with the frightful dilemmas of war and peace today, the best any man can do is to make his personal choice in the agony of his own conscience, convinced that whatever he does he will be in some sense wrong, that, like Pascal, he is making a desperate wager in the dark and that no one will forgive him if he proves to have been in error.

To me, this tone—the civility of it, the humility of it, the humanity of it—added immeasurably to the force of Hughes's argument. It did not make that argument right, nor did it prove that nuclear pacifism itself was intrinsically more humane than deterrence. Thanks to a tiresome paradox of human nature, nuclear pacifists, like pacifists in general, were often—as I had by now had ample occasion to discover—unattractive people who could be as violent in character and savage in argument as they were pacific in ideology. But Hughes was an exception, and for me this in itself gave a greater credibility to his position than it might otherwise have had.

At no point did I feel more strongly about this than in the other major public debate generated by Hughes's article—a round-table discussion held in 1961 under the auspices of *Commentary*. This time my own role was that of moderator, with Hughes himself as a participant along with Sidney Hook, Hans J. Morgenthau, and C. P. Snow. It made for a very interesting mix. Morgenthau was known in those days as the most distinguished exponent in America of the so-called *Realpolitik* school of thought, which stressed power and self-interest as the decisive forces in international affairs. Snow, just then at the height of his prestige as one of the few literary figures in the world who could also speak with authority on technical scientific matters, had recently made head-lines by predicting that atomic bombs would "go off" within ten years (he even said that this was a "statistical certainty"); and Hook was then probably the most consistent upholder of the liberal anti-Communist consensus in the intellectual community.

As might have been expected, the real heat of the discussion came in the exchanges between Hook and Hughes, with Morgen-thau and Snow taking positions somewhere in between Hook's unshaken confidence in the necessity and desirability of maintain-ing a nuclear deterrent and Hughes's equally strong belief in the necessity and desirability of unilateral nuclear disarmament.

I doubt that anyone present that day, or any disinterested reader of the edited transcript, which later appeared in *Commentary* under the title "Western Values and Total War," would have thought that Hughes emerged victorious from these exchanges with Hook. Hughes was a good enough debater, but he was no match for Hook who, in addition to being a highly skillful polemi-cist, had devoted a large part of his energies to political debate and came equipped with thirty years of experience in all the radical wars. A lifelong socialist, he always spent so much time attacking the betrayers (as he saw them) of socialism on the Left, and then defending the United States and the other Western democracies against the assaults of these same ideological forces, that many people would snicker privately whenever he declared himself to be a socialist.

What Hook saw in Hughes that day was the latest variant of the fellow-traveling liberalism he had been fighting since the mid-thirties, and probably the most insidious. In the thirties, at least, the fellow-travelers had defended the Soviet Union and sub-scribed to outright lies that could be exposed by the patient accumulation of evidence. Now, however, people like Hughes who for all practical purposes wanted, as Hook charged, "to surrender the world" to Soviet control not only denied that this was their objective but even competed with anti-Communists like himself in denouncing the evils of the Communist system. Evidence was not enough to refute a position like that. In fact, it was a position almost impossible to expose without calling the sincerity or the motives of those holding it into question; and this is what Hook did with Hughes ("Mr. Hughes maintains that he'd rather be red than dead, and then tells us that of course he's prepared to die fighting against Communism"). Combined with his normally abrasive manner in debate—a manner which gave no hint of how kindly a man he could be in personal relations—these sarcastic *ad hominem* thrusts made a very bad impression on me and almost everyone else in the audience, especially as contrasted with the dignified and good-natured way in which Hughes responded.

To the extent that the point was to debate the case for a unilateral renunciation of nuclear weapons by the United States, Hook won and Hughes lost. But to the extent that the issue was the continued viability of nuclear deterrence, it was Hughes who won and Hook who lost—and not only because of Hook's manner. Hook's restatement of the liberal consensus was very effective, but Hughes was also very effective in exposing its weaknesses. In this he had support from both Morgenthau and Snow who, as he rightly pointed out, agreed with him in "describing the present situation as impossible" even though they stopped short of accepting his solution.

That, as I have said, was exactly where I stood too—highly critical of the liberal consensus on nuclear deterrence but not persuaded by the case for unilateral disarmament. I had no solution of my own to offer, but for the time being it seemed enough, and more than enough, to expose "the present situation as impossible" and to encourage the exploration of radical alternatives. Even if—like miscegenation or unilateralism—these radical ideas ultimately proved unable in their own turn to withstand careful critical scrutiny, they at least served a temporary purpose in stirring things up against the established liberal wisdom on the kind of society we ought to have and the kind of role that society ought to play in the world at large.

But so far as the cold war in general was concerned, an issue was at that very moment just beginning to emerge which would soon put an even greater strain on the relations between the new radicalism and established liberal opinion than the problem of nuclear arms: Vietnam.

By the time the last American soldier had left Vietnam in 1975, there was hardly anyone in the United States of any political persuasion who still thought that American intervention into the affairs of that country had been a good idea. By that time too, almost everyone who had ever had anything to do with that intervention, either actively or by supporting the policies behind it, had long since deserted the sinking ship. Some had the good grace to fade away into silence and discretion, but many others did everything they could to convey the impression that they had opposed the war from the beginning or at least from early on, and had been working against it from the inside. Yet very few Democrats who held high office during the Kennedy and Johnson administrations were able to make the grand claim George McGovern made about being "right from the start" without doing at least some violence to the truth. Not that this stopped them from trying. Indeed by 1972 there were so many early opponents of the war among the people who had been running things in Washington in the Kennedy and Johnson years, and so few supporters, that it was hard to understand how or by whom the war had actually been waged.

The fact is that at the "start" very little opposition of any kind was mounted within the liberal community to American intervention in Vietnam for the simple reason that hardly anyone within that community doubted the need to prevent any non-Communist country from being taken over by the Communists if it was possible to do so at reasonable cost.

To be sure, there was a certain measure of disagreement over the relative effectiveness of military as distinguished from political means in holding the line against Communist advances. But it is important to realize that the people—mostly liberals—who favored an emphasis on the political aspect of the struggle against Communism tended, if anything, to be *more* interventionist in their proposals than the military-minded cold warriors. What the military-minded generally favored was sending arms to non-Communist regimes, and letting them tend to their own defense. But the politically-minded, who believed that Communism thrived in situations of social injustice, wanted to force these regimes into adopting reforms which would in their judgment deprive Communism of its breeding ground; and they were only too willing to tell other countries exactly how to organize their political and economic institutions to this particular end.

Another reason for the relative scarcity of opposition to intervention in Vietnam at the start was that in the first year or two of the Kennedy presidency, Vietnam was only one of many "underdeveloped" countries in the news and by no means the most prominent. Late in 1961 a political scientist from Pittsburgh named Joseph J. Zasloff, who was then a visiting professor at the University of Saigon, sent me a paper he had written on the situation there, which eventually appeared in the February 1962 issue of *Commentary*. Here is how it began:

> While Laos and then Berlin and then Katanga have been dominating the front pages in recent months, a situation of equally critical proportions has been building up in South Vietnam, where the government of President Ngo Dinh Diem is struggling for survival against well-organized strongly sustained guerrilla forces—the Vietcong—inspired and supported by the Communist Viet Minh government of the North.

But not only did the situation in Vietnam seem less worthy of front-page coverage than the Berlin crisis or the civil war in Katanga or even the comic-opera war (as Arthur Schlesinger would later describe it) in neighboring Laos; it even struck many people as hardly worth reading about. Some years later, in 1965, when Robert Lowell and Dwight Macdonald themselves became worthy of front-page coverage—Macdonald for circulating a protest against the war in the very midst of a reception at the White

House to which he had been invited by Lyndon Johnson, and Lowell for refusing to attend—I found myself recalling with wry and somewhat bitter amusement the night they had both cornered me at a party and demanded to know why *Commentary* was carrying so many "boring" articles about Vietnam.

Admittedly Lowell and Macdonald were a special case when it came to the problem of Communism. In the early fifties Lowell issued a public denunciation of Yaddo, the artists' colony, for harboring Stalinists, and despite the fact that Lowell was then suffering from one of the psychotic episodes that plagued him all his life, Macdonald rushed to endorse the attack. My guess is that Macdonald did not realize that Lowell was insane at the time, since he always had great difficulty in recognizing insanity when he saw it, at least in poets. Thus on another occasion, after he and I had spent an entire evening together listening to Delmore Schwartz explain that his publisher was conspiring with T. S. Eliot to prevent him from collecting a legacy of millions of pounds that had secretly been left to him in England by Siegfried Sassoon, Macdonald chided me for saying that Delmore had gone completely crazy. Schwartz had, to be sure, brought all his famous wit and brilliance to bear on the spinning of this paranoid fantasy, but that did not make it any the less psychotic, and it amazed me that Macdonald refused to see this.

But whether or not Macdonald had experienced a similar blindness in the case of Lowell, he did take part at Yaddo in what he himself a few years later might well have considered an act of McCarthyism. In any event, the night Macdonald complained to me about the "boring" articles in *Commentary*, his days as a hard anti-Communist were past and his days as an antiwar activist were still in the future. For the moment his interests had become almost entirely cultural, and politics left him cold.

As for Lowell, his periodic bouts of insanity apart, he had a peculiar relation to politics altogether. He was always getting involved in political battles, but in my opinion the only thing that was real to him was poetry, and it was only through poetry that anything else ever became real. He once said to me in answer to certain criticisms I had made of the poetry of W. H. Auden in the course of a quiet conversation: "After all, if not for Auden we wouldn't have known about the Second World War." At first I was puzzled by the remark, and then it struck me that he meant it literally: if *he* had never read about the outbreak of the war in Auden's poem "September 1, 1939," if he had only read about it in a newspaper, he would never have believed in its reality. No wonder, then, that he too was bored by all those articles in *Commentary* about Vietnam which, whatever their other virtues, were certainly not poems.

Yet special though Macdonald and Lowell were, their indifference to Vietnam seemed to be fairly representative of the general mood among intellectuals in the early sixties. Zasloff's article scarcely attracted any notice, and neither did the other two pieces on Vietnam Macdonald and Lowell were referring to—both of them by Hans J. Morgenthau.

Like Zasloff, Morgenthau criticized the emphasis in American policy on military means and urged that we resort instead to "manipulative skills" in promoting "the restoration of a viable political order which constitutes the only effective defense against Communist subversion." He did not shrink from acknowledging that such a policy "required the elimination of Diem"—a conclusion which the Kennedy administration also reached a little later when it acquiesced, or perhaps cooperated, in the "elimination" of Diem by assassination.

But Morgenthau was prescient in a better way too. Writing when only a small number of American military advisers had been sent to Vietnam, he warned against a deeper military commitment; and in the course of doing so, he established probably as good a claim as anyone to have been "right from the start" on Vietnam:

> If the present primarily military approach is persisted in, we are
> likely to be drawn ever more deeply into a Korean-type war, fought

under political and military conditions much more unfavorable than those that prevailed in Korea and in the world a decade ago. Such a war cannot be won quickly, if it can be won at all, and may well last . . . five or ten years. . . . Aside from the military risks to which it will give rise . . . , such a war would certainly have a profound impact upon the political health of the nation. McCarthyism and the change in the political complexion of the nation which the elections of 1952 brought about resulted directly from the frustrations of the Korean war. The American people are bound to be at least as deeply affected by the frustrations of a Vietnamese war.

Morgenthau made his own share of mistakes in those pieces. Like the Kennedy people, he thought that the North Vietnamese and the Vietcong were, in effect, agents of Mao Tse-tung and that the fall of the South to Communism would for all practical purposes represent a dangerous extension of Chinese power. A few years earlier, when China had been entirely subservient to the Soviet Union and when Communism was still a worldwide movement controlled by and directed from Moscow, such a victory would have been indistinguishable from a Russian advance. But when the first American military advisers were sent into Vietnam, the split between China and the Soviet Union had already become visible. This meant that the interests of the Russians and the Chinese no longer necessarily coincided, and to that extent it might have been reassuring. The trouble was that the Chinese took a much more aggressive line than the Russians on "wars of national liberation" (of which they considered the one in Vietnam a prime example) and on the duty of the Communist nations to foment and support such revolutionary uprisings against the "imperialist bloc" led by the United States. And in general, while the Russians spoke of "peaceful coexistence" (Khrushchev's term for what in the time of his successor Brezhnev would be called "détente"), the Chinese stressed the need for and even the positive desirability of revolutionary violence in the struggle against "capitalism" and "imperialism."

Consequently, the Chinese acting on their own seemed more

dangerous than when under the presumably restraining influence of the Russians, whose own ideological moderation was thought to stem from the fear that great-power involvement in local conflicts could escalate and ultimately lead to a nuclear war (which, by the way, they knew they were bound to lose because of the great superiority of the United States in nuclear weaponry during the early sixties). The Chinese, as they often proclaimed, did not share the Russians' "cowardly" fear of nuclear war—a fear that only served to inhibit revolutionary zeal and to retard the victory of Communism throughout the world.

The issue, then, was whether the United States ought to commit itself to the containment of China in Southeast Asia as we had committed ourselves to the containment of the Soviet Union in Europe and then Korea. Adlai Stevenson, who was Kennedy's ambassador to the United Nations, once, in answering an appeal by a group of his supporters who were against the war, put the case as clearly as anyone would ever put it:

> The period from 1947 to 1962 was largely occupied in fixing the postwar line with the Soviet Union. . . . We have no such line with the Chinese. Since they are in an earlier, more radical stage in their revolution, it may be more difficult to establish one. Should we try? And is the line we stand on halfway across Vietnam a reasonable line? Should we hold it? . . .

The answer, he went on, depended on one's assumptions about Chinese power and Chinese intentions; in his judgment the Chinese were "very aggressive" and the war in Vietnam was an instance of Chinese expansionism. "My hope in Vietnam," Stevenson concluded, "is that relatively small-scale resistance now may establish the fact that changes in Asia are not to be precipitated by outside force."

Stevenson, who died in 1965, never lived to see the "relatively small-scale resistance" in Vietnam grow into its full dimensions as a major military commitment. Nor did he live to discover that an American defeat in Vietnam would lead in the late seventies to a split between Communist Vietnam and Communist China, and to the encouragement of Soviet rather than Chinese expansionism. As for Morgenthau, his foresight—which was so much greater than Stevenson's or almost anyone else's with regard to the chances of a successful American military intervention and the domestic political consequences such an effort would bring—did not extend to the geopolitical implications of Vietnam at all. He shared the general view among liberals that China was the issue in Vietnam, and he shared the general fear of Chinese power. Where he differed was in believing that it was impossible to apply the same strategy of containment to China as had been followed so successfully in Europe against the Soviet Union.

To me Morgenthau's analysis was entirely persuasive, and I adopted it as my own, leaning heavily on it in debate, both public and private, as the deepening American involvement in Vietnam during the Kennedy years made the issue more and more visible and less and less boring to more and more people (though not yet to the likes of Macdonald and Lowell, who really got interested only after the United States under Lyndon Johnson began bombing North Vietnam in 1965).

These debates that I was now having over Vietnam were two-edged. On the one side I found myself arguing with my anti-Communist friends against American military intervention; and for that purpose Morgenthau's line could be very effective. The reason for its effectiveness was that it rested on prudential considerations, saying that Vietnam (to cite a slogan that later became very popular) was the wrong war in the wrong place at the wrong time—wrong not morally but in the sense of being an impossible war to win. This was, in other words, an approach by which it became possible to oppose American military intervention without surrendering one's anti-Communist perspective.

Morgenthau himself, to be sure, did not think of it in those terms. As a member of the *Realpolitik* school of thought on international affairs, he tended to see ideologies like Communism, and for that matter democracy, as subordinate to power and other material interests in the behavior of nations. He spoke of China and the Soviet Union and the United States, not of Communism and anti-Communism, as the actors in the current conflict. Nevertheless, unlike the more ideologically oriented centers of opposition to American policy, which often depended on benevolent interpretations of what the Communists—whether the Chinese, the North Vietnamese, or the Vietcong—were after in Vietnam, Morgenthau's approach was, true to its name, politically realistic in expecting the worst of the Communist forces.

It was for this reason that, even as I engaged in missionary work among my anti-Communist friends and acquaintances, trying to convert them to the oppositionist camp, I also found myself getting into arguments with my friends and acquaintances on the other side, within the peace movement, over their own grounds for opposing American policy; and here the Morgenthau line was not effective at all. The problem was that many of the people connected with that movement were against American military involvement not because they thought it would fail but because they feared it would succeed. What they wanted, in short, was a Communist victory in Vietnam.

Among these people were some of the self-proclaimed pacifists associated with *Liberation* who wanted a Communist victory so much that they were willing to sacrifice their pacifist principles to it. Thus they developed a theory according to which a pacifist could approve of the resort to armed violence in the case of colonial uprisings or wars of national liberation. This perversion of pacifism had originally done duty as a justification for supporting Castro, and it was now applied with even greater fervor to the struggle of the Vietcong against the government in Saigon.

But not everyone in the peace movement who supported the Vietcong was quite so bloodthirsty as this particular school of "pacifists." There were those whose support took the more conventionally pacifist form of urging a cessation of armed hostilities and the setting-up of a coalition government in which the Communists would be included (and which, as most proponents of such a coalition fully expected but rarely said, the Communists would inevitably come to dominate). This position may have been politically disingenuous or even cynical, but it was at least truer to the principles of pacifism than the position of those "pacifists" who—as Norman Thomas, himself a pacifist, memorably said—loved the Vietcong more than they loved peace.

Norman Thomas did not love the Vietcong more than he loved peace. In fact, he did not love the Vietcong at all. And it was on that basis that he refused to join in a march on Washington organized by Staughton Lynd and Dave Dellinger in 1965 to protest American military intervention in Vietnam. This was one of the earliest of the demonstrations that would come to be known as "antiwar," although they were not against the war at all but only against one of the two sides fighting it.

The Staughton Lynd who was now marching in support of the Vietcong was the same Staughton Lynd who had written a piece a few years earlier for *Commentary* on "How the Cold War Began." In that piece he had taken an evenhanded, almost neutralist, stand as between the United States and the Soviet Union on the question of who had been responsible for the conflict between them. The article had provoked many angry protests suggesting that Lynd's article was nothing more than an elegantly written apology for the Soviet line. In defending himself Lynd had responded by saying that his way of looking at the cold war, as "a tangled situation to which both sides contributed," held out the hope of future accommodation, whereas seeing "the conflict between America and Russia as a struggle of good with evil" made "the unimaginable horrors of nuclear war more likely."

I had used similar terms in defending my decision to publish the article when some of my anti-Communist elders attacked me for it: it was unfair, I said, to accuse so balanced an article of being one-sided or, more bluntly, pro-Soviet. But a talk with Lynd in my apartment one night which lasted almost until dawn left me feeling worried. One of his critics had said that the "sobriety and balance" of his article were only a "patina," covering over a "grossly tendentious reading of history," and by the time our conversation was over, I found myself having to admit that there might well be more to this charge than I had thought the article alone justified. It was not that Lynd was pro-Soviet; if anything, he seemed to be leaning toward the Chinese line in the Sino-Soviet dispute. But his attitude toward Communism was much more benevolent than I had realized, and his ideas about the American role in the world much more hostile.

I marvel today that this was not as fully apparent to me at first as it was to some of my anti-Communist elders. But the truth is that I was blinded by a great wish to believe that the new radicalism which Lynd and I had been working together to create would be new in nothing so much as its freedom from the illusions about Communism that had corrupted the last great wave of radicalism in America. The illusions about Communism in the thirties had mainly been embodied in a false and lying picture of what was going on in the Soviet Union. Now the focus was shifting to the underdeveloped world where, it was said, Communism represented a protest against the "corrupt" (always corrupt) feudal or right-wing governments which owed their power to Western imperialism. In those countries, ran this view, many so-called Communists were not Communists at all; they were nationalists fighting for freedom from colonial domination and for the overthrow of oppressive backward regimes. Instead of siding with such regimes, as it always did, the United States ought to be helping these "Communists" in struggling against them.

I had no quarrel with the idea that many of the non-Communist regimes in the underdeveloped world were oppressive and corrupt. Nor did I disagree with the contention that the United States was wrong in throwing its support to dictators like Diem in South Vietnam or Rhee and then Park in South Korea. And I certainly shared the view that Communism in those countries often fed on nationalist passions and the desire for social reform. But I differed from Lynd and many others in the peace movement in their willingness—indeed their eagerness—to believe the best of the Communist parties and the Communist guerrillas in the underdeveloped world. After all, the Chinese Communists had once been represented in similar fashion as harmless "agrarian reformers," and yet they had turned out to be even more militantly Communist than the Soviet Union itself. What was this support for the Vietcong and its North Vietnamese allies but a new form of the old illusions about Communism—an updated version of the naïveté and the outright lying about the Soviet Union that had destroyed both the intellectual and moral credit of radicalism in the 1930s?

Even though Lynd had used tellingly soft language in describing the Soviet system (he had called it, much to George Lichtheim's disgust, "authoritarian socialism"), he had at least not tried to portray Stalin's Russia as a democratic society or as a worker's paradise—and in my wishful state of the moment that had been enough for me. But not even this much ambiguity attached to his sympathy for the Vietcong. There was no way I could blind myself any longer to the fact that Lynd and his friends and allies in the peace movement were not interested in creating a new radicalism that would be free of the old illusions about Communism. And that was putting it at a minimum, since some of them clearly—and, with the water getting warmer, more and more openly all the time—thought that the illusions were on the other side: that the real villain in the conflict between "authoritarian socialism and democratic capitalism" was not now and never had been the Soviet Union but rather the United States and its allies and clients all over the world.

If Lynd's point of view had been the only one within the peace movement, my hopes for the new radicalism would have been dashed a lot sooner than they actually were. But there was also Norman Thomas. Still, the presence of an old socialist did not exactly hold out any great hope for a new radicalism either. I usually agreed with Thomas's views (except on the Middle East, where his sympathies were too pro-Arab for comfort), but no more than his younger comrade Irving Howe did he have anything new or anything especially radical to offer. There was, however, one prominent figure in the peace movement who did seem to stand for something as new as it was radical. His name was Robert Pickus, and he headed an organization called Acts for Peace (which later became Turn Toward Peace, then Negotiation Now, and finally the World Without War Council). Pickus was a pacifist—a full-time professional activist on behalf of the pacifist cause—but he was a pacifist with a difference. Unlike most of his fellow pacifists, he was very hardheaded in his political thinking. He was not unctuous or sanctimonious; he had no sentimental ideas about human nature or about the role of love in political life; and he understood and accepted what he himself called "the realities of power and the validity of conflict."

That was the first thing that was new about him. The second was his anti-Communism, which stood in very sharp contrast to what he once described as the "vulgarized quasi-Marxist political analysis" accepted by most other pacifists who located "the problem of twentieth-century international conflict wholly in the structure of the American economy and the evil motivations of an American power elite."

All this was new indeed. To me it was also very appealing—so much so that I supported Pickus in one way or another in almost all the organizational work he did throughout the sixties. I could never fully share his faith in the possibilities of "a world without war"—pacifism, even in this hardheaded version, seemed unreal to me. Nevertheless Pickus, more than any other political activist I had yet run into, embodied my own idea of how a new radicalism might look and the kind of things it would find to say.

Pickus was so energetic, so intelligent, so articulate, so confident, that it was possible at first to believe that the future would belong to him—not him personally, but his way of thinking, his point of view—rather than to Staughton Lynd and his friends and allies, and their way of thinking and their point of view. Alas, it was not to be; and again, if I had not been misled by a wishful heart, I would have known a lot earlier that it was not to be. It was not that I was blind to the many signs already in evidence from the very beginning that the new radicalism was destined to develop in a direction that I would be unable and indeed unwilling to follow. I saw the signs, or anyway some of them, but for a long time I continued to believe that all was not yet lost, and that the burgeoning movement now coming to be known as the New Left could be saved from the old corruptions by the efforts of Pickus and others to influence, to teach, to persuade.

The term "New Left" was, if I am not mistaken, imported into the United States from England by C. Wright Mills, who taught sociology at Columbia and who in the fifties wrote several books challenging the liberal analysis of American society from a radical point of view. Much of what Mills was saying in the late fifties came very close to ideas I had been mulling over during those same years in my own growing dissatisfaction with the liberal analysis, but I disliked and disapproved of his stridency. His book *The Power Elite,* for example, drew what seemed to me a wildly exaggerated picture of the control exercised by a small number of corporations over the American political system, and *White Collar* gave an equally overdrawn and even hysterical account of the dissatisfactions of middle-class life. Responsive though I was becoming in those days to criticism of American society, I was put off by the hostility and even hatred that gave such a charge to Mills's prose (and a very good writer he was, especially for an academic sociologist). And I was put off even more by his attitude toward the Soviet Union. He was not pro-Soviet, but he seemed to think that the Soviet Union was not much worse than the United States, and that the two countries were in any case growing more alike with every passing day.

This was known as the "theory of convergence," and it was neither unique to nor invented by Mills. But unlike Staughton

Lynd, who also subscribed to it, Mills took a malicious pleasure in the idea, which for him extended all the way to the drawing of parallels between the anti-Communist intellectuals of America ("the NATO intellectuals," in his characteristically pungent formulation) and the defenders of "socialist realism" in the Soviet Union:

> In Uzbekistan and Georgia, as well as in Russia, I kept writing notes to myself at the end of recorded interviews: "This man talks in a style just like Arthur Schlesinger, Jr." "Surely this fellow is the counterpart of Daniel Bell, except not so—what shall I say?—so gossipy"; and certainly neither so petty nor so vulgar as the more envious status-climbers. Perhaps this is because here they are not thrown into such a competitive status-panic about the ancient and obfuscating British models of prestige.

Then, finally, there was the romantic and uncritical attitude he took toward Castro and the revolution in Cuba, in a book called *Listen, Yankee!* Here again Mills was not alone. In fact, a great many people, liberals as well as radicals, had at first seen Castro as a hero—"the first and greatest hero to appear in the world since the Second War," according to Norman Mailer—and had taken him at his word when he claimed to be fighting to replace the military dictatorship of Batista with a system of "Jeffersonian" democracy. Even after Castro had come to power in 1959 and had begun establishing a dictatorship of his own, and one moreover in which the Communist party was playing a larger and larger role all the time, a great effort was made to deny or apologize for these developments. There was no Communist influence in Cuba, it was said; the whole idea was a right-wing myth. And if Castro was becoming friendly with the Soviet Union, it was because American hostility gave him no choice. In any case, he was neutral as between the Americans and the Russians. He represented an alternative to capitalism on the one side and "authoritarian socialism" on the other—a "new humanist socialism" which might yet prove a model for the entire underdeveloped world. Then, in 1961, came the Bay of Pigs invasion, which only served to in-

crease sympathy for Castro and which gave greater credibility to
the contention that he had been moving closer to the Soviet
Union not because he was really a Communist but because
American enmity—fueled by corporations fearing for the loss of
their profitable investments in Cuba—had driven him into
Khrushchev's arms.

This was more or less how Mills saw it in *Listen Yankee!* and yet
between the time he wrote that book in 1959 and the time it was
published in the fall of 1960, Castro himself had given the lie to
his apologists by aligning Cuba unambiguously with the Soviet
bloc and by proclaiming that he had secretly been a dedicated
"Marxist-Leninist" all along.

12

"If anyone was the intellectual father of the Movement," said Paul
Jacobs and Saul Landau in one of the first of the many books that
would be written about the New Left, "it was C. Wright Mills."
This being so, it was only proper that he should have been wrong
about the Cuban revolution. For it was that revolution which
"provided the first significant test of the values and political intelligence of the amorphous entity, the 'New Left.' "

Those words appeared in the introductory section of an article
by Dennis H. Wrong in the February 1962 issue of *Commentary*
(the same issue, by the way, which carried Joseph Zasloff's piece
on Vietnam). Wrong's article dealt with the response of the entire
spectrum of left-wing opinion in America, not just the New Left,
to Castro and his revolution. But his main concern was how the
New Left (still so new as a recognizable entity and so amorphous
that the name had to be enclosed in quotation marks) had met this

"first significant test" of its values and its political intelligence. After refuting the various justifications of the New Left for the absence of democracy in Cuba, Wrong came to a devastating conclusion: that some of Castro's New Left supporters in the United States "seem in an equally short time to have traveled from a fresh rebellious idealism, sorely needed after the confusions and timidities of the fifties, to a fascination with populist totalitarianism that is scarcely distinguishable from that of the latter-day Communist apologists of the late thirties and early forties."

I shared this view—and not only because of Cuba. In fact, there was something about the New Left, or the Movement, as this entire phenomenon was getting to be called, that had been bothering me from some time now.

There was first of all the low intellectual quality of the thinking in New Left circles. Long before the term "New Left" had come into currency—indeed just about the time that I had come to *Commentary* and begun openly to call myself a radical—I had also begun following the work of a new group of young Marxists. They were mostly graduate students at the University of Wisconsin and a few other places who had been trying to revive a long-dormant tradition of Marxist thought. As such they had at first seemed to be an important sign of the kind of intellectual development without which any new radicalism would be unable to make its way.

Yet with rare exceptions, the writings of these young scholars were disappointing. It was easy to forgive the turgidity of the articles they had begun to publish in such new Marxist journals as *Studies on the Left,* but it was not so easy—not for me, at any rate —to swallow the hysterically overdrawn characterizations of American life that served as the common coin of their social criticism. In this—if not in the prose they wrote—these young Marxist intellectuals were true disciples of C. Wright Mills, whose vision of an America manipulated by a corporate elite and filled with robots fit for nothing but consumption and war they had taken over as their own. They had also taken over Mills's attitude toward Communism, or more precisely toward anti-Communism, which they considered an evil almost as great as, and perhaps even greater than, Communism itself. As can clearly be seen from the way Mills talked about Daniel Bell and Arthur Schlesinger in the passage I quoted earlier, the hatred here was not directed exclusively or even primarily at right-wing anti-Communism or at McCarthyism; it was *liberal* anti-Communism that served as the main target—the kind, in other words, that prevailed in the universities and the intellectual world generally, where right-wing anti-Communism or McCarthyism was pretty much confined to a single magazine, *The National Review.* But the usual tactic was to break down any such distinctions by trying to show that liberal anti-Communism functioned merely as a polite justification for an oppressive status quo both at home and abroad.

Like so much Marxist analysis, all this seemed to me crass and reductive. Reading Mills and his disciples on America, I simply could not recognize the country I lived in. At their worst they sounded like people writing about a place they themselves had never actually seen or at least hardly knew. And no wonder, since their starting point was not the evidence of their eyes and ears but the abstractions of an ideological system to which they were committed and which allowed them to see only those "realities" that served its own moral and political purposes. They were like Trotsky, who while he was living in the United States once rose to address a rally with the words, "Workers and peasants of the Bronx . . ."—except that their distortions were neither innocent nor funny.

Nor did I see anything innocent or funny in the way they talked about Communism and anti-Communism. Careful as they usually were to dissociate themselves from the Communists, the blandness of their criticisms of Communism as compared with their heated denunciations of anti-Communism showed at the very least a lack of intellectual balance. Some of this could be explained away as a reaction to the strength of anti-Communist sentiment in the United States, and particularly the role played by such sentiment in inhibiting radical thought and action. Even allowing for that, however, there was still something intellectually superficial, not to say morally disturbing, in the analysis.

But crude and superficial as much of the thinking of these early young Marxist scholars seemed to be, it was formidable by comparison with the pamphleteering of the New Left. In the winter of 1962, I was sent a long manifesto which had been drafted (largely by a young radical activist named Tom Hayden) for the meeting in Port Huron, Michigan at which Students for a Democratic Society, or SDS, was for all practical purposes born. In view of the fact that SDS was soon to become a kind of flagship of the New Left—the one organized group within that otherwise amorphous "Movement" that everyone could recognize and identify —and considering also that the "Port Huron Statement" almost immediately achieved the status of a historic document, the decision I made against running it, at least in a shortened version, might easily be considered the worst judgment of my entire editorial career. Certainly I was tempted. I think—though memory may be playing tricks on me here—that I even suspected while reading this long single-spaced manuscript that I was in the presence of something potentially historic. If so, I would have been responding to its own sense of itself. "We are people of this generation," it began, "bred in at least modest comfort, housed now in universities, looking uncomfortably to the world we inherit. . . . Our work is guided by the sense that we may be the last generation in the experiment with living."

Nevertheless, historic or not, the Port Huron Statement simply was not on its intellectual merits worth publishing. Here again were all the criticisms of American life that had been made and repeated many times over by Paul Goodman, David Riesman, C. Wright Mills, and others to the point where they were losing their freshness and beginning to take on the dreary aspect that afflicts all clichés even when they contain important elements of truth. In fact, seeing some of these ideas as filtered through the mind of Tom Hayden, stripped of all complexity, qualification, and nuance and expressed in callow and derivative language, forced me to begin wondering how much truth they really contained even, so to speak, in the original.

No doubt it was unfair to blame the authors of an idea for its subsequent vulgarizations; Karl Marx himself had once said, on reading the work of certain of his self-proclaimed disciples, that he was no Marxist. But the trouble in this case was that no one whose influence could be detected in the Port Huron Statement seemed to be criticizing, let alone repudiating, it.

Years later, when the low intellectual quality that bothered me in the Port Huron Statement had grown so pronounced among the radical young in general that Paul Goodman at least began turning against them, he would complain after a lecture tour of the college campuses that they "hectored" him with words he himself had put in their mouths without even knowing where the words had come from (the origins, he said, had been lost in the recesses of prehistory, author Anon.). But in the early sixties, almost everyone concerned, including Goodman (though in his characteristically patronizing way), was singing the praises of SDS and of the Port Huron Statement. The young people of this new movement were everywhere described as the brightest members of a generation which was itself more and more taken to be the best crop of young people America had ever produced. But for all the talk that was going around about the extraordinary intelligence of the new generation of student radicals, and about how much better educated they were than any generation that had ever been seen before, it was not primarily their intellectual gifts or attainments that they were celebrated for. It was their "idealism," their commitment to humane values, their vision of the future. The Port Huron Statement even became the standard by which the radicalism of the later sixties would be judged and found wanting by older allies and sympathizers who then fell away. For example, Nathan Glazer, writing in 1970 about his own "deradicalization," ruefully described the Port Huron Statement as "a model of humanist radicalism," from which SDS and the student Left in general had unfortunately departed in the later stages of their development.

Goodman and Glazer were undoubtedly right in saying that the SDS of 1962 had a very different tone from the snarling and violent revolutionism of the SDS of 1968 to which "humanist" was perhaps the last word anyone would have thought to apply. Yet the seeds of 1968 were present in 1962. Taken at face value the Port Huron Statement was an expression of love for humanity: "We regard men as infinitely precious and possessed of unfulfilled capacities for reason, freedom, and love." But below the surface there flowed a steady current of moral smugness and self-satisfaction. Thus: *We* believe in everything good—in "fraternity," "brotherhood," "selflessness," "generosity," et cetera, whereas everyone else, including most of our fellow students, cares only about "business as usual, getting ahead, playing it cool," and above all power. *Our* values are "rooted in love, reflectiveness, reason, and creativity," while everyone else's are "rooted in possession, privilege, or circumstance." And so it proceeded. On every point in the analysis, the ideas and values of the SDS radicals were placed in the most attractive light while the "system" and its defenders were portrayed in morally repugnant and politically cynical terms.

There was on the one side, then, according to the statement, a saving minority of students who had "in the last few years . . . demonstrated that they at least felt the urgency of the times," who had "moved actively and directly against racial injustices, the threat of war, violations of individual rights of conscience," and who had succeeded "in gaining some concessions from the people and institutions they opposed, especially in the fight against racial bigotry." On the other side, there was apathy, cynicism, brutality, war, all embodied in the "system" and perpetuated by the privileged few who benefited from it. In the middle were the masses of "ordinary people," powerless and resigned "before the enormity of events." To be sure, "some would have us believe" that these ordinary people "felt contentment amidst prosperity." But this was a delusion. The contentment most Americans appeared to experience was in truth "a glaze above deeply felt anxieties about their role in the new world." Though many had been seduced by the system into imagining that they were reasonably well off, the truth was that they were afflicted by "loneliness, estrangement, isolation." They were afraid of change, but they were also moved by a "yearning to believe . . . that something *can* be done" to make things better. The job of the new student radicals was to bring this yearning to consciousness and to guide it in the proper direction.

It was here that the seeds of later developments could be seen, for in addition to being morally smug and self-satisfied, this kind of thinking was inherently authoritarian. Hayden and his friends congratulated themselves over and over again on their commitment to freedom and democracy and on their faith in the "people," among whom they said they wanted to live and work, but what they were actually saying was that *they* knew what was best not only for themselves but for everyone else as well. They had a better sense of how other people felt than those people did themselves, and they also knew exactly how to cure the ailments that other people did not realize they were suffering from.

At this stage they were willing to limit themselves to persuasion in the hope of appealing to the spark of unconscious yearning for change they were sure existed in the hearts of most Americans. In the search for "truly democratic alternatives," they were against coercion and they found "violence to be abhorrent." But as I uneasily sensed even as I read the Port Huron Statement (helped along in this perception by personal contact with a number of young radicals whose dogmatism consorted incongruously with an almost ostentatious show of gentleness), the rejection of force and violence was more conditional than principled and wholehearted. It depended on the innocent conviction that the mass of Americans really were as discontented with life and with the present arrangements of American society as the radicals thought, and that they really could be led into voluntary support of a new political movement. But what would happen if and when it should turn out that this movement was incapable of attracting a significant popular following?

All the indications were that what would happen in that case is what in fact did happen—and within the space of only a few years. By 1968 SDS had moved from argument and example to shouting down speakers with whom it disagreed on the ground that only the "truth" had a right to be heard. And it had also changed its position on violence. The Port Huron Statement denounced violence as an instrument of social change because "it requires generally the transformation of the target, be it a human being or a community of people, into a depersonalized object of hate." By the late sixties SDS was speaking with open hatred about the "community of people" it now called "Amerika" (spelled that way to suggest an association with Nazi Germany), it had become an advocate of violent revolution as the only road to "social change," and a number of its members had gone beyond advocacy to actual practice in the form of bombings and other varieties of terrorism.

I cannot say that I saw all this coming, but I can say that SDS and the New Left generally were a far cry from the new radicalism I had been hoping might now emerge in the United States. Still, I remained reluctant to write it off without giving it a chance, and this reluctance was deepened by some of the attacks that were beginning to be launched against the entire Movement.

One of the earliest of those was a piece submitted to *Commentary* in 1964 by the eminent sociologist Lewis Feuer. The occasion was a student strike at Berkeley, where Feuer was then teaching, organized by a radical group called the Free Speech Movement (FSM) to protest a university regulation against political activity on a certain part of the campus. But this narrow little issue was almost immediately swamped as the Berkeley strike—the first in an almost endless series of campus demonstrations and uprisings to come—began to be taken as an immensely important development. Now, for the first time, many people, especially within the liberal community, who had regarded the new radicalism as an insignificant phenomenon confined to a tiny minority of disaffected intellectuals, began wondering aloud whether there might not after all be more to this movement than they had previously thought. Obviously something was going on. But what? Who were these students? What was bothering them? What did they want? What (to use a phrase that was to be parroted *ad nauseam* in the years ahead) were they trying to tell us?

Although the students themselves were by no means inarticulate or shy about telling "us" what they wanted—they wanted, said the leader of the Berkeley rebellion, Mario Savio, to "stop the machine"—one commentator after another flew into print to interpret the message. Not surprisingly, almost every one of those commentators discovered that the students were trying to tell us whatever it was he himself wanted to hear; and what he wanted to hear was invariably what he himself had been trying to tell us, often unsuccessfully, in the past about the deficiencies of the American educational system and about the sins of American society in general. But the particular details of the various analyses were much less important than the almost universal agreement that "our" young people were turning against "us"—that "alienation" and "rebelliousness" were spreading from the poor and the dispossessed to the privileged and to the future leaders of American society. To most liberals, this could only mean that something was seriously wrong with the "system." But no such conclusion followed for Lewis Feuer, who dismissed the idea that the grievances of the students at Berkeley were justified in objective terms or were caused by deficiencies in the system. Instead, he argued, the entire episode had to be understood in Freudian terms as an Oedipal rebellion against authority in general.

I turned down Feuer's article because I found it reductive. Even though I was offended by the increasingly vociferous descriptions in the press and elsewhere of the younger generation as an "oppressed majority," as a "prophetic minority," as "the party of hope," as "the new aristocrats," and even as a new and better species, I objected to Feuer's psychologizing approach as well. Whatever side one might be on in the Berkeley dispute, or in the larger ideological conflict of which Berkeley was perhaps the first nationally noticed example, there were issues and ideas to talk about, in their own terms and on their own merits, and I did not believe that these issues and ideas should be dismissed as nothing but superficial symptoms of a deeper psychological reality.

Feuer's article was eventually published in *The New Leader,* and when Jason Epstein discovered that I had rejected it, he expressed amazement at my failure to realize what a journalistic coup I could have scored by running it. But his amazement at me was as nothing compared with my amazement at him. For while my enthusiasm about the new radicalism had been cooling steadily, his had been growing hotter and more intense.

In addition to having become more convinced than ever before of the truth of the radical critique of American society, he had also been persuaded by the surprisingly large sales of *Growing Up Absurd* and other such signs that radicalism was acquiring a substantial following, that it was becoming more popular and more powerful every day. Since Berkeley was so clearly a product of the new radicalism, and since it was also so dramatic a confirmation of Jason's judgment that this new radicalism was becoming a force to be reckoned with, and even perhaps the wave of the future, he had every reason to detest Feuer's piece. After all, Feuer's purpose was to make light of the ideas of the new radicalism and to ridicule their potentiality for power. I did not altogether understand then, and I do not fully understand now, why Jason responded so perversely from his own point of view to this assault on his political beliefs. But whatever the reason, it was to be the last perverse inconsistency he would permit himself for a very long time where the new radicalism was concerned.

There was another article about Berkeley that touched on my relations with Jason, but in almost exactly the opposite way. Only a short time before the uprising, Jason had acted as the prime mover in the launching of a new magazine, *The New York Review of Books,* of which his wife Barbara became co-editor and in the running of which he himself participated informally. Inevitably this meant that I too, as an intimate friend, would have close relations with *The New York Review.* And in fact, I had taken an active part in the early discussions that led to its birth, and there had even been talk of my leaving *Commentary* to become the editor of the new magazine. In the end, however, I decided that I wanted to stay with *Commentary* and the job was offered to Robert Silvers, who had been associated with *The Paris Review* and then with *Harper's*. I cannot remember whether it was I who suggested Silvers to Jason, though it may well have been since I myself had offered him a job at *Commentary* three years before. In any case, his appointment strengthened my already strong connection with *The New York Review.* Nor did the fact that I had a magazine of my own to edit interfere with this connection. Since *Commentary* and *The New York Review* shared a similar point of view and similar literary and intellectual standards, they would naturally find themselves relying on many *Commentary* writers. But since they only intended to run book reviews, there was no serious problem of competition; and far from objecting to the existence of another outlet for the perspective we shared and for the writers I valued, I considered it an advantage.

Or rather I did until the day I telephoned Nathan Glazer in Berkeley, where he was then teaching, to ask him for an article about the student uprising only to discover that he had just promised such an article to Bob Silvers. Naturally I felt certain misgivings over this discovery that the ally I had thought I was helping to create was now branching out to become a competitor and a rival. But I needn't have worried. In the end, Glazer's article wound up in *Commentary* after all—not because of any amicable agreement among us regarding the division of editorial territory but because *The New York Review* turned it down on the pretext that it was "too long," but on what I was convinced were really political grounds.

The division, then, was turning out to be political rather than editorial, and it represented the first sign of a split between the two magazines that would in the next five years grow wider and wider and finally end in an open and bitter break. Since we were all friends, this split was bound to put a great strain on our personal relations; and it did. But since all of us were also responsible for running two of the leading magazines within the intellectual community, the split acquired a significance that went far beyond personal relations, important as these were to the individuals concerned. Many other people outside our immediate circle in New York were drawn in, while the issues that divided us broadened and deepened as time went on to a point where they could only be imperfectly understood if approached in narrowly political terms, and still less in merely personal ones.

For the moment, however, the issue was only Berkeley, and the only issue that really interested anyone about Berkeley was whether—when all was said and done and when all the complicated details of the conflict had been sorted out and sifted and analyzed—one sided with the students leading the uprising or whether one opposed them. To oppose them of course meant to deny the legitimacy of their grievances, as Lewis Feuer had done. But it also entailed minimizing their claim to represent the student body of Berkeley, let alone the entire student generation of America or even the younger generation as a whole; and this too Feuer had done. Despite Jason's criticism of me for turning down Feuer's article, I cannot imagine that *The New York Review* would, if given the opportunity, have published it. To have published such an article so early in its history would have been an act of self-definition. It would have suggested that *The*

New York Review was hostile to the radical forces stirring in the land, which would have been untrue as well as damaging to its rapidly burgeoning reputation as a fresh new voice within the intellectual community.

Indeed, far from wishing to convey any such impression to the world, Silvers and Barbara Epstein, joined in this by Jason, were unwilling to risk identifying their magazine with any position that fell short of complete solidarity with the Berkeley radicals. This was why they rejected Glazer's article (not, by the way, an easy thing for an editor to do in the case of a commissioned piece by an important writer who is also a personal friend).

In contrast to Feuer, Glazer sympathized with the student radicals on many points, he granted the legitimacy of many of their grievances, he agreed with many of their criticisms of the university and of the society at large, and he even took their feelings and ideas as widely representative of the sentiments of their entire generation. He did all this, but he also definitely refrained from an unqualified endorsement. He raised several questions about their ideas, about their tactics, and about what he called in a subsequent defense of his piece "the moral quality" of their actions, and especially the techniques of civil disobedience they had taken over from the civil-rights movement and adapted to the very different situation at Berkeley. "A great wave of energy has been released here," he said, but he also warned that "no movement in this world is immune from the threat of distortion and corruption, even a movement working for the good and the just. . . . These are possibilities; and at times they have come close to realization on the Berkeley campus."

An article on Berkeley written in the spirit of those words was not what *The New York Review* wanted. What it wanted, and what it got, was an article by two other members of the Berkeley faculty, Sheldon S. Wolin and John H. Schaar, who endorsed the rebellion wholeheartedly. Looked upon in the context of Berkeley itself, the uprising, they said, was a protest against the failures of the university—or the "multiversity," as very large institutions like Berkeley were then being called—to educate properly. Striking a note that would soon be more stridently sounded by a young radical in a pamphlet entitled *The Student as Nigger,* Wolin and Schaar said that the students were comparable to the poor of the "Other America"; they were "ill fed, ill housed and ill clothed not in the material sense, but in the intellectual and spiritual senses." But Wolin and Schaar also placed Berkeley in a wider context as a protest against "the phony slogans and spiritual tawdriness of so much of the public rhetoric and action of our time." As for the tactics that worried Glazer, there had been a few "regrettable, but understandable, and not unjustifiable" excesses, but except for these, the students had conducted themselves "with admirable dignity and calm . . . and showed a clearer appreciation than their elders of the moral burdens involved in the use of pressure tactics." Finally, on the issue of how representative the Berkeley student leaders were of their generation, Wolin and Schaar ridiculed Feuer's view that only a handful of radicals, many of them not even genuine students, had stirred up all the trouble. The truth, they said, was that the "vast majority of the students shared the goals" of the radicals, which in any event "consisted in little more than devotion to some traditional principles which their elders had taught them, plus that impatience with the conservatism of the old that the young ought to have."

By rejecting Glazer's article and publishing the one by Wolin and Schaar, *The New York Review* for all practical purposes announced that it was signing on with the new radicalism as a concrete political movement. Conversely, by both rejecting Feuer's article and publishing Glazer's, *Commentary* was in effect saying that it now had serious reservations about the new radicalism.

Neither Glazer nor I had as yet come anywhere near to giving up on the Movement, but we were both developing anxious misgivings about it. Looking back I can see more clearly than I did at the time that Glazer and I were less consistent than Silvers and the Epsteins. All of us had in varying degrees been calling for a new radicalism. We had all helped in one way or another to build the intellectual foundation for a fundamental critique of the current condition of American society, of its legitimating ideas and of its leading institutions. We had all written and caused to be written and published and promoted articles and books paving the way for SDS and the Port Huron Statement and for FSM and the Berkeley uprising. A few years later, when Columbia erupted, Lionel Trilling, thinking of the "subversive" and "adversary" attitudes toward modern society he had inescapably propagated through the teaching of modern literature, ruefully reflected that the demonstrators he found himself opposing were in a profound sense his own students: where else had they learned the language of "alienation" from American society but in his own classroom? Yet Trilling had less reason to feel that way than Nathan Glazer did, and certainly less than I myself did. He, after all, had at first strongly resisted the ideas that led to the new radicalism, whereas by developing and spreading those ideas we had done everything in our power to bring the new radicalism into being. In celebrating its emergence, *The New York Review* was doing what *Commentary* might also have been expected to do and, again, with greater reason, *Commentary* having been in the field long before *The New York Review* even existed.

Nevertheless—speaking now for myself alone, since I, as usual, went a bit further than Glazer though, also as usual, sharing his views almost to the last detail—I did not feel vindicated by Berkeley, any more than I had felt confirmed by the Port Huron Statement. The vulgar caricature of ideas I myself had subscribed to in the Port Huron Statement had made me wonder about their validity, and the translation of those ideas into action at Berkeley was deepening my doubts.

There was very little actual violence at Berkeley but there was a great deal of rhetorical violence in the speeches and manifestos and even in such apparently responsible analyses as the article by Wolin and Schaar. The violence that was done, in other words, was precisely to language and to ideas. Everything was simplified into slogans, fit for shouting and chanting; rational argument was replaced by "direct-action" tactics based on the assumption that there was no longer anything to argue about except the choice of means to an end already known with great certainty to be just. Applied to the fight against segregation in the South, such tactics made sense. But what sense did they make in the context of a university, one of the greatest and most liberal in the country? The answer of the radicals and their apologists was to deny that there was any significant distinction between Berkeley and Montgomery, Alabama; and in that answer lay their first act of violence against language and ideas.

And there were many other such acts of violence committed at Berkeley and in the approving literature it spawned. Violence was committed against the distinction between the black poor of the ghettos and the privileged and prosperous young on the campuses *(The Student as Nigger)*; violence was committed against the distinction between the oppressions of a tyrannical state and the disciplines of an academic community, with required courses and grades being cavalierly compared to prisons and chains; and violence was committed against the distinction between one political position and another, as when Wolin and Schaar maintained that the Berkeley radicals were merely trying to uphold the traditional values of American liberalism.

As an intellectual, I would have found it hard to stomach open contempt for distinctions under any circumstances and under any aegis. I had been trained to regard such contempt as simple philistinism—an expression of hatred for intellectual values and for the pursuit of truth (which, in the words of a wonderful French epigram, always "resides in nuance"). So had my friends on *The New York Review*. Berkeley thus resolved itself into a conflict of loyalties—loyalty to radicalism as against loyalty to intellectual standards. As I saw it, they were willing to sacrifice intellectual values to their radicalism, whereas I was choosing to break political ranks rather than betray what I regarded as my responsibilities to the intellectual community and the intellectual vocation.

They of course denied that their wholehearted and uncritical support of the Berkeley students involved a betrayal of intellectual values. In fact, they asserted the opposite. What the students wanted, wrote Wolin and Schaar, and what they were being denied by the "architects of the multiversity," was precisely an education that would inform their lives "with the values of the intellect, preparing them to serve as the guardians of society's intellectual honesty and political health." Yet Wolin and Schaar, like the students themselves, and the legions of their other adult apologists and fellow travelers, belied this claim of devotion to intellectual values both in their ludicrously overheated characterizations of the virtues of the students ("They take ideals seriously, and are quick to detect evasion, posturing, and doublethink . . . [They have] a plenitude of spirit, open and vital . . . [They are] a university's most valuable resource") and in the indiscriminate brutality of their ideological assaults on the university and all other established institutions.

I know for a certainty now, and I even had a glimmer of it then, that this split over Berkeley was the beginning of a process that bore a very striking resemblance to the struggles of the *Partisan Review* circle over Stalinism in the 1930s. In its original incarnation, *Partisan Review* had been an organ of the Communist party. That it was a devoted one can be seen from an author's note in one of the early issues: "Tillie Lerner is at work on a novel of mining life. . . . Last year she took a leave of absence from the Young Communist League to produce a future citizen of Soviet America." (Tillie Lerner's offspring did not become a citizen of Soviet America, though she herself, under her married name of Tillie Olsen, did become a venerated heroine of the women's movement nearly half a century later.) But Phillips and Rahv soon ran into trouble with their superiors in the party and they broke —not over such momentous events as the Moscow Trials or the Nazi-Soviet pact, but over their refusal to accept dictation on matters of literary taste and judgment. As Communists, they discovered, they were expected to subordinate their literary and intellectual values to the party line. They were not, for example, supposed to publish or praise any writer who had the wrong political views or who wrote in any but the officially approved "proletarian" style, no matter how good a writer he might be. Confronted with a choice between loyalty to the party and loyalty to literature, they chose literature.

Now, the radicalism of the 1960s differed in several major respects from the radicalism of the 1930s. The most important of these was the presence in the 1930s, and the absence in the 1960s, of an organization like the Communist party which made policy and could force its members (and even, though to a much lesser extent, its sympathizers) to accept and support whatever the line might be on any given issue. There could be no question in the thirties of disagreeing with the party line and remaining a member of the party; anyone who could not accept party discipline either resigned or was expelled. Nothing like this existed in the sixties. The Communist party was still alive, but it was infinitely weaker than it had been in the thirties; and in any case, it no longer occupied the center of the radical movement. But neither had it been succeeded by any other organized group. There were many groups and many parties. From time to time, one of them—SDS, FSM, SNCC, the Black Panthers—would move to the center of the stage, but few ever tried to exercise the kind of power over their members that the Communists did, and those who tried invariably failed.

Yet decentralized though the Movement of the sixties was, and chaotic though it may have been in its organization, it was nevertheless amazingly successful in establishing a powerful claim to loyalty over amazingly large numbers of people. For a long time almost anything done by the Movement or in the name of the Movement could at the very least count on widespread support and would often be celebrated, as Berkeley was, in the most glowing terms. Like the "working class" in the thirties, the "young" and the "blacks" in the sixties could do no wrong, and to oppose them was to be accused of opposing the forces of political and social health.

On Berkeley, *The New York Review* decided to follow the "party line." Obviously I did not believe then, nor am I suggesting now, that *The New York Review* was taking orders from above; if anything, it was the other way around, since the appearance of so enthusiastic an endorsement of the student radicals in a magazine already noted for its commitment to high literary and intellectual standards undoubtedly helped to legitimize their uprising and everything it purported to represent. But what I did believe then, and what I am suggesting now, is that *The New York Review* was deceiving itself and others as to the meaning of the events at Berkeley. It was lending itself to political propaganda when it should have been exercising the critical function it had promised to perform in its very first number, and it was thereby betraying the values of the intellectual tradition in which it implicitly claimed a place.

That tradition was the tradition of critical independence that had been established, or reaffirmed, by *Partisan Review* in its break with the Communist party. In describing it, William Phillips said it was a form of "dissidence" that "made itself felt through a criticism of crude, agitational, populist slogans," and it was precisely this kind of dissidence and this kind of criticism that in my judgment was now called for once again. In the case of Berkeley, this meant refusing to romanticize or sentimentalize the "young" merely for political advantage or because they seemed to be on one's own side. And that in turn meant refusing to go along with "crude, agitational, populist slogans" even if they seemed in the short run to serve one's political purposes.

In breaking with the Communist party, the *Partisan Review* intellectuals had not seen themselves as breaking with radicalism. They still considered themselves the embodiment of "a free-floating radical spirit," as Phillips put it, in conflict with "a historical force that both channeled it and throttled it." This was not exactly how Glazer and I felt in our growing disaffection from the radical movement of the sixties, but we certainly did not see ourselves as becoming conservative or moving to the Right either. In taking a critical stand on the Berkeley uprising, we did not deny the reality of the grievances against the university that had presumably caused all the trouble. Nor did we deny the need for changes in the way Berkeley, and the American educational system in general, operated. That would have been the conservative or right-wing position. What we did deny was that the situation had become so bad that nothing less than a revolution could possibly do any good. We thought that Berkeley was a fundamentally sound institution that should and could be improved without resort to "tactics of force and disruption" and the rhetorical violence that always seemed to accompany tactics of that kind. And we also believed—as Glazer put it in answering an attack by one of his colleagues, Philip Selznick, whose views were almost exactly the same as Wolin's and Schaar's—that a "time of potential change" would be "perverted and aborted" if the student leaders failed to "recognize how such a wide-ranging discussion concerning the character and future of the university should be conducted."

For taking this position, Glazer was privately denounced by Jason Epstein as a "fink." Since I had published Glazer's piece, and since I both agreed with and admired it, I too should have been tarred with the same brush. But I was given at least a temporary reprieve, possibly because Jason was not yet ready to quarrel with me seriously, possibly because in Jason's eyes my credentials as a radical were less suspect than Glazer's (Glazer had, after all, managed to maintain suspiciously friendly relations with the likes of Irving Kristol, and even Lewis Feuer). In addition to following the Movement party line, then, Jason was serving notice that to deviate from it, even gently, was at a minimum to risk abuse and to open oneself up to the most insulting interpretation of one's motives.

This too was reminiscent of the experience of our intellectual elders in the thirties. No sooner had they begun voicing the mildest doubts about the wisdom of the Communist party on what might have seemed the relatively safe issue of literary taste and judgment than they began to find themselves vilified as traitors preparing to sell out for some form of personal gain. The bitter joke was that far from gaining as a result of a break with the Communist party, they stood only to lose. For the literary-intellectual world they lived in was so heavily influenced by the Communists at the time that breaking was more dangerous to a young intellectual's chances of personal gain than staying in. To be sure, things were not as bad in New York as they were in Hollywood, where (as Louis Berg, who spent many years covering the movie industry for a mass-circulation magazine, once told me) the head of one of the big studios was driven to circulate a memo informing all personnel that it would no longer be enough to be a Communist in order to be employed there and that doing a bit of work would now also be required. But even in New York, young anti-Stalinist intellectuals like Mary McCarthy and Philip Rahv had trouble getting books to review in the thirties from literary editors like Malcolm Cowley of the then fellow-traveling *New Republic;* and many book-publishing houses in those days were equally cold to writers of the "wrong" political persuasion.

In the sixties things were a bit different, but what some of us were later to think of as the "terror" also came into play then. The word "terror," like everything else about the sixties, was overheated. No one was arrested or imprisoned or executed; no one was even fired from a job (though there were undoubtedly some who lost out on job opportunities or on assignments or on advances from book publishers they might otherwise have had). The sanctions of this particular reign of "terror" were much milder: one's reputation was besmirched, with unrestrained viciousness in conversation and, when the occasion arose, by means of innuendo in print. People were written off with the stroke of an epithet—"fink" or "racist" or "fascist" as the case might be—and anyone so written off would have difficulty getting a fair hearing for anything he might have to say. Conversely, anyone who went against the Movement party line soon discovered that the likely penalty was dismissal from the field of discussion.

Seeing others ruthlessly dismissed in this way was enough to prevent most people from voicing serious criticisms of the radical line and—such is the nature of intellectual cowardice—it was enough in some instances to prevent them even from allowing themselves to entertain critical thoughts. The "terror," in other words, could at its most effective penetrate into the privacy of a person's mind. But even at its least effective, it served to set a very stringent limit on criticism of the radical line on any given issue or at any given moment. A certain area of permissible discussion and disagreement was always staked out, but it was hard to know exactly where the boundaries were; one was always in danger of letting a remark slip across the border and unleashing the "terror" on one's head. Better, then, not to take a chance. Of course one could recant and be forgiven; or alternatively one could simply speak one's mind and let the "terror" do its worst. Yet whatever one chose to do, the problem remained.

Berkeley was only the beginning, a kind of warning shot across the bow. A little later there would be Vietnam and Jason would act as an instrument of the "terror" among his own friends and acquaintances and associates, revealing as he did so the virulence that lay beneath the generally genteel and sober surface of *The New York Review* but that only occasionally showed itself fully in print. Once, for example, in the course of what had been a civil discussion among a group composed entirely of people who thought that the United States should never have intervened in Vietnam and all of whom agreed that the United States should get out as soon as possible, someone expressed anxiety over the likelihood that the Communists would take over if the United States withdrew, at which point Jason turned on him and snarled: *So you like to see little babies napalmed.*

The group was stunned by the injustice of this remark but when I saw how few of them protested, I realized that something more was going on here than another eruption of the kind for which Jason was famous among all who knew him. They were afraid of what might be said about them, not just by Jason but in general, and not only to their faces but behind their backs when they would be unable to defend themselves and when, as they knew all too well from their own reluctance to defend others against such insulting charges, there would be no one else to stand up for them either.

I myself did not take the "terror" seriously for a very long time. I knew that it was there, and I detested the sight of it in action, but I suppose I thought that I personally had nothing to fear from it. Certainly I was not afraid of Jason. I never hesitated to cut him off when he began making outrageous statements about others, and once I even made a drunken public scene in a restaurant when he compared the United States to Nazi Germany and Lyndon Johnson to Hitler. This comparison was later to become a commonplace of radical talk, but I had never heard it made before, and it so infuriated me that I literally roared in response. He was taken aback and so was I, and when we both calmed down a bit, I told him that he had better be careful about saying such things because if he really meant them he ought to leave the country or join a revolutionary party, and if he didn't really mean them he had no business trying to persuade others who might be more serious than he was and who might therefore feel impelled to act on what they believed.

That evening Jason backed down, but he and *The New York Review* went on to engage in just such efforts of irresponsible persuasion. On the issue of Vietnam in particular, *The New York Review* more and more stridently pushed an interpretation according to which the United States was indeed the moral equivalent of Nazi Germany, and the clear implication of which was that almost any action to overthrow so evil a system was justified. The war was the most visible expression of this evil "Amerikan" system, but it was not the only one. There was also the "dehumanization" of the young in the universities, and to this process demonstrations, even if they involved more actual physical violence than occurred at Berkeley, were, also by clear implication, the proper response. And there was, finally, the oppression of the blacks. Here violence was not only a justified and a proper but a necessary response. *The New York Review* rarely published anything openly advocating such violence—it was a little too cautious for that—but there was no doubt as to where its sympathies lay on this matter. In the summer of 1967, just after a series of bloody riots in the black ghettos of the North had broken out, *The New York Review* published on its cover a diagram showing how to make the firebomb known as a Molotov cocktail; inside the same issue there was an article by the young radical journalist Andrew Kopkind declaring that "Martin Luther King and the 'leaders' who appealed for nonviolence . . . *are all* beside the point"—the point now being that "Morality, like politics, starts at the barrel of a gun."

This was too much even for some previously uncritical admirers of the Movement and of *The New York Review.* Yet what mainly drew their protests was the open celebration of violence, not the despairing analysis both of the condition of blacks in the North and of the possibilities for improving that condition which made violence appear to be the only possible answer. On the contrary: that analysis was now beginning to seem persuasive to large numbers of liberals whose optimism about black progress had been shattered by the riots.

With an irony getting to be familiar, just as liberal opinion was becoming radicalized on this issue, my own views were moving in the opposite direction—away, that is, from the perspective of the new radicalism. The process had started long before the riots. Thus by an interesting coincidence, the very same number of *Commentary* (February 1965) which carried Glazer's article on Berkeley featured a piece entitled "From Protest to Politics" by Bayard Rustin calling for a change of direction by the civil-rights movement. Rustin's argument was that the tactics of "protest"—civil disobedience, nonviolent demonstrations, and other forms of "direct action"—which had worked so well in the fight against segregation were unsuited to the struggle for economic and social equality. What was needed in order to undertake that much more difficult struggle was political action to enact programs going beyond civil rights as such—"programs for full employment, abolition of slums, the reconstruction of our educational system, new definitions of work and leisure." To enact such programs, a coalition had to be formed "of Negroes, trade unionists, liberals, and religious groups" who could work together as they just had in electing Lyndon Johnson by a landslide margin over the forces of racism and reaction united behind Barry Goldwater in 1964.

It was a tribute to the prestige which the idea of revolution had already acquired by 1965 that Rustin should have insisted on applying it to a program and a strategy that were the opposite of revolutionary in the usual sense. I would even go so far as to say that the whole point of Rustin's article was to deny that there was any need for a revolution in America. Why resort to revolution when, by working directly within the established political system and according to its own already established rules, it was possible to bring about a "qualitative transformation of fundamental institutions . . . to the point where the social and economic structure which they comprised can no longer be said to be the same"?

What Rustin was saying about the problems of the blacks bore a striking similarity to what Glazer was saying about the problems of the young: that they could be solved by working peaceably through the normal processes of an already functioning system. But if that was true, it meant that the system was basically sound and worth preserving. And it also meant that it was irresponsible, and worse, to compare the United States to Nazi Germany, or even to encourage the idea that desirable change could never be effected within the going social terms or the established political rules.

Beneath all the particular disagreements over one detail or another, it was on this large question of the nature and character of American society that I found myself more and more parting company with the Movement in general and *The New York Review* in particular. Not only did I reject the view that the United States was as evil in its way as Nazi Germany had been; I even objected to the idea that it was evil in any degree. That there were many things wrong with the country I had been saying for a long time now. But *evil?* Beyond redemption? In need of and deserving to be overthrown by force and violence? I could not believe that the condition of the blacks, let alone of the young, justified any such apocalyptic verdict. And I even felt the same way about Vietnam. I had opposed American military intervention into Vietnam from the beginning as a piece of arrogant stupidity and I continued to support an American withdrawal, if at all possible through a negotiated settlement that would keep the Communists from taking over in the South. But I did not and could not see the American role in Vietnam as evidence that the United States and its leaders were evil. In fact it seemed to me closer to the truth to say that the United States was fighting in Vietnam out of an excess of idealism—making good on John Kennedy's famous promise in his inaugural address that we would "pay any price and bear any burden" to hold the line against Communist expansionism—rather than out of the will to conquer or dominate others.

Nothing could have been more offensive to the radical party line than a favorable attitude of this kind toward the United States. To be pro-American in the sixties was like being anti-Soviet in the thirties, for just as radicalism then had been tied to support of the Soviet Union as the center of socialist hope, so radicalism now increasingly defined itself in opposition to the United States as the major obstacle to the birth of a better world. Here too, then, in dissenting from the anti-Americanism of the new radicals, I thought I was adapting the example of my elders who in the thirties had refused to accept the equation of radicalism with support of the Soviet Union.

13

As I certainly should have known, all this was bound to unleash the "terror" on my head, just as the obversely analogous process had on theirs. And so, despite all my illusions of invulnerability, it finally did—when my book *Making It* appeared in the winter of 1967/68. In fact it started even before the book actually came out, with my own literary agent and my own publisher serving as its first instruments.

My agent read the manuscript and decided that she would rather forfeit a substantial commission and a client hitherto considered valuable than represent such a book. My publisher read the manuscript and decided that he would rather lose the substantial advance he had already paid me than put his imprint on such a book. They reacted, as I said at the time, the way their Victorian counterparts might have reacted to a work of sexual pornography. So did another publisher to whom the manuscript was then submitted by my new agent. Nor was the response much better among my friends. Lionel Trilling advised me not to publish it at all, warning that it would take me ten years to live it down. Jason Epstein agreed. No amount of money, he said, was worth what "they" would do to me when this book came out.

Was there nothing I could do? Were there no revisions I could make? Nothing, said my original publisher. Nothing, said my original agent. The trouble was not with this or that chapter or with the execution of the scheme; it was in the book as a whole, in its very conception. Lionel and Jason, however, were a bit more helpful: I could, each said independently, add a new chapter at the end taking back everything I had written before.

I decided to disregard all this advice, lovingly offered though it was by friends and associates who were sure that they had my best interests at heart. The idea that a writer should suppress his own book struck me as bizarre, and all the more so in a case like this. For far from thinking I had disgraced myself by writing *Making It,* I was proud of the book and the last thing I wanted to do was disown it or throw it away. Not that I was so supremely self-confident as to be certain that I was right and everyone else was wrong; on the contrary, I was full of pain and full of doubt. But I believed that even if *Making It* really was as bad as almost everyone seemed to think, I would be doing myself a greater damage by suppressing it than by publishing it.

In the end it was the firm Jason himself worked for that published *Making It,* though (by our mutual agreement and to our mutual relief) he had nothing whatever to do with the process. When it finally came out the critical response was not as uniformly bad as had been predicted; there were a few mixed reviews and even a few favorable ones. But by any measure other than the dire expectations Jason and Lionel had aroused in me, the response was very nasty indeed. In an article about *Making It* and its reception that was itself none too friendly to the book, Norman Mailer summed up the critical response as "brutal—coarse, intimate, snide, grasping, groping, slavering, slippery of reference, crude and naturally tasteless." But, he added, "the public reception of *Making It* was nevertheless still on the side of charity if one compared the collective hooligan verdict to the earlier fulminations of the Inner Clan." By the "Inner Clan," Mailer meant the community of New York literary intellectuals I myself had called the Family. According to Mailer, what they had been saying in private about *Making It* even before it was published made the "horrors" of the public reception seem charitable and kind. "Just about everyone in the Establishment"—i.e., the Family—was "scandalized, shocked, livid, revolted, appalled, disheartened, and enraged." They were "furious to the point of biting their white icy lips. . . . No fate could prove undeserved for Norman, said the Family in thin quivering late-night hisses."

Having of course read all the reviews, I could confirm for myself the accuracy of Mailer's characterization of the public reception of *Making It,* but it was hard for me to tell whether his description of the private reaction was exaggerated. Not many of those "thin quivering late-night hisses" had I actually heard with my own ears, and the few members of the Family who had the courage to tell me what they thought about *Making It* did so, or pretended to do so, in the measured tones of serious literary criticism and more in sorrow than in anger.

Still, I had every reason to trust Mailer's account. For one thing, there was independent confirmation. In one of the weekly news magazines it was reported that in recent weeks *Making It* had replaced Vietnam as the main topic of conversation at dinner parties in New York; and the author of the report clearly thought that as an evil to be deplored the book was a reasonable substitute for the war. Rumors also reached me from time to time about the extraordinary animosity "everyone" seemed to feel toward *Making It.* A few compassionate souls even did me the favor of quoting particularly choice examples, and they came very close to justifying Mailer's lurid imagery: "they spoke after midnight," he said, "in voices like snakes and beetles and rats, hiss and titter, prick and sip."

The book that provoked this reaction told the story of how I had moved from a childhood in the slums of Brooklyn to a position at the center of the New York literary establishment, and of what I had learned in the course of this journey about the way success is achieved in American society and about "the contradictory American attitude toward the ambition for and the pursuit of worldly success." Though autobiographical, it was not exactly an autobiography since it confined itself very strictly to a single aspect of my life, my career, and ruthlessly excluded any details that did not bear directly on that single theme.

Nor was it exactly a success story. Certainly, as I said in the preface, it resembled "the traditional success story in tracing the progressive rise of a young man up from poverty and obscure origins." In contrast to the traditional success story, however, its purpose was not "to celebrate that rise, but rather to describe certain fine-print conditions that are attached to the successful accomplishment of what the sociologists call 'upward mobility' in so heterogeneous a society as our own." In addition to this, it differed from the traditional success story in being "a confessional work." That is, it deliberately set out to expose "an order of feeling in myself, and by implication in others, that most of us usually do our best to keep hidden, from ourselves as well as others."

The feeling I was referring to here was the lust for success which I said (borrowing a phrase from D. H. Lawrence) had replaced sexual lust as the "dirty little secret" of our time, especially for the writers, artists, and intellectuals among whom I lived and worked. In writing *Making It* I was betraying the dirty little secret and thereby opening myself up to charges of self-inflation and tastelessness. "So be it," I cavalierly declared; I was willing to offend against certain current standards of tastefulness for the sake of bringing the dirty little secret out into the open and thus weakening its power to shame.

Except for its virulence, then (since charges of self-inflation and tastelessness were the least of the accusations hurled at *Making It* and at me personally), the response to the book was foreseen in the book itself. By violating a taboo, I had asked for trouble, and my request had been enthusiastically granted. So clearly did this response confirm my own theory about attitudes toward success in the literary world that I might even have taken a certain bitter satisfaction in the reflection that *Making It* could only have been warmly received if it had failed to accomplish what it had set out to do—if, that is, it had played false with its declared intention of bringing a dirty little secret out into the open, if the dirty little secret were not really a dirty little secret at all, or if I had only pretended to be revealing a shameful truth while reassuringly winking at the reader and then taking the whole thing back at the end (as both Lionel and Jason had indeed urged me to do).

There was a good deal of talk about politics in *Making It,* but it was not a political book in the narrow sense. Nor was the opposition to it mainly provoked by the political views it explicitly expressed. When I wrote *Making It* I still considered myself a member, and even in some sense a leader, of the radical movement, but the uneasiness I have been describing here over the direction the Movement had begun to take was also evident there.

Thus I said at one point that I was worried about "a certain tone or emphasis" that was becoming visible in the Movement on questions like the cold war, Vietnam, and civil rights. In the course of spelling this out I provided ammunition enough for any number of political attacks on the book—but not enough to account for the extraordinary virulence of those that were actually made. What provoked them was not this doubt about or that disagreement with the radical party line. It was the informing idea of the whole book—an idea implicit in the title and summed up toward the end in the statement that the pursuit of success was not necessarily "a corrupting force in American culture."

This may not sound like a political statement, and in an ordinary political climate it would not automatically be read as one. But in the climate of 1967 any statement about American culture was taken as political, and, conversely, all strictly political statements, while important and interesting to many people in their own right and on their own terms, became even more important and interesting for what they revealed about the nature of American culture. Vietnam, for example, was by now seen universally among radicals and more and more widely among liberals not as a mistake but as a crime—and not as the crime of an otherwise innocent nation with a previously spotless record but as an entirely characteristic act differing from similar acts in the past only by virtue of the nakedness that had made detection possible. Now at last the truth about this master criminal posing as a law-abiding philanthropist could be uncovered for all the world to see. The truth was that the United States had for the past twenty years been pursuing the goal of world domination and had been using the illusory specter of a Communist menace as the excuse. Its foreign policy, pretending to be guided by an opposition to Communist aggression, was in fact ruled by aggressive purposes of its own, and there was virtually nothing it would not do to achieve those purposes. It would bomb, it would assassinate, it would subvert—and all for the sake of imposing on the rest of the world a system that was in itself evil at the core.

This was where the issue of race came into the picture. As Vietnam had stripped the benign liberal mask from the face of American foreign policy to reveal the criminal imperialist who had been hiding behind it all along, the course of the civil-rights movement in the North had exposed the evil built into the very foundations of the American system.

Ideas like these, once confined to small or marginal groups, were now becoming fashionable in the most conventional and respectable circles. Around the time *Making It* was published, a professor of philosophy at Columbia declared that "Anyone who still imagines that the United States is the land of opportunity and the bastion of democracy is a candidate for a mental hospital. . . ." What a sane person according to those lights believed was summed up in the same period by the science editor of CBS television:

> We are a nation with the blood of genocide on our hands. For those who think that America cannot go the way of Nazi Germany, we have only to recall that we have already been down that road. That's what makes the whole black-white situation so frightening. Will white Americans somehow find their way back to the rationale of destroying whole peoples in the name of God, capitalism, and law and order?

As is clear from statements like those, Vietnam and the race issue were now being seen—and not only in small centers of radical opinion—less as political problems that needed to be addressed and could be solved than as links in the chain of evidence proving that the United States was now and always had been an incorrigibly evil country.

But the case against America was not confined to these indictments of its political system, its treatment of the blacks, and its behavior in the world at large. It also reached directly down into the cultural (or what in another age would have been called the spiritual) foundations of the country: that "exclusive worship of the bitch-goddess SUCCESS" which, as William James had said more than half a century before, was "our national disease."

This idea that the worship of success lay at the root of the sickness of a "sick society" became the central, the organizing theme of the strictly cultural arm of the Movement, variously known as the "youth culture," "the new culture," and the "counterculture." For the culture against which the "young" were said to be rebelling, the old culture with respect to which theirs was "new," the established culture to which theirs was a "counter"—this old established culture was what had once been called "bourgeois" and what was now more generally called "middle-class." So far as the counterculture and its apologists were concerned, "bourgeois" or "middle-class" culture meant puritanism in sex and philistinism in the arts; in some versions of countercultural thought it could also embrace science, industrialism, and technology. But what it stood for above all else was the "exclusive worship" of success defined in terms of money and material things.

And it was above all else because it challenged this idea about success in America that *Making It* provoked such a storm. *Making It* denied, in the first place, that American culture was entirely given over to the worship of success. One could, I said, argue that the truth had been more complicated even in the heyday of bourgeois self-confidence fifty or a hundred years before, but whatever might have been the case then, it was certainly more complicated now. Scarcely anyone could be found any longer who had a good word to say for the pursuit of success or its attainment; not even businessmen seemed willing to preach the old "gospel" according to which the ambition for success was the highest virtue and the amassing of riches its just reward. America was now a country where other qualities besides worldly ambition and other things besides money were more and more widely valued. In this connection, I pointed to the rising status of the intellectual class and the growing appetite for the arts in the population at large.

In saying such things I was moving uncomfortably close to the "complacent" view associated with the "American Celebration" of the fifties, which was bad enough, especially coming from someone who had helped to weaken the grip of that view on the intellectual community. But what was far worse than this assertion that success was no longer worshiped in America to the exclusion of all else—not even by businessmen—was the converse contention of *Making It* that neither was it entirely despised —not even by intellectuals. Intellectuals did not, of course, admit this—it was their dirty little secret. Nevertheless it was true and moreover there was nothing in it to be ashamed of. The old idea that the pursuit of success was corrupting in itself may once have been largely valid, but things had changed in America to the point where this was no longer automatically or necessarily the case. Nor could it any longer be taken for granted that the achievement of success was in itself a mark of corruption. There had been a time, for example, when the presence of a novel on the best-seller list almost certainly meant that it was a bad book, but this had long since ceased to be so, and nothing but "hypocrisy and cant" followed from denying the change.

In saying these things, *Making It* did more than fly in the face of the radical party line on the spiritual condition of American society; it also undermined the claims of the intellectuals to represent a higher and better alternative. For those claims rested on the assumption that the educated or intellectual class was intrinsically superior—superior by nature—to the business class. The business class was "materialistic," the intellectual class was "idealistic"; the business class valued the "lower" things of life, the intellectual class cared only about the "higher"; and so on through all the usual dualisms and all the invidious indices. Merely by suggesting that this picture was an oversimplification, I had given aid and comfort to the "enemy" and had for all practical purposes become a traitor to my class.

Naturally that is not how I regarded myself. In my own view I was being more loyal to my class by trying to tell the truth—even if it meant being critical of myself and my fellow intellectuals— than my friends at *The New York Review* and on the Left in general with their uncritical celebrations of anything that seemed to serve their political or ideological position. That the tribe of "yahoos and muckers" (in Mailer's pungent phrase) who did most of the reviewing in the middlebrow press would be incapable of understanding such a thing, I fully expected, especially as most of them had become fellow travelers of the Movement and so obedient to the radical party line on all issues that they could not even recognize it as a line. (They thought it was the simple truth and self-evident to all reasonable minds.)

I even expected that a certain number of my "relatives" in the Family would have trouble with the book; they were the ones who were "capable of the most brutal honesty in other areas" but who "would at the mention of the word 'success' suddenly lift their eyes up to the heavens and begin chanting the most horrendous pieties imaginable." But not William Phillips, who in breaking with the Communist party as a young man had set the example I saw myself as following. And not Norman Mailer, whom I had described as "the only man in America . . . capable of perfect honesty on the subject of success" and who had in *Advertisements for Myself* produced "one of the great works of confessional autobiography in American literature." And not Lionel Trilling, who had "taught me more than he or I ever realized" about the very complexities of American culture I was trying to describe and unravel. Each of these men, in addition to having influenced me in a way that bore directly on the writing of *Making It*, was a close friend. Thus I had every reason to believe that they, at least, would understand the book. Yet all three were in varying degrees hostile to *Making It.* And while they were all prevented by a lifelong belief in the principle of the autonomy of art from admitting, perhaps even to themselves, that the objection was political, there could be no doubt that it was.

Phillips, for example, had so much trouble explaining to me what he thought was wrong in strictly literary terms with *Making It* that I was unable to understand what he was saying then and I am unable to remember it now. What I do remember, though, is a series of conversations with him both before and after *Making It* came out, in which it was evident that he had become very uneasy with my increasingly critical attitude toward the new radicalism.

There was an ironic side to this, since he had several years earlier been very uneasy about my enthusiasm over the potentialities of a new radicalism in America. Then he had accused me of overestimating Norman Mailer, he had expressed bewilderment over my excitement about Norman O. Brown, and he had disapproved of my sponsorship of Paul Goodman. He was all for being critical of American society, but he was still enough of a Marxist at heart to regard the utopianism of such writers as a form of infantile leftism.

So too on issues of foreign policy. In the late fifties and early sixties he was still enough of an anti-Communist to look with suspicion on a peace movement that took so benign a view of Soviet intentions and that contained so many old Stalinists and fellow travelers; even on Vietnam, he leaned at the beginning more toward support of American policy than opposition to it. What worried him about the new radicalism of the early sixties was that it seemed uncomfortably reminiscent of the old radicalism of the early thirties against which he himself had rebelled and whose leading ideas and attitudes he had spent so many years fighting. Even as late as the mid-sixties it was possible to cite him as someone who doubted that the New Left was quite as new as it claimed to be. Indeed in *Making It* itself I was able to write the following sentence: "William Phillips once told the New Left-minded English critic Kenneth Tynan that he could not argue with him about politics because Tynan's arguments were so old that he, Phillips, could no longer remember the answers."

Yet even as I was writing that sentence it was turning from a good joke into a sorry literal truth. At first Phillips had been unable to remember the answers, but he had at least known why answers were necessary. By the time *Making It* came out he seemed even to have forgotten that. At any rate, he was in the process of changing his mind about the new radicalism. Now instead of cautioning me as he had done earlier about getting mixed up with a political movement that might turn out to be the latter-day equivalent of the Stalinism of his youth, he was warning me against going too far in my criticisms of that very same movement. "They're *not* like the Communists," he insisted heatedly when I tried to draw a parallel between his break with the Communist party and my own growing disillusionment with the New Left. Paradoxically, when the New Left had several years before, in the early sixties, really looked as though it represented a departure from the Communist tradition, he had mainly noticed the similarities; and yet now, in the late sixties, when the New Left was becoming less and less professedly "humanist" and more and more openly Leninist, he was suddenly overwhelmed with a sense of the differences.

Like so many other academics, William Phillips (who had become a professor at Rutgers in 1963 when that university took over the sponsorship of *Partisan Review*) grew radicalized precisely at the point when the new radicalism was reaching the height of its power in the universities. For by 1968 radicalism was so prevalent among college students that any professor who resisted it at the very least risked unpopularity and at the worst was in danger of outright abuse. Indeed it was in the universities that the "terror" first appeared and where it operated most effectively. But there was also a more positive pull in the idea that if so many of the "best" students were becoming radicals, then the new radicalism must surely be that "wave of the future" the Communist party had only seemed to be in the days of one's own youth.

In short, I think that William Phillips was radicalized by a desire to get on what looked like the winning side. From one point of view he was a little late in joining a movement already several years old. But from another point of view, he was in the forefront of a "wave" that was to sweep past the universities and other intellectual enclaves such as the one he and I inhabited in New York. Soon it would engulf even the city of Washington, where one politician after another would desert the liberal consensus which had governed the foreign and domestic policies of the country under the Kennedy and Johnson administrations and would begin betting their political fortunes on this new power in the land: what they called the "young."

Perhaps the first of these was Eugene McCarthy, who in 1968 challenged a sitting president, Lyndon Johnson, for the Democratic nomination, with Vietnam as his leading issue. McCarthy had not previously been a rebel or a maverick. He was a Democratic senator from Minnesota who had made a quixotic speech nominating Adlai Stevenson at the 1960 Democratic convention —the convention which ultimately nominated John F. Kennedy— and his name had subsequently been on the list of candidates being considered by Johnson as running mates in 1964. In the end Johnson chose the other senator from Minnesota, Hubert Humphrey, and it was often said to be his bitterness over this that led McCarthy into the effort to topple Johnson four years later.

I have never believed that theory. But neither have I ever believed that McCarthy took the extraordinary step of challenging a sitting president of his own party—a step which in those days, when there was still such a thing as party discipline and party leaders still had the power to punish a disloyal act, meant risking his own political career—entirely out of opposition to American policy in Vietnam. After all, we had already been fighting in

Vietnam in 1964 and that had not deterred McCarthy from wishing to run *with* Lyndon Johnson. Moreover, it is extremely unlikely that, had he been chosen, he would have behaved any differently from Humphrey who as vice-president was given the job of holding on to the support of his fellow liberals for the war.

Not that Humphrey was being insincere. He was a liberal—and none more militant—at a time when liberalism and anti-Communism still went comfortably together. But between 1964 and 1968 the marriage of liberalism and anti-Communism began to break up, largely because of the deepening doubts among liberals about Vietnam which made Humphrey (and would almost certainly have made McCarthy, if he had succeeded in becoming Johnson's vice-president) unpopular with his own political community.

In an interview on the occasion of his appointment in 1966 to Lyndon Johnson's White House staff, John Roche (a former president of Americans for Democratic Action, who like Humphrey had remained in the anti-Communist "church" and unlike Humphrey would stay there to the bitter end) told the reporter Jimmy Breslin, then an enemy of the antiwar movement but soon to be converted and radicalized by a sniff of the prevailing wind, that the only opponents of the war were a few "jackal bins" on the Upper West Side of Manhattan. No one could figure out what this mysterious term meant until it was explained as a typographical error for "Jacobin." I have always suspected that the typesetter was being blamed for Breslin's ignorance in transcribing a word he had never heard before. But be that as it may, both Roche and Breslin, in denigrating the strength of antiwar sentiment were certainly wrong about the trend within the liberal community, and they may even have been wrong about the state of affairs in the country at large.

On a trip with Willie Morris to his hometown in Mississippi, for instance, I was amazed to discover that even in the Deep South, in a place where sympathy for the military was strong, and which had gone overwhelmingly for Goldwater in 1964, no one seemed to be enthusiastic about the war. They were not against it exactly, but neither were they for it; mostly they were against the kind of people who were against it. And if support for the war was thin and passive in the Mississippi Delta, it was becoming altogether nonexistent in the universities, and among intellectuals generally. I say "becoming" because, contrary to the usual impression, here again it was a matter of liberals changing their minds and going over to the radical view.

As late as 1967, Noam Chomsky, perhaps the most influential radical critic of the war, could write, and *The New York Review,* then in the process of turning itself into the main center of such criticism within the intellectual community, could publish, a piece attacking the "intellectuals" and the academic community as apologists for American foreign policy in general and the war in Vietnam in particular. By the time this piece, "The Responsibility of Intellectuals," appeared, it was no longer true that the "intellectuals" were in favor of the war; the balance of opinion had shifted dramatically from the early sixties and by now even a few of those Chomsky singled out by name (Arthur Schlesinger and Daniel Bell) either had changed or were about to change their minds. Yet only a short while before, there would have been nothing especially outlandish in saying that the "intellectuals" or the "academic community" were an important constituent of the liberal consensus on foreign policy that had in some sense led to American military intervention into Vietnam.

In turning against the war, many of these liberal intellectuals no doubt thought that they were responding to the force of evidence and argument, and this may indeed have been the case with some. But I have always found it hard to believe that it was the case with most. In those days the argument over Vietnam in the universities was characterized less by the appeal to evidence and reason than by the shouting of slogans, the mounting of mass demonstrations, the threat and the occasional resort to physical force, and the actuality and ubiquitousness of rhetorical violence and verbal abuse. Admittedly there were "teach-ins" on Vietnam staged at many campuses, where reasoned arguments were offered and both sides were heard; and many articles and books were produced by opponents of American policy in which the case was developed and documentation amassed. But a point was soon reached where speakers supporting the war were either refused a platform or shouted down when they attempted to speak. A speaker whose criticisms were insufficiently violent could even expect a hard time, as I myself discovered when a heckler at Wayne State in Detroit accused me, to the clear delight of the audience, of not being "that much" against the war because in expressing my opposition to the American role I had also expressed my usual reservations about the virtues of the Communist side.

As for the literature, although some of it may have been intellectually persuasive, much of it was so aggressive in tone and abusive in language that the only way it was likely to change a reader's mind was through intimidation. This was even true of many pieces that looked at first glance as though they were engaging in an effort of rational persuasion.

Chomsky, for example, drew on his training in the field of linguistics to create an impression of scrupulous reasoning and meticulous scholarship; on the surface his political articles bore all the marks of responsible scholarly discourse, including—always including—large numbers of footnotes. But all this served only to legitimize a ferocious assault on anyone who disagreed with his own line (including other opponents of American policy whose opposition was based on a different set of assumptions) as —again the comparison that had so shocked me when I first heard it made—no better than Nazi war criminals.

"In no small measure it is attitudes like [theirs]", he wrote at the conclusion of "The Responsibility of Intellectuals," "that lie behind the butchery in Vietnam, and we had better face up to them with candor, or we will find our government leading us toward a 'final solution' in Vietnam, and in the many Vietnams that inevitably lie ahead." And in case the association of the phrase "final solution" with Nazism had not registered with sufficient force, Chomsky proceeded to quote a German soldier who had worked in one of the Nazi death camps and who had burst into tears upon being told that the Russians would hang him: "Why should they? What have I done?" This question, said Chomsky, was "one that we [i.e., the intellectuals] may well ask ourselves, as we read each day of fresh atrocities in Vietnam—as we create, or mouth, or tolerate the deceptions that will be used to justify them."

Language like that was not meant to persuade, nor could it do so; it could, however, incite supporters and frighten opponents, and that is exactly what it did. Those already convinced were encouraged to believe that no other view deserved to be tolerated; those who still disagreed but who lacked either very powerful conviction or very great courage lapsed into prudent silence; those who continued speaking up in favor of American policy were isolated and even excommunicated by students and colleagues alike; and those who had been wavering were pushed into joining the righteous—and winning—side.

14

It was to this rapid shift in the consensus on the war, I would guess, that Eugene McCarthy was responding when he first conceived the idea of challenging Lyndon Johnson for the Democratic presidential nomination in 1968. But in making the guess I have something more than mere speculation to go on.

One day either late in 1967 or early in 1968, I received a call from a mutual acquaintance who said that Senator McCarthy was coming to New York and would like to have lunch with me. Knowing that McCarthy occasionally did some writing, I assumed that he had a manuscript he wanted me to publish. As it turned out, he was not submitting a manuscript but testing the waters for his possible candidacy, and the only written matter he was carrying with him when he arrived at the restaurant was a volume of poems by Robert Lowell. Later he was to become famous for his literary propensities, but on that day it struck me as odd; no other politician I had ever met would have been interested in, or possibly even capable of, reading a difficult modern poet like Robert Lowell.

It was not that I thought that all politicians were stupid. On the contrary: if my experience of them was any guide, they tended as a breed to be much more intelligent than they were generally thought to be, especially by intellectuals.

To be sure, my experience of politicians was still very limited, but thanks to my friend Richard Goodwin it had also been intense. I had met Goodwin at a conference in 1961 when he was working in the White House as a speechwriter for John F. Kennedy. By 1965, after various detours through the federal bureaucracy, he was back in the White House working in the same capacity for Lyndon Johnson—one of the few Kennedy people to have joined Johnson and, of those few, one of the still smaller number who had been able to do so without incurring the wrath of the Kennedy family and its entourage. How he had managed this difficult feat I do not know, but there he was—one of Johnson's most important assistants and yet a close friend of Robert Kennedy, Jacqueline Kennedy, and (or so it seemed) everyone else who formed part of what some people were already calling the "government in exile." Johnson, who was bothered by the invidious comparisons always being made between him and John Kennedy and worried about a possible challenge in 1968 from Robert Kennedy, was evidently happy to have a Kennedy man like Dick Goodwin working for him. At the same time he must have been unsure of Goodwin's loyalty. Whatever the precise content of Johnson's suspicions, Goodwin was well aware of them, and he considered it the better part of wisdom to keep his relations with Kennedy as quiet as he decently could.

As for his relations with me, they were based, I think, on affection and sympathy, but there was also something less personal for him in our friendship. He was fascinated by the world of the New York intellectuals; it was a milieu he very much wanted to penetrate. I was by no means the only New York intellectual he had ever met or who could have introduced him around, but I was perhaps better placed than most in those days to perform this service. In the climate of the early sixties, before all the political battles that were to embitter my relations with so many former friends and acquaintances (including ultimately Goodwin himself), I knew and was on good terms with "everyone" in New York and I gave and went to large parties all the time. I remember taking Goodwin to such a party at Norman Mailer's apartment overlooking the harbor in Brooklyn Heights, where he not only inaugurated what would be a long friendship with the host but where he met many other writers and intellectuals for the first time. And so it went.

But the transaction was not at all one-sided. He in turn introduced me and some of my friends to Jacqueline Kennedy when she moved to New York, and he then arranged an extraordinarily heady day in Washington in the course of which we had a long lunch with Robert Kennedy at his home in McLean followed by a four-hour visit with Lyndon Johnson in the White House and finally a dinner party attended by George McGovern and various other Washington notables of the period.

I came away from that endless day in Washington with a new respect for the intelligence of politicians. Of the three I had been exposed to in such concentrated doses, the most impressive by far was Johnson and the least was Kennedy, but they all seemed more formidable than I had been led to expect by the conventional wisdom on this matter. McGovern, of whom I would in later years come to have a very low opinion indeed, struck me on that day as highly articulate and much more quick-witted than his gravely deliberate style of speaking might suggest. I was also surprised by his grasp of the ideological implications of foreign-policy questions that in Washington always seemed to be discussed as though they had no wider context or meaning at all. (I would have been less surprised on both counts if I had known that he had a Ph.D. in American history and that he had supported Henry Wallace for president in 1948.)

This favorable impression of McGovern was reinforced a year or so later, in 1966, when he came to New York to participate in a *Commentary* symposium on Vietnam in which he (together with Bernard Fall, an academic specialist on Vietnam), represented the antiwar position, while Dick Goodwin (soon to switch sides) and John Roche (who never would switch sides) spoke, in effect, on behalf of the Johnson administration. There was a party afterward, at Lillian Hellman's, where McGovern was made so much of by people who lived, as it clearly seemed to him, at the very center of intellectual influence and social glamor that it might well have occurred to him for the first time that the presidency might not be altogether beyond the reach even of such a man as he, a relatively obscure young senator from an unimportant midwestern state.

He and I left the party together at about 1:00 A.M., and we stood chatting briefly on the corner of Madison Avenue and Eighty-second Street before going our separate ways, I to the Upper West Side, he to the Plaza Hotel. Pointing down toward the Carlyle Hotel, where John F. Kennedy had always stayed when visiting New York and where—it was rumored—he had set up arrangements for women to slip in without being noticed, I teased McGovern about having to spend the night in New York alone. When he responded with a wry and self-deprecating gesture, I turned serious. Didn't he realize that opposition to Vietnam had been growing to the point where he, as one of the war's earliest and most outspoken critics, would soon find himself becoming very popular and much in demand—not only in New York and on the campuses, but in many other places too?

His eyes widened, almost imperceptibly, at this prediction. He himself believed—he had said so at the symposium that very afternoon—that strong support did not exist in the Senate for the policy we were now following in Southeast Asia. But he also knew that very few of his colleagues in the Senate, or in any other branch of the government, were willing to go public with their doubts.

In Washington the antiwar position had not yet become entirely respectable, let alone popular, so that anyone who looked at the world from the perspective of Washington was bound to misread the mood in New York, where the balance of power had been shifting toward the antiwar position since 1965. Of course, as Washingtonians never tired of pointing out, New York was not the country; sometimes they implied that it was not even an integral part of the United States. That New York was the center and the source of fashion—not only in such superficial areas as dress and manners but in the more serious realms of art and morals—everyone was willing to acknowledge. But it was not yet clearly recognized in Washington that politics itself was increasingly becoming a creature of cultural fashion, and that this development made what was happening in New York a significant portent for the political future—not, to be sure, as significant as the currency values in the galleries of Fifty-seventh Street were for the future of art, but significant enough to be weighed very carefully indeed in the balance of any new political calculation.

George McGovern was intelligent enough to make an impressive case for his point of view, but he was not intelligent enough to grasp the degree to which that point of view was being carried into the ascendant by the movement of culture—of ideas and attitudes shaped in the universities and the intellectual magazines and disseminated through the channels of communication centered in New York. And when he finally did come to perceive the workings of this new influence of culture on politics, he would go all the way over to the opposite mistake and wildly exaggerate its force.

Neither of the other two politicians I met that day in Washington understood the new role of culture in American politics any better than McGovern did, though it would soon drive the one out of the White House and might well have carried the other in if not for an assassin's bullet. In Lyndon Johnson's case, this failure of understanding could not be attributed to a lack of intelligence, since he was, on the evidence of what amounted to a four-hour monologue punctuated by an occasional question from me, a man of the highest intelligence. I say this now, and I said it then, in full awareness of how easy it is to be overly impressed when in the presence of the president of the United States.

Before meeting Johnson, the only other president in whose presence I had ever been was John F. Kennedy. On that occasion I was one of a group of about twenty who had just come from a conference—the one at which I had first run into Dick Goodwin and which Arthur Schlesinger, then also working at the White House, had attended as well. Goodwin and Schlesinger had arranged for the entire group to meet with the president at the conclusion of the conference, and we had all accordingly gathered on a clear and brilliantly sunny afternoon in the Rose Garden to await his arrival. Suddenly and with no advance warning the french doors opened and Kennedy emerged with a grin on his face as clear and brilliant as the day itself. The sight had an amazing and altogether unexpected effect on me. Staring at him while he circulated among us shaking hands, I felt a nearly ungovernable awe.

It was a humiliating experience. Here, after all, was a man I did not admire. Indirectly he had even made trouble for me when one of his people had asked a delegation of American Jewish Committee leaders why, if they were as enthusiastic about the president's policies as they were claiming to be, "their" magazine was being so unfriendly to him. (No great respecter of the principle of editorial independence, the assistant was unimpressed when they answered that *Commentary* was only "their" magazine in the sense that they subsidized it but not in the sense that they controlled its editorial policies.) That this assistant was acting in a way consistent with the president's feelings in the matter of editorial freedom became entirely clear when Kennedy himself complained to the publisher of *The New York Times* about his "young man in Saigon," David Halberstam, with the evident intention of getting him reassigned or maybe even fired; the effort failed, but no thanks to Kennedy.

Yet in spite of how I felt about Kennedy, I was awed by the sight of him, as though he were an absolute monarch and I his subject. Fortunately for my pride, I could see that I was not the only one of the group affected in that way. My friend Robert Rossen, an ex-Communist who still considered himself a radical, nearly fainted with pleasure when Kennedy responded to the sound of his name by saying, with the subtlest possible emphasis, "Very pleased to meet *you*, Mr. Rossen."

Others in the group too, including some who had seen a president or two before, were visibly overwhelmed. It was almost impossible not to be when in the presence of the most powerful man on earth, no matter what one might think of him as an individual or of how well he was doing his job. Even people who saw the president all the time—members of his own cabinet, for example—seemed vulnerable to the majesty conferred on him by the office. I would later be invited to a state dinner in the Johnson White House and what would strike me as unique about the occasion was that it was the only party I had ever attended where every single guest, including members of the cabinet, was unequivocally honored and delighted to be there.

Of course this was in the days of the "Imperial Presidency"—before Nixon and before Watergate; things would be a little different under Ford and Carter. (Indeed they would begin, thanks to his escalation of the war in Vietnam, to be different even under Johnson, as witness the singularly unawestruck action of Dwight Macdonald who, as a guest at a White House Festival of the Arts in 1965, circulated that petition against the president's policies in Vietnam and—*sic transit ingloria mundi*—the Dominican Republic.)

But escalation and its effects were still in the future on the day Dick Goodwin brought me to the Oval Office for what was supposed to be a brief introduction to the president and turned into an entire afternoon's visit. Johnson was just then at the high point of his confidence and his popularity. He had already proposed and was pushing through the most far-reaching program of liberal domestic legislation that had been seen since the legendary first hundred days of Franklin Roosevelt's New Deal. What was even better for his reputation than this great new "war on poverty," however, was the new boost he was giving to civil rights. Since his accession to the presidency, the Civil Rights Act of 1964 had already been passed, and only twelve days before my meeting with him he had delivered an address to a joint session of the Congress urging passage of a new civil-rights act that would guarantee the right to vote to the Negroes of the South.

That speech, read in a voice that remained heavily redolent of the Old South despite his awkward efforts to temper an accent of which he seemed ashamed now that he had become the president and therefore a national rather than merely a regional figure, made an enormous impact—and all the greater because in incorporating Martin Luther King's famous phrase "We Shall Overcome" it seemed to be lifting the civil-rights forces out of the marginal status of a dissident movement and placing them at the very center of American political life.

Everyone had praised the speech and the man who made it— in editorials and articles in the press and in hundreds of thousands of calls, letters, and telegrams to the White House. Understandably, then, Johnson, a naturally exuberant personality, was even more exuberant than usual the day I happened in on him. Almost the first thing he did was to order his assistant Jack Valenti to bring out some of his fan mail, which he proceeded to read aloud without the slightest embarrassment even though all the letters and telegrams more or less agreed that the speech had been the greatest statement of its kind by an American president at least since Abraham Lincoln; and there was a long telegram from John Steinbeck even more fulsome than that. Oddly enough bragging in this way did not detract from his dignity. Nor did his loud and deliberately, even ostentatiously, crass manner. Nor did the elaborate acts of mimicry he performed—speaking in falsetto, walking mincingly around the office—as he told one anecdote after another about his political career and gossiped about life in Washington.

This "vulgarity" of his was soon to become famous, or rather notorious, among the "government in exile" and its sycophants in the press who delighted in leaking stories about obscene remarks Johnson had made or about actions such as his alleged habit of receiving visitors while sitting on the toilet or insisting that they join him for a swim in the nude in the White House pool. The purpose of these leaks was to create an impression of Johnson's unfitness for the presidency based not on his policies (which were after all a continuation and extension and fulfillment of the proclaimed objectives of the Kennedy administration, emphatically including its objectives in Vietnam, despite all the self-serving subsequent propaganda to the contrary) but on his character. To the Kennedy court, Johnson was a usurper. I doubt that anyone in that court accepted Barbara Garson's insinuation in her much-acclaimed play *MacBird!* that he was a usurper like Macbeth —that is, that he had stolen the throne through murder. But despite the fact that he had just been elected in his own right by a landslide vote, they did seem to believe that he lacked legitimacy and that only a restoration of the Kennedy dynasty could set things right again.

If the power to arouse awe in his immediate presence were the mark of a president's legitimacy, then I would have to agree that John Kennedy had it and Lyndon Johnson did not. There was no awe in me when I entered Johnson's office and shook his hand. Nevertheless I was enormously impressed by him, and his "vulgarity" contributed to rather than detracted from a royal aura all his own. Kennedy may have been a king in the mold of Prince Hal become Henry V, but Johnson was more Henry VIII than

Macbeth: large, loud, full of gusto and appetite, and luxuriating in the freedom—a royal prerogative indeed—of uninhibited self-display.

At any rate that was how he struck me that day, and how he seems to have behaved in private much of the time. In public, and especially when delivering presidential statements, he tended to grow stiff and awkward, striving for a colorless and artificial dignity against his natural accent and his natural character. This made him seem false and itself did as much to create the "credibility gap"—the euphemism that began circulating for lies told by the president and other government officials—as anything he ever actually said.

Was, then, the fact that I found Johnson so extraordinarily intelligent another form of bending the knee in the presence of the king? I think not. Even as I sat there listening to him, I made a conscious effort to resist confusing my response to the royal aura with my judgment of the mind that was revealing itself in so rich and full a display. It was a mind attuned more to the concrete than to the abstract; it had a novelist's feel for the significant detail. Like a novelist too, Johnson possessed the mysterious gift of bringing a character to life in the act of telling a story about him. Through his monologue in the Oval Office that day passed a parade of Texas politicians led by the late Speaker of the House Sam Rayburn, from whom he had learned his trade, and a crowd of Washington personalities led by Richard Nixon, who, he said, surprisingly to me, was "perceptive as a cat" but whom he had delighted in outwitting, when he, Johnson, had been majority leader and Nixon as vice-president under Eisenhower had presided over the Senate and had been forced by Johnson through intricate parliamentary maneuvers to vote time and again against "widders and orphans." In describing these maneuvers, Johnson conveyed a better sense than I had ever been given of what American politics was like, and of what the art of party government consisted of at the highest levels and when practiced with the broadest and yet the subtlest skills.

Such skills were often denigrated as "wheeling and dealing," but in Johnson's hands they obviously involved intelligence of a very considerable order. It was not the "pure" intelligence most valued by intellectuals—the kind that is most at home with ideas and abstractions; it was a practical intelligence shot through with mother wit about human nature and a sense of how people actually behave in their daily lives. But it had also been trained and sophisticated by many years of experience in government. He was the last person of whom it could have been said, as he himself said of Estes Kefauver, another famous politician from the South, that he would never succeed in mastering the procedures of the Senate no matter how long he served there. Johnson sounded like an east Texas farm boy, and he never lost that knowledge of the ways of the earth that a rural upbringing can leave in the bones; yet long before becoming president he had developed into one of the great senators of modern times, and so powerful and influential in that role that his willingness to accept the lesser position of vice-president under a man like Kennedy, who had been his junior and his inferior in the Senate, came as a great surprise to many. What came as no surprise was how wretchedly unhappy he then turned out to be as vice-president. The office provided nothing for him to do that was commensurate with his talents and his energies, and as if this were not enough, he was systematically frozen out and (by all accounts) humiliated by Kennedy and his people. But now he was president, and the talents and energies he had displayed and developed in the Senate were being exercised in the White House, and so effectively that his administration ("The Great Society") already made Kennedy's "New Frontier," with all its talk of boldness and vigor, seem timid, thin, and pale.

The general opinion has always been that it was Johnson's decision to push ahead with the war he had inherited from Kennedy that destroyed him and ruined his chance to "solve" the problem of race in America and also to abolish poverty. In this view, by trying to win the war in Vietnam, he lost the war on poverty and on racial discrimination in America. But without denying that Vietnam was the major cause of Johnson's downfall, I would say that the two domestic "wars" he was waging also had something to do with the drastic decline in his political fortunes between the landslide victory of 1964 over Goldwater and his announcement four years later that he would not be running again. For if the war in Vietnam was going badly and becoming more and more unpopular within the liberal community, so too were the wars on poverty and racial discrimination.

The riots that broke out in the mid-sixties in the black ghettos of many northern cities came as a traumatic shock to the liberal community. Up to that point the general liberal assumption had been that progress toward racial justice and harmony was being registered all the time. Yet now, in spite of the Civil Rights Act of 1964 and the Voting Rights Act of 1965 and the dozens of poverty programs that had spawned a whole new acronymic language— OEO, VISTA, CETA, et cetera—things suddenly seemed to have grown worse rather than better. Following the first of these riots— the one that erupted in Watts, the black ghetto of Los Angeles, in the summer of 1965—the governor of California, in what was becoming a characteristic gesture of the sixties, appointed a commission to investigate the causes and to recommend remedial action for the future. The commission's report spoke sympathetically of the rioters and of their need for better schools, better housing, and more and better jobs, but it still reflected confidence in the power of the system to supply these needs. For this it was attacked by Bayard Rustin in *Commentary:* "Like the liberal consensus which it embodies and reflects, the commission's imagination and political intelligence appear paralyzed by the hard facts of Negro deprivation it has unearthed. . . ."

Rustin was speaking here as a socialist exposing the inadequacy of liberalism to deal with the conditions to which the Watts "manifesto," as he called the riot, were a response. But soon liberals themselves, including highly placed members of the American political establishment, were beginning to say the same kind of thing. Evidently the problems of race and poverty could not be solved by the traditional liberal strategies of abolishing discrimination and establishing equality of opportunity. Either these strategies did not go far enough, or they were pointed in the wrong direction. Perhaps what was needed was a degree of government intervention far beyond anything that had already been attempted to accelerate the integration of the races, and to build new schools, new houses, new neighborhoods, even new cities, while also creating enough new jobs to put everyone in America to work. Alternatively, the answer might lie in a different strategy altogether, aimed not at wholesale integration and a level of federal economic intervention amounting in effect to socialism, but rather at the creation of self-governing black communities in control of their own schools and their own economic affairs.

This alternative was sometimes known as Black Power and sometimes as community control, and it came to be sponsored by no less prominent a leader of the liberal establishment than McGeorge Bundy. Bundy had been a dean at Harvard and had then gone to Washington under Kennedy, where he became one of the key figures behind the American military intervention into Vietnam; unlike many of his friends and colleagues, he stayed on under Johnson and he also remained firmly committed to the waging of the war, which he not only supported but helped centrally to direct. Nor when he left the Johnson administration in 1966 to become president of the Ford Foundation did he do so in protest against the war. But if he thereby remained loyal to the old liberal consensus on foreign affairs, he deserted it altogether in the area of domestic affairs, and especially on the issue of race, by backing the radically different approach of community control.

On the other hand, the fact that he backed this approach could even be interpreted by a slight stretch of the imagination as in itself an implicit repudiation of the policies to which he remained explicitly committed where Vietnam was concerned. For one of the things community control involved in practice was the turning over of power and patronage to a new breed of black leader—the kind, to put it bluntly, who lived on the ghetto streets and who led riots rather than the kind who came in from the outside and tried, unsuccessfully, to stop them once they had started. Having discovered how hard it was to win in Vietnam by fighting a guerrilla insurgency like the Vietcong, Bundy was now seeking out its domestic analogue and giving it a grant.

In this he anticipated exactly what many other repentant hawks like Cyrus Vance would do ten years later, when under Jimmy Carter they would re-import the Bundy approach back into foreign affairs and throw American support behind Marxist guerrillas in Africa instead of trying to prevent their accession to power. The "guerrillas" to whom the Ford Foundation, together with liberal mayors like John Lindsay in New York and liberal organizations like the Urban Coalition, gave their support were not Communists or even, except for a few, Marxists; most of them were black nationalists of one variety or another. But they did resemble guerrillas in their use of violence and the threat of violence (Tom Wolfe's "mau-mauing") to achieve their political objectives.

Their opponents within the black community—socialists like Rustin, liberal integrationists like Roy Wilkins—saw the new prominence being given by the white liberal establishment to such people and their separatist ideas as a sinister maneuver designed to frustrate any further progress toward integration. They also thought that it was a way of pacifying the black community on the cheap, community control being so much less expensive than the $100 billion "freedom budget" that the great black labor leader A. Philip Randolph, Rustin, and their allies were recommending as the only possible solution. No doubt there was something in these suspicions, but the real significance of the new turn in liberal opinion was to be found less in the positive appeal of community control than in the loss of faith it revealed in the liberal consensus. From that perspective, the increasing volume of support for Rustin's approach (socialism in all but name) was part of the same development. It too became more and more popular as the rioting spread after 1965 from Watts to Newark and Detroit and a dozen other cities, convincing more and more liberals that the war against poverty and racial injustice could no more be won by means of the traditional liberal strategy embodied so fully in the domestic policies of the Johnson administration than the war against Communism could be won by the traditional liberal strategy embodied with equal fullness in its policies in Vietnam.

Obviously Lyndon Johnson knew that opposition to a continued American involvement in the Vietnam war was growing in volume and intensity from 1965 on. He could hear the demonstrators chanting, "Hey, hey, LBJ, how many kids did you kill today?" He knew that members of his own cabinet risked being mobbed and shouted down if they tried to speak on a college campus, assuming they were even invited to speak at all. And he knew that former supporters of the war, including some who had participated actively in the decision to send American troops to Vietnam, were turning against it. But because all this opposition amounted numerically only to a small minority, he persisted in believing that while it had great nuisance value, it had very little political power—that is, the power to reward and punish candidates running for election. In the strictest sense this was true. Except in a few areas where the "jackal bins" were concentrated (parts of Manhattan, university towns like Ann Arbor and Berkeley), antiwar sentiment remained numerically weak; and the fact that its most visible face was the extremist one—hirsute and foul-mouthed youths waving Vietcong flags—put off a great many people who might otherwise have been persuaded. (So at any rate my own branch of the antiwar movement thought, and that trip to Mississippi with Willie Morris in 1968 convinced me that the pro-Communist and anti-American elements within the movement were doing more to isolate us politically than to further the cause of a peaceful settlement.)

Yet what Johnson failed to understand until it was too late was that this issue would not be settled by numbers alone. The deeper truth was that in the debate over Vietnam, the opposition was winning. By 1965 it had already triumphed in the intellectual world, where the general anti-Communist rationale for conducting it had for years been suffering a steady pounding at the hands of radical critics. Thus it was now very difficult to defend American policy by appealing to a consensus on the need to draw a line against the advance of Communism. This need might have seemed self-evident to most liberals in the past—they had, for example, hardly challenged it during the Korean war—but it no longer did. Yet even many for whom the need did remain clear ran up against the very good case that could be and was made by Hans J. Morgenthau, Walter Lippmann (the most respected of all American newspaper columnists), and even George F. Kennan, the architect of the policy of containment himself, against Vietnam as "the wrong war in the wrong place at the wrong time."

And to make things still worse for its defenders, Vietnam was a guerrilla war and therefore could only be fought in ways that were bound to seem, and sometimes actually were, immoral and atrocious. To defend the American role in Vietnam put one in the position of appearing to justify such horrors as the bombing and napalming of innocent civilians mistaken for Vietcong, the deliberate destruction of crops and the defoliation of forests to deprive the enemy (operating in *South* Vietnam, the country we were fighting to save) of food and cover, and the large-scale bombing of the North. No matter that equivalent horrors occur in all wars and that the United States had done terrible things in World War II without public protest or revulsion; no matter too that many of the charges of immorality and criminality against the American forces in Vietnam were (as the political scientist Guenter Lewy would later put it in a careful study of the record) "based on a distorted picture of the actual battlefield situation, on ignorance of existing rules of engagement, and on a tendency to construe every mistake of judgment as a wanton breach of the law of war." In spite of all this, the burden of the horrors of Vietnam weakened the defenders and dragged their arguments down.

Robbed of a convincing justification, the war lost its legitimacy and could only go on being waged because those who were waging it had the power to do so. They had the power because they were in office and because they had the votes to remain there. But lacking legitimacy, they would be unable to exercise that power effectively; they would, in other words, be unable to govern. When Lyndon Johnson finally realized this, he stepped down, defeated not by numbers but by culture—by ideas and attitudes shaped in the centers of intellectual life and disseminated through the press, through television, and through the mass media in general.

15

What Johnson may never have realized, however, was that the domestic policies in which he took so much pride were also losing liberal support. It has often been said that the Tet offensive of 1968, when the North Vietnamese mounted a major assault that reached almost to Saigon, convinced everyone in the American political establishment that we were incapable of winning the war and that the only remaining questions were how quickly and by what means to withdraw. Something analogous happened to the climate of opinion as a result of the riots in Detroit and in Newark in 1967. "The civil war and the foreign one have contrived this summer to murder liberalism—in its official robes," exulted Andrew Kopkind in the notorious Molotov-cocktail issue of *The New York Review.* This was an exaggeration, and the revolution Kopkind saw coming was never remotely possible. But there was more than a grain of truth in his announcement that the "liberal elites" had been rudely shoved off "center stage" by the "insurrections of

July" and that the old liberal order had been, if not as he said "shattered," at least very severely shaken. And his diagnosis of what it was that had shaken the liberal elites was also very shrewd. They, like everyone else, now knew that "even if all Martin Luther King's programs were enacted, . . . and the Great Society . . . materialized before our eyes, there would still be the guerrillas."

In short, by 1968, both the old liberal consensus on foreign affairs and the old liberal consensus on domestic affairs were breaking apart. In foreign affairs, the consensus had centered for exactly twenty years—since the enunciation of the Truman Doctrine and the enactment of the Marshall Plan—on the containment of Communism, by political means where possible and by military means where necessary. Now, as a result of its failure in Vietnam, it was growing more discredited by the day. The consequence was that those who had opposed it from the beginning— unreconstructed Stalinists and their equally unreconstructed fellow travelers within the liberal community—could claim, with a plausibility they had never dreamed they would ever again be able to achieve in public debate, that their position was at last being vindicated.

Sometimes these people spoke in their own voices, silenced for so long by the combined effects of demoralization from within and intimidation from without. But more often they spoke through the voices of their children. Thus although no idea of the sixties was more universally accepted than the idea that a gulf had developed between the young and their parents so wide as to be almost unbridgeable—the eminent anthropologist Margaret Mead said that the two generations were like citizens of two different countries speaking two different languages, while the wildly brilliant literary critic Leslie Fiedler characteristically went her and every other social commentator one better by declaring that the two generations were actually members of two different species—the truth was that in political attitudes at least there was no "generation gap" in the sixties at all. Study after study revealed that the vast majority of young Americans held the same political views as their parents, and far from being an exception, the young radicals—as two separate studies sympathetic to them, one by Kenneth Keniston and the other by Richard Flacks, confirmed—were if anything closer politically to their parents than young Republicans or young Democrats. They were, Keniston and Flacks agreed, "red-diaper babies"—the children of "radicals" who differed from their parents, if at all, not in their political values but in working more boldly and actively "to fulfill and renew the political traditions of their families."

There was a certain caution in such formulations, a certain resort to euphemism. Thanks to the legacy of McCarthyism, the word "Communist" was no longer generally used even to describe self-proclaimed members of the Communist party. If they were black, like Angela Davis, they would be referred to in the press as "militants," and if they were white, like Dashiell Hammett, they would simply be called "radicals." And if the use of the word "Communist" to describe a Communist was interdicted as a species of McCarthyism, it was almost unthinkable to employ such subsidiary concepts as "fellow traveler" or "Stalinist" or "Stalinoid" to describe people who were not members of the Communist party but whose outlook had been largely shaped or influenced by its ideas and values.

Without the help of this vocabulary, Keniston and Flacks were unable to be as clear and precise as they might have been about the "political traditions of the families" of these "red-diaper babies" who dominated the New Left. Yet as one read about the student radical leaders in the press—celebrity or even stardom having been conferred on many of them—one kept coming upon scions of what could be called the First Families of American Stalinism. Then as the New Left grew more and more violently hostile to everything about America—its political system, its economic system, its culture—I found myself joking mordantly that it was in the end turning out to be a movement by the children of McCarthy's victims to avenge their parents on the flesh of the country which had produced him.

Joke or no joke, the tables were now being turned. For twenty years anti-Communist liberalism had been riding high and fellow-traveling liberalism had been lying low. Now fellow-traveling liberalism was once again in a position to make its bid, and it naturally proceeded to do so. This time, however, the issue was not the Soviet Union; it was the United States. Indeed many and perhaps most of the old fellow travelers, and certainly most of their newer and younger allies, had long since given up on the Soviet Union. They might still pin their hopes on other "socialist" countries—Cuba one day, Chile the next—but the Soviet Union no longer claimed their allegiance, and they no longer found themselves burdened with the crippling need to defend or apologize for its every move. This was a great change and it involved an admission that they had been wrong about the Soviet Union, or at least about its domestic character. But they could and did still claim to have been right about the United States— right in having blamed it for starting the cold war, and right in believing that it was fundamentally an evil country. As they had been put on the defensive in the past because of the crimes of Stalin, they now sought to put the anti-Communist liberals on the defensive by focusing on the "crimes" of the United States.

Of course if the old Stalinists and their children had been alone in making this effort, very little would have come of it. Even in their best of times, the 1930s, they had been a relatively small group, and they were much smaller now. But many other people with no personal or family history of Stalinism, and some indeed with a history of anti-Stalinism, were independently and for reasons of their own cooperating in this turning of the tables.

One of these was my old friend Jason Epstein who, in response to the revelation that the CIA had been secretly financing the Congress for Cultural Freedom and its many magazines around the world, wrote an article for *The New York Review* attacking the anti-Communist "faction" within the intellectual community and comparing its relations to the CIA with the relations of an earlier generation of intellectuals to the Communist party. The anti-Communist intellectuals of the postwar period, he suggested, were no different from and no better than the Communist intellectuals of the past. Not only had the anti-Communists violated their responsibilities as intellectuals by accepting the covert sponsorship of the CIA; they had also turned themselves into slavish apologists for an America which was at least as "sinister" as and probably more dangerous than the Soviet Union under Stalin for which the Communist intellectuals had apologized. So slavish were they, indeed, that there seemed to be no "aspect of America's fight with Communism" that they found "intolerable." (By this he meant McCarthyism and Vietnam; the fact that all the people he was attacking, including Irving Kristol, had been opposed to McCarthyism and that many of them were also opposed to the war affected his argument only to the extent of forcing him into a self-protective qualification or two and the substitution of insinuation for direct accusation at certain strategic points.)

In declaring that the perspective of the "Left faction" within the intellectual community had been vindicated by Vietnam (and other developments as well), Jason was talking not about Stalinism or fellow-traveling liberalism but about the new radicalism of the sixties. Yet as was clear from his own piece, in the field of foreign affairs this was by now a very fuzzy distinction. Whatever might have been the truth about the origins of the cold war and whether Stalin had entertained aggressive designs against Western Europe or not, he said, the "real trouble was not any longer Stalinism, and it had begun to seem that it probably wasn't Communism either." What was "poisoning" the world today was not Communist but capitalist expansion, not Soviet but American imperialism: the effort by the United States "to impose its national obsessions on the rest of the world."

This perspective, encouraged by Vietnam but going beyond it to the question of the American role in the world in general, and given greater currency by a new generation of "revisionist" historians of the cold war who were establishing themselves in the universities, was making more and more headway all the time within the liberal community at large. And this meant that it was also making more and more headway within the Democratic party. By 1968 no one in the Democratic party, not even John Roche, would have dismissed it any longer as confined to a few Jacobins or to the Upper West Side of Manhattan. But neither as yet did anyone know for sure how far it had traveled—except perhaps Eugene McCarthy.

That first time I met him, the day he showed up for our lunch appointment carrying a volume of Robert Lowell's poems, he indicated that he was thinking of challenging Lyndon Johnson for the presidency in the New Hampshire primary on the issue of Vietnam, and he wanted to know what I thought of the idea. My initial response was surprise. No doubt it was my own ignorance, but I hadn't, I said, been aware that he felt so strongly about the war. No, he answered, with the slightest touch of pique, it wasn't my fault; it was the fault of the press. He had only recently made a major speech against the administration, but the papers had given it no play. In any case, the time had come to do something more than make a speech. No one else seemed willing, not Robert Kennedy, of whom he had a low opinion, and not any of the Republicans, of whom his opinion was even lower. Kennedy was at least a Roman Catholic, not a truly literate one as (he suggested with a mischievous little smile but did not actually say) he himself was. But had I ever noticed how many of the leading Republican candidates had been raised in young and newfangled religions— Nixon as a Quaker, George Romney as a Mormon, Charles Percy as a Christian Scientist? I had not noticed and I was impressed by the fact that he had so keen an eye for that kind of detail. And still more was I impressed by the brilliantly witty lecture, half-humorous, half-serious, he proceeded to deliver on why such people were bound to be more superficial than members of more ancient churches and religions.

This obviously sophisticated interest in culture—in religion and poetry and the world of ideas—was what made McCarthy's intelligence so different from Lyndon Johnson's and George McGovern's. Highly intelligent as they both were, they both also had minds that were focused too narrowly on conventional electoral politics to sense what was happening in the culture and how it was already beginning to impinge on the sphere of politics itself. But McCarthy, uniquely attuned among politicians as he was to the culture and its relation to the electoral process—why else had he sought out a person like me for advice?—saw before anyone else that a new wave was sweeping through the liberal community that might even turn out to be powerful enough to wash Lyndon Johnson's administration away; and he decided to ride it.

Robert Kennedy—the third of the major politicians I met on that heady day Dick Goodwin had arranged for me in Washington—had a much slower mind than McCarthy's; he seemed earnest and plodding and unimaginative by comparison. Possibly there was something about me that put him off, but both on our first meeting and on several subsequent occasions, mostly social gatherings, I found him obtuse. He would ask me a question, he would listen intently to the answer, and then he would say something that left me with the distinct impression that he had missed the point I had been trying to make.

For example, having been told that I had written a highly provocative piece on the subject, he wanted to hear my "ideas" (his word) about the "Negro problem." Trying to comply with this request, I said that in my judgment anti-integrationist sentiment was much stronger both among whites and blacks than was generally thought to be the case, and that this sentiment was almost certain to frustrate the established liberal strategy for dealing with the problem. No sooner had I begun to develop the theme than he grew restless. He had asked for my "ideas," yet what he wanted was not a historical or sociological analysis but a series of practical suggestions that could be put into effect tomorrow. I knew that in the very home in which we were now having lunch and this frustrating conversation, he had in the days of "Camelot" made a practice of inviting eminent intellectuals to give lectures and conduct seminars for him and other members and friends of the Kennedy administration. But talking to him now I realized that the fact that one of these seminars had reportedly been punctuated by Kennedy's ordering his wife to "can it" when she began hectoring the lecturer during the question period, was not the only reason they had become something of a joke and an embarrassment to the speakers who had participated. If Robert Kennedy had any interest at all in "ideas" that were not immediately translatable into a ten-point program, it could only have been as an additional luxury of the rich and the powerful or as a means of self-improvement. In neither case was a serious intellectual likely to leave the scene without feeling that his dignity as an intellectual had been compromised, however much his social status might have been enhanced.

If, moreover, Robert Kennedy had been as interested in the world of ideas as he sometimes pretended to be or imagined he was—as interested as Eugene McCarthy really was—he would not have had to wait until McCarthy's impressive showing in the New Hampshire primary had exposed Johnson's vulnerability before entering the race for the presidency himself. Not even Dick Goodwin, who by 1967 had broken with Johnson and thought he could be beaten, had succeeded in persuading Kennedy to run. Only a little while earlier Goodwin had twitted me patronizingly for saying that the United States could not win in Vietnam, and he had been almost as derisive as his colleague John Roche about the power of the intellectual community. Nevertheless, like McCarthy and unlike almost everyone else working in Washington or caught up in its perspective (and this included such academics as Roche and Schlesinger, who seemed compelled to denigrate the political weight of the intellectual community to which they themselves belonged as a way of demonstrating their hardheadedness to the Washington professionals), Goodwin grew so interested in the intellectual community that he could scarcely prevent himself from taking it more and more seriously. First he changed his mind about Vietnam and then he changed his mind about what he called, in a piece for *Commentary* in 1967, the entire "shape of American politics."

In that piece he mounted so forceful an attack on the growth of centralized power that several conservative ideologues who had been railing for years against the very same thing as the keystone of Democratic-party liberalism not unreasonably thought that Goodwin had become a convert to their position. But while they were right in interpreting "The Shape of American Politics" as a break with the old liberal consensus on domestic affairs, they were wrong in thinking that it represented a move toward the Right. In breaking with the old liberalism which he had faithfully been serving, Goodwin had moved to the Left and was now speaking not as a conservative but as a sixties radical. He referred approvingly to Norman Mailer's characterization of modern life as a "plague," and he offered what he himself called "utopian" proposals for what he also did not hesitate to call "radical changes in ideology—and consequently in action" to help cure the disease.

A few years earlier, while working on one of Johnson's State of the Union messages, he had telephoned me and asked jocularly, "What's really hot in social criticism these days?" "Community," I had said, telling him about Paul Goodman and other proponents of decentralization whose ideas were at the center of the new radicalism. Robert Kennedy, not yet seeing any way he could exploit all this, would probably have been bored, but not Goodwin. A proposal to use federal power to preserve and nourish relatively autonomous local communities wound up, suitably edited, in the mouth of Lyndon Johnson. That it would be difficult for local communities to be independent while living in a condition of dependency on Washington evidently did not bother Johnson. But neither did it bother Goodwin enough to sour him on the idea when he came to develop it under his own name.

Indeed, in nothing so much was Goodwin now a true radical of the sixties as in the utopian belief that all contradictions could be resolved if only there were a will to resolve them.

But he had also become a true radical of the sixties in another sense: he now believed that the new radicalism was the wave of the future and that it was already displacing the old liberalism as the ruling ideological force in the land. In addition, then, to taking the ideas of the intellectual community with such great seriousness, he saw that community as a barometer of changes soon to come, first in the Democratic party and then in the general political weather. Translated into the terms of concrete political action, this meant that Lyndon Johnson—who now embodied and represented the old liberalism more perfectly and more fully than any single figure in American public life (with the possible exception of his own vice-president, Hubert Humphrey)—could be deprived of the nomination in 1968 by a challenger sensitive to these new developments.

Because he was personally close to Robert Kennedy, and because Kennedy had great popular appeal simply as a Kennedy and quite apart from the deeper question of where the country was moving, Goodwin would have preferred him to become the candidate. But Kennedy, assuming in the conventional way that a sitting president could not be successfully dislodged, refused to run. Consequently Goodwin turned to McCarthy, who at least knew enough to know that challenging Johnson was worth a try. It seemed unlikely that McCarthy himself could ever reach the White House. But what did not seem at all unlikely was that he might push Lyndon Johnson out of it. Arriving in New Hampshire to join McCarthy in his fledgling campaign, Goodwin told him that the two of them and his portable typewriter were going to destroy Lyndon Johnson. And so they did, simultaneously bringing Robert Kennedy into the race with the claim that McCarthy's constituency rightfully belonged to him. In trying to win that constituency over, Kennedy naturally had to join it, which is to say that he had to move to the Left—or rather even further to the Left than he had already moved since becoming a senator from New York in 1964.

Kennedy too then grew more and more radicalized as radicalism looked more and more like the winning side. Having been one of the architects of the war in Vietnam and a great believer in resistance to Communist power in general, he now managed to suggest that he opposed these policies both in the small and in the large; and having as attorney general been the symbol to many blacks of caution and timidity in the enforcement of civil rights, he now managed to present himself successfully as a greater champion of the blacks even than Lyndon Johnson. Of course he could not go as far, nor could he be quite as explicit in the positions he took, as intellectuals like William Phillips who were following an analogous course. Being a politician, he was constrained and inhibited by the fear of driving off nonradical groups of voters whose support he had to attract in order to get elected. Nevertheless he did go far enough to win over a party-line New Leftist like Jack Newfield of *The Village Voice* and even so prominent a Movement celebrity as the Yippie leader Abbie Hoffman. And this in itself was a mark of how far the new radicalism had traveled in the roughly ten years of its existence. Beginning as a tiny dissident movement within the intellectual community, it had swept through that community itself and had then grown so influential within the much larger community of educated liberals as to have become very nearly capable of a serious bid for control of the Democratic party.

I myself had been there at the start, and I was still there in 1968. I encouraged McCarthy to run, I arranged for him to meet other people in the intellectual community, and I broke a rule I had made for myself against active participation in electoral politics when I began to campaign for him. But just as I had been feeling uneasy about the way the Movement proper had been developing since the days of its infancy, I now found myself afflicted with similar feelings toward this translation of it into the terms of practical electoral politics.

If in the case of the Movement proper, I had been bothered by a lowering of intellectual standards, what troubled me about the McCarthy campaign was a lowering of tone. There was an air of unseriousness that seemed to infect almost everything about it, at least after the triumph in New Hampshire.

The term "radical chic" had not yet been invented by Tom Wolfe, but the phenomenon it described with immortal perfection already existed; and nowhere could its operations be more clearly observed than in Eugene's. This was a Manhattan nightclub named for McCarthy and established to attract both money and support for his campaign. I do not know whether anyone had ever before thought of opening a nightclub for such purposes, but I doubt it. In any case, Eugene's was situated with unconscious symbolic significance in the premises that had previously housed El Morocco, one of the most famous watering holes of what had once been called "café society." Now, night after night, alumni of that society gathered with their more up-to-date "jet-set" counterparts—also now known as the "Beautiful People"—to demonstrate their opposition to the war by buying drinks and watching a floor show which frequently consisted of a panel of intellectuals discussing one of the great issues of the day. Foreign visitors would also show up, especially from the upper reaches of English Bohemia with its mix of titled young women, slumming aristocrats, and fashionable literary types, all of whom of course held only the most advanced—that is, left-wing—political opinions. ("Think Left, Live Right" was a maxim invented in France, but like many Parisian fashions, it had spread to London and now New York as well.)

It was in front of just such an audience, a packed house, swelled by an unusually large contingent from Columbia and other centers of New York intellectual life, that I performed one night together with Irving Howe and Dwight Macdonald. They were the speakers and I was the moderator (though under the circumstances master of ceremonies would have been a more accurate title), and it accordingly fell to me to inaugurate the proceedings by standing up at the microphone and calling the crowd to attention. The trouble was that I had put away so many double shots of Jack Daniel's while waiting to go on that I could hardly stand up at all. Consequently I sat (as I had seen professional nightclub performers do) on a high barstool while holding on to the microphone for additional support. This worked well enough to get me through the first crisis, and much experience of managing under the influence of alcohol got me through the rest without any major mishap.

It seems clear to me in retrospect that I allowed myself to get that drunk because I was secretly feeling contempt for the occasion, for my own participation in it, for what had become of McCarthy's brave initiative. Feeling that way, I could, I suppose, have followed the example of Goodwin and many other early supporters of McCarthy who had switched to Kennedy when, with the count in New Hampshire scarcely completed, he announced his own candidacy. Yet even if I had not been outraged by what seemed to me a cynical act of political theft, an effort to cash in on the courage of another man, going over to Kennedy would have been as effective a way of escaping from radical chic as going from Eugene's to Le Club. For Kennedy's campaign was pervaded by it too.

16

All things considered, then, 1968 was no time for a book written from within the premises of the new radicalism but expressing mixed feelings about it—a book, that is, like *Making It*. The new radicalism was riding so high that it was in no mood for anything but allegiance, praise, and flattery. This had been enough, and more than enough, to frighten William Phillips. But what was more surprising and more significant, it was even enough to intimidate Norman Mailer, whom Phillips commissioned to write the piece for *Partisan Review* about *Making It* from which I have already quoted.

Before writing his piece, Mailer told me how good he thought *Making It* was and how unfair and even incomprehensible he found the malicious talk about it which had been going the rounds. But in the piece itself the kindest thing he called the book was "a not altogether compelling memoir," and he now blamed the extraordinary ferocity of the response to it on its own faults and failures.

Mailer's only explanation to me for what I had every reason to regard as a betrayal by my "old dear great and good friend," as he described himself in the piece, was that he had read the book again and had simply changed his mind. I had a different explanation that I found rather more convincing, which was that when confronted with the full force of the opposition to *Making It,* and realizing that in defending it he would in all probability unleash the "terror" against himself as well, he simply lost his nerve.

He himself, ten years earlier, had spoken in *Advertisements for Myself* of his own ambitions for success, and he had been punished for it. But that had been at a low point in his career, and since then times had changed and he now had much more to lose. As the bad boy of American letters—itself an honorific status in the climate of the sixties—he still held a license to provoke and he rarely hesitated to use it, even if it sometimes meant making a fool of himself in the eyes of his own admirers. But there were limits he instinctively knew how to observe; and he observed them. He might excoriate his fellow radicals on a particular point; he might discomfit them with unexpected sympathies (for right-wing politicians, say, or National Guardsmen on the other side of a demonstration) and equally surprising antipathies (homosexuality and masturbation, for example, he insisted on stigmatizing as vices); he might even on occasion describe himself as (dread word) a conservative. But always in the end came the reassuring gesture, the wink of complicity, the subtle signing of the radical loyalty oath.

Making It contained no such gesture, no such wink; and it ended not with a reaffirmation of radical loyalties but with what amounted to a declaration of defiance. The next-to-last paragraph described the "very dangerous" book about success I had once thought I might try to write, and the last paragraph consisted of only three words: "I just have." This paragraph, "as indigestible in its brevity," said Mailer, "as a plastic peanut," was a fitting conclusion to the "blunder of self-assertion, self-exposure, and self-denigration" that *Making It* represented as a whole.

That I had committed a blunder in writing *Making It* was certainly true in the sense that such a book published at such a time could not conceivably have brought its author the rewards of success for which it constituted a self-proclaimed "bid." But "plastic"? In Mailer's vocabulary "plastic" was a big, significant word; it stood for the principle of anti-nature, the violence done by the machine to the true sources of being. How could he have applied it to a sentence like the one with which *Making It* ended? For what made that sentence "indigestible" was precisely its fidelity to the natural: a "plastic" conclusion taking it all back by saying in the manner of the reformed sinner or of the ex-alcoholic at an A.A. meeting that I had learned the error of my ways and the treacherous falsity of my ideas about success would have gone down as smoothly as a bowl of cream.

Mailer himself would not have done it that plastic way ten years earlier, but that is how he would have done it in the climate of the late sixties, with a newly solidified popularity to protect. Of course he would have done it cleverly, flattering the attitudes of his audience while seeming to offend it; or, more cleverly still, actually saying offensive things while protecting himself from the wrath of the audience by playing to it as a fool to the king. The fool is free to speak the truth to the king, but only because, being a fool, he need not be taken seriously except at the pleasure and convenience of the king. Nor do the truths he speaks constitute any threat to the king and his power. On the contrary, to play the fool is in itself a form—a somewhat complicated form—of servile obeisance to power.

Though Mailer's instinct in the matter of the limits of permissible dissent from radicalism was usually very sound, it was not infallible. Once in a while he would misjudge the toleration of his audience and wander irrepressibly or distractedly off the reservation altogether, only to discover that even an old radical loyalist like him was subject to party discipline. Whenever that happened, he would quickly scurry back into line, salvaging his honor with roguish confessions of weakness which, while seriously intended, and taken, as placatory gestures, still left open the possibility that the whole thing might be—in one of his own favorite phrases— a "put-on."

The clearest example of this process was the way he collapsed before the onslaughts of the radical feminists in the early seventies when they charged him (and justifiably from their point of view) with sexism. At first he was amused and a little patronizing. But then he finally saw that the women's movement really meant business. This was, I think, borne in upon him at a raucous forum on Women's Lib in which he participated together with Diana Trilling, Germaine Greer of London, and Jill Johnston of *The Village Voice* (whose contribution to the proceedings consisted largely of necking and petting with a female lover who walked onto the stage at the conclusion of her incomprehensible speech). Pounded from all sides that night, Mailer realized that the new feminism was neither a transient fashion nor an interesting though insignificant eruption of the bad temper and hysteria he was so familiar with from his (to date) four marriages and (probably) dozens of love affairs. It was becoming a real force on the radical scene. At that point he ceased for all practical purposes to criticize and began to cajole and flatter it—treating it not as he would an angry woman he was trying to pacify but rather the way he always treated any element within the radical culture that had shown itself to be truly powerful: by backing down through playing the fool.

Something similar happened with *Making It*. The first time he read the book, Mailer had not realized how subversive it was of the radical party line both in its relatively benign view of middle-class American values and, even more seriously, in its denial that the intellectuals—and the educated class in general—represented a true or superior alternative. Then, having become convinced by a study of the reaction that *Making It* really had overstepped the line, and wishing to dissociate himself from so dangerous a connection without seeming to behave in a cowardly fashion in his own eyes (and mine), he attacked me for ruining "a potentially marvelous book" not by having gone too far but by having failed to go far enough in exposing what he himself called the new Establishment of the Left.

Why so "charitable" a portrayal should have won me the Establishment's wrath instead of its applause was a question Mailer understandably had great trouble in trying to answer. But behind the fog of speculation generated by the effort, and with the help of a prose style so baroque that it became the rhetorical equivalent of the cap and bells of the fool, he managed simultaneously to turn his back on a friend, convicted now of treason to the cultural ruling class, and to pretend to the courage of even greater acts of treason against it while in reality submitting to the terrible power it had shown itself capable of wielding in its treatment of *Making It*. The fact that Norman Mailer—a founding father and patron saint of the "Left Establishment" and, though not perhaps quite so brave as he thought he was, much less cowardly in this respect than most—should have felt himself forced into a maneuver like this was all the proof anyone could have needed that the "terror" had become pervasive and efficient enough to make strong men quake and to leave no one feeling safe.

And indeed Mailer had plenty of company. In 1974, in a round-table discussion at the Rockefeller Foundation, the transcript of which was subsequently published in *Commentary* under the title "Culture and the Present Moment," one of the participants, Hilton Kramer, observed in talking of the sixties that certain figures had paradoxically become "heroes of high culture" by attacking high culture. Among the figures Kramer had in mind was Marshall McLuhan, who had begun as a literary critic and who had then achieved great fame—or rather celebrity—through a series of books demonstrating without too much regret that literature was becoming obsolete and that print would be entirely superseded in the future by television and other electronic media. Another prominent defector Kramer mentioned was Susan Sontag, who had also begun as a serious literary critic and had then repudiated the entire tradition of serious criticism—which she identified with the interpretation of texts—as overly rationalistic and therefore inimical to the full experience of art. Like several other critics Kramer did not mention—for example Leslie Fiedler and Richard Poirier—Susan Sontag also attacked the idea of "high culture" itself as in effect snobbish or "elitist" (to use a word they themselves rarely employed but that came into wide currency during the sixties to express a point of view they certainly did everything they could to justify).

What followed from this was a newly respectful attitude toward popular or mass culture that stood in the sharpest possible contrast to the contempt for "kitsch" so characteristic of the avantgarde critical tradition out of which all these suddenly anticritical critics and anti-intellectual intellectuals had come. Susan Sontag may have been "against interpretation" (this was indeed the title of her first collection of essays) where the difficult texts of the avant-garde or "modernist" literary canon were concerned, but the ban on interpretation did not seem to extend to movies or to popular music. She herself was especially high on a singing group called the Supremes, while Poirier more conventionally favored the Beatles, in writing about whom he brought to bear the same solemnity and all the heavy critical artillery with which he had been trained to approach James Joyce and Henry James. McLuhan, for his part, liked writing about television programs, and Leslie Fiedler—again, as always with him, taking things to their extreme limits—made a specialty of comic books, which he explicated with the same ferocious and unmodulated brilliance he had exercised in writing at an earlier stage of his career on the classics of American fiction or on Dante or on Ezra Pound.

In addition to thus denigrating literature, serious criticism, and high culture both explicitly and implicitly, many literary intellectuals—mainly in the universities but also outside the academic world—began preaching or at least acquiescing in a notion of "relevance" which for all practical purposes wiped out any writer of the past who did not immediately interest students or readers of the present. In the name of this notion, for example, a professor of English at a major university argued against teaching the poetry of John Milton to American students, and far from being discredited in the eyes of his colleagues for taking this impious position, he was elected national president of their professional organization, the Modern Language Association. And if being great did not satisfy the new criteria of relevance, neither did literary inferiority rule a writer out. Reading lists that had once consisted of universally acknowledged classics were now crowded with contemporary works of little or no literary value but whose very popularity with students was taken as evidence of their relevance.

But relevance soon came to mean more than the capacity to catch the attention of a class of students who (touted though they were everywhere as the brightest and best-educated generation ever to appear on the face of the earth) were bored by Milton and baffled by Yeats. Like everything else in the sixties it was politicized to the point where what certified a book as relevant was less its ability to entertain an easily bored and ill-prepared reader than its usefulness to a given political purpose. The purpose might be to promote black nationalism or feminism, or it might more broadly be to further (whether directly through indoctrination or indirectly through formal experimentation) the "revolution" against bourgeois civilization. In either case, literary values and literary considerations became, well, irrelevant by comparison with political values and political considerations. In fact, in the eyes of some, they became worse than irrelevant: "Good writing," said a radical feminist of the period, echoing something Lenin had said about music, "is counterrevolutionary."

All this was undoubtedly what Hilton Kramer was thinking of when he referred to the assault on high culture from within which had been mounted in the 1960s. But what mainly concerned him, he said, was the response of "serious intellectuals" to this "attack on mind" and "on the high functions of mind." "I think one could say that there was, to invoke an old phrase, a kind of failure of nerve, an intellectual abdication in the face of pressure."

In making this particular charge, Kramer was not thinking primarily of academic English departments or of the *Publication of the Modern Language Association*. He was talking about the New York intellectuals and *Partisan Review,* once the very symbol and bastion of "high culture" and its associated belief in "the high functions of mind," but now dominated by the spirit of Susan Sontag, several of whose key essays had appeared there, and Richard Poirier, who had replaced Philip Rahv as co-editor along with William Phillips.

There had been many reasons for Rahv's departure after so many years from the magazine he had helped to found and that he had perhaps been more closely identified with than any other single individual—including even Phillips, who was just as important but who had a somewhat less vivid personality. Since taking a teaching job at Brandeis in the fifties, Rahv had been living in Boston, and being so far away from the office had made it difficult for him to exercise as much influence over the magazine as he would have wished. Since Rahv was a man with a great appetite for power, this would in itself have been bad enough even if he had approved of the direction in which Phillips seemed to be steering *Partisan Review.* For even in that case, being absent from the scene would still have deprived him of the pleasures of conspiring with junior members of the staff against Phillips and even against his own writers.

Magazine editors naturally identify with the material they publish, and will invariably stand behind their contributors in public, whatever private misgivings they may feel about the writer or his work. But as I mentioned earlier, Rahv was unique among all the editors I have ever known in consistently running down the contents of his own magazine and ridiculing his own literary protégés. There were those who thought he did this because, as someone who had great difficulty in writing anything from a short book-review to the major works on Dostoevsky and Tolstoy that were still being awaited from him at his death in 1973, he envied anyone who could actually complete a piece or a story—especially if it was good enough to appear in *Partisan Review*! While I myself would not dismiss this explanation out of hand, I think that Rahv's destructive will was larger and more powerful than the petty malice and spite usually associated with envy. Wherever it came from, it had so much force behind it that it might even have interested his beloved Dostoevsky, who would not have reduced a compulsion of such dimensions to the operation of mere envy.

"Stay away from him," I was once warned in the early days of my own friendship with Rahv, which went back to 1953 when I was only twenty-three and beginning to write for *Partisan Review*. The warning came from William Barrett, who had himself just recently been working under Rahv as an associate editor. "Stay away from him," Barrett repeated melodramatically, in his cups and under a full moon in the middle of the night on a Cape Cod beach, "he killed me and he'll kill you too." Barrett was wrong. No doubt Rahv really had tried to "kill" him, but obviously the attempt had failed. Since leaving *Partisan Review* Barrett had gone on writing and would continue to do so, producing a series of highly original works whose originality consisted not least in their being virtually the only books produced in America since William James by a distinguished professional philosopher who was also entirely at his ease in the arts and a master of English prose to boot. (Barrett would even make use of that mastery twenty years later in writing marvelous memoirs of Rahv himself and of their days together on *Partisan Review.*)

But to return to the sixties: if moving to Boston would have made life as an editor of *Partisan Review* difficult for Rahv under the best of circumstances, it became intolerable to him under the circumstances that were actually coming to prevail. He had long since lost whatever respect or affection he had felt for Phillips when, as very young men, they had met at the John Reed Club, the literary society of the Communist party, and had joined together to found *Partisan Review;* or when, a few years later, they had again joined together to break with the Communists and to refound their magazine on a new political footing; or when, a few years after that, they had once again joined together against their co-editors Dwight Macdonald and Clement Greenberg in taking the position that the Allied side in World War II deserved the support of a socialist magazine; or when, in the period after the war, they had yet again been together in supporting American policy toward the Soviet Union while also forcing the resignation of James Burnham from their editorial board because he had gone all the way from Trotskyism to support of Joe McCarthy.

Yet by 1953, when I met Rahv, his relations with Phillips— which had already come to resemble nothing so much as a bad marriage being held together for the sake of the child—were also beginning to suffer for the first time from a weakening of the old bonds of political or ideological solidarity that had remained firm over two decades through so many personal and public upheavals. The problem was that Rahv felt less comfortable about being "pro-American," as he himself called it, than Phillips did. In this he was closer to Irving Howe than to Phillips; and indeed it was Rahv who encouraged Howe to write the famous attack on the new "conformity" of the intellectuals for *Partisan Review.* By "conformity" both Howe and Rahv said they meant the growing tendency among intellectuals to adopt a positive attitude toward American society, but this was disingenuously general. What they were really complaining about was something more specific: the turn away from socialism in the intellectual community. In an effort to reverse this drift, Howe founded *Dissent,* which unlike his article on conformity or the magazine in which it had appeared, was frankly and explicitly socialist in orientation.

As the fifties wore on, however, Rahv became more and more frankly and explicitly socialist himself, more and more hostile to American society, and less and less sympathetic to anti-Communism. In short, he was moving back to the radicalism of his youth; and since Phillips at first responded to the resurgence of radicalism in the late fifties and early sixties with suspicion and resistance, he and Rahv now found themselves politically at odds in a serious way for the first time in nearly thirty years. And to make matters still worse from Rahv's point of view, Phillips, being in New York, had control (as they used to say in a less affluent period of American radicalism) of the mimeograph machine and was failing to seize on the opportunity presented by the appearance of the New Left to shift the magazine from its "pro-American" track of the fifties back onto the old radical course.

But there was a complication here. For while Rahv thought that Phillips was too slow and hesitant in embracing the political attitudes of the new radicalism, he also thought that Phillips was too eager to sponsor the cultural aspects of the Movement. What Rahv wanted was indeed to return to the radical position of his youth, when he had been both a revolutionary socialist and a partisan of high culture, and he imagined that he could do this by becoming a supporter of the New Left and a critic of the New Sensibility and the counterculture. In other words, he saw the New Left as the legitimate heir of the revolutionary socialist tradition—he even once praised it as the most significant radical movement ever to appear in the United States—and the counterculture and the New Sensibility as heretical distortions and even cheap commercializations of the revolutionary modernist tradition in the arts. To develop this perspective he started a new magazine of his own, *Modern Occasions,* which he obviously considered a more faithful embodiment of the true *Partisan Review* heritage than *Partisan Review* itself.

The trouble was that despite certain strains, the New Left and the counterculture were by now so intertwined that any effort to distinguish between them was bound to fail. Together they formed a single movement—the Movement, as it was for this very reason known to itself and almost everyone else—and when Rahv tried to separate them out, he was engaging in a strictly academic exercise with virtually no bearing on the realities of the case.

Nevertheless Rahv was now what might be called a "born-again" radical (or as the critic Frederick Crews would have it, a "born-again Leninist"). As such, he repented so wholeheartedly of his former anti-Communism that he even attacked his old ally of the fifties, Irving Howe, for "still fighting off the dread specter of Stalinism" and for failing to grasp that "anyone continuing with this line is lost to genuine radicalism." Without denying that the Soviet Union was still "authoritarian, still dominated by a single party," he denied that it was a totalitarian state; and without quite defending it as a worker's paradise, he compared it favorably in this respect with the United States:

> It is ridiculous . . . to believe that a country . . . as bent on military domination as the U.S. is in this era, will somehow benignly evolve . . . into a peaceful welfare state. . . . In fact, there is more "welfare" in the Soviet Union right now, with free education and free medical care guaranteed to all, than there is here. . . .

While railing against Howe for betraying "genuine radicalism" in politics by being too hard on Communism and the Soviet Union, Rahv railed against Susan Sontag and Leslie Fiedler for betraying genuine radicalism in the arts in failing to expose the counterculture as a "degeneracy . . . masquerading as the boldest and bravest spirit of experiment and liberation."

On the other hand, his hatred of "the hip youth-scene" that Leslie Fiedler and Susan Sontag were celebrating did not prevent Rahv from setting up the young as cultural arbiters or from allowing political considerations to influence his own literary judgments. For example, having helped in the 1940s to restore the reputation of Henry James as a great novelist "after its long decline," he now turned against James as "patently deficient" in the qualities "the young people" of today supposedly wanted from literature. In addition to lacking these qualities, James also had the wrong ideas. He was, Rahv charged, conservative in taking "the social order of his time too much for granted" and he also entertained a "preposterously" sympathetic attitude toward the American character. But these were the very "faults" for which James had been denigrated in the past and against which Rahv had defended him in arguing with his critics, expecially those of a Stalinist cast. Thus having found his way back to a radicalism which, if not precisely pro-Communist or pro-Soviet, could live on comfortably fraternal terms with Communism and the Soviet Union, he eventually also found his way back to the old Stalinist ethos in which writers were valued in accordance with their conformity or usefulness to the correct position of the moment and were otherwise abused or shunted aside.

It was as though Rahv felt he had been given a second chance to repent of the twin defections from the radicalism of his youth and that he had determined to do so, first making his peace with Communism and then surrendering to its ideas about the relation of art and politics—the ideas in opposition to which he had so many years before been led astray and onto a road that had taken him away from "genuine radicalism" altogether.

Rahv, then, just as surely suffered a failure of nerve in the face of the new radicalism as Mailer and Phillips did, although the motive and the way the failure expressed itself were different in each of the three cases.

17

Even more surprising than what happened to contemporaries of his like Phillips and Rahv, however, was the fact that Lionel Trilling too retreated in the face of the radicalism of the late sixties. But Trilling's retreat took a much more complicated form than theirs. At the forum on culture I quoted from earlier, after Hilton Kramer had invoked the phrase "failure of nerve" to describe the abdication of the intellectuals in the face of pressure, I raised the question of why such a failure of nerve had taken place and I answered it by offering an explanation "expressed in moral language: there was an epidemic of cowardice, together with an enormous panic to get on the right side of what looked like a triumphant revolution." To this, Trilling, who was also participating, made the following response:

> There is a reason to say cowardice in individual cases, but as a general explanation of the situation Norman Podhoretz refers to I think the word "cowardice" might lead us astray. One has to conceive of it rather in terms of fatigue. . . . Subjects and problems got presented in a way that made one's spirits fail. It wasn't that one was afraid to go into it, or afraid of being in opposition—I suppose I am speaking personally—but rather that in looking at the matter one's reaction was likely to be a despairing shrug.

It was, as Hilton Kramer later said to me in private, an astonishing confession. I agreed. We both knew that Trilling had not been in the forefront of resistance to the Movement, and that even when Columbia, his own university, had been overrun by it in 1968, he had taken a highly cautious attitude toward the students ("I find," he had told an interviewer at the time, "that, contrary to my first expectations, I have great respect for them and that their demands at least begin to make sense"). On the other hand, I had heard him voice great indignation against Archibald Cox (the Harvard law professor who had been invited in to investigate the Columbia uprising and was later to achieve greater fame for his contribution to the toppling of Richard Nixon when as a special prosecutor he defied the president during the Watergate investigation) for beginning his report on the uprising with the statement: "The present generation of young people in our universities is the best informed, the most intelligent, and the most idealistic this country has ever known." Cox claimed that this was "the experience of teachers everywhere," but it was not, Trilling told me, his experience as a teacher at Columbia. Having said this, he then proceeded, with more heat than was usual in his conversation, to denounce his present students as much less literate, much less intellectually curious, and much less intelligent than the students of my own generation.

This doubleness was entirely characteristic of Trilling. He was a liberal, but more often than not he would use the word in a pejorative sense; he believed in and celebrated society and its restraints, but he also wrote with great sympathy about the yearning for an "unconditioned" life; he loved literature above all things, but he was capable of complaining about how much he hated to read. Everything, always, was "complicated" to him. (I can hear him now pronouncing the word, as I heard him do a thousand times as teacher and friend—but of course a complicated one—over a span of more than twenty-five years: the voice a bit thin, lovingly lingering over the first syllable.) Yet for most of his life he did not rest in complication; nor would he use the complexity of the world and his responses to it as an elegant excuse for trimming or remaining neutral. Ultimately he would always take a stand, and the stand he took would become the more persuasive and credible as it was seen to emerge out of so much awareness of the obstacles—in himself, in his mind and in his feelings, as well as in the world—that he had worked through and had finally overcome to arrive at where he now so clearly stood.

Kramer and I realized that the stand he had taken in relation to the new radicalism of the sixties had been much less clear and even less forceful than might have been expected from the man who more than any other single member of the intellectual community had instructed our own generation in the errors and dangers—especially to culture and to the life of the mind—of the old radicalism of the thirties. What we had not realized before—but what I, who knew him so much better than Kramer, should have understood all along—was how poignantly aware he himself was of the weakness of his own response. It was not, he said, "speaking personally," his nerve that had failed but his spirits; it was a matter not of cowardice but of fatigue. This was a real distinction, and yet he himself went on to blur it when Kramer pressed him on the point:

> Kramer: Surely you wouldn't deny that there were cases in which people were terrified to find themselves on the wrong side?
>
> Trilling: Yes, there were indeed. But if you look at the thing from a large historical perspective, cowardice isn't quite the answer, it doesn't quite explain the movement of an entire class. Something has happened to make cowardice a possibility.

In the case of the "entire class" of intellectuals who were "terrified to find themselves on the wrong side," the "something" that had "happened to make cowardice a possibility" was, according to Trilling, "disaffection . . . from its own life." In his own case, however, what had made his "spirits fail" was the way "subjects and problems got presented."

In this he differed sharply from his wife Diana. She was so energized by finding herself once again called upon to attack the radical Left in the name of true liberalism that she produced a twenty-eight-thousand-word essay on the Columbia uprising. Of course, Diana had always been the more vigorous polemicist of the two, and the more forthright in stating the political views they both shared. Indeed, while she had in the past written pieces on the Oppenheimer case and other controversial political subjects, he had restricted himself to writing mostly about literature and literary issues, rarely dealing with politics or political issues as such.

Nevertheless his work was drenched in politics. With the possible exception of T. S. Eliot, he had the most highly developed sense of context possessed by any contemporary critic, and almost everything he ever wrote emerged from and was directed back into the surrounding atmosphere—a prevailing idea, a current attitude, a fashionable taste that needed correction or modification or qualification. It was not, however, *any* contemporary idea or attitude or taste that he addressed himself to in writing about literature. The context out of which his essays came and back into which they were sent was contemporary American liberalism. More concretely, it was the liberalism that had been shaped intellectually by the nineteenth-century heritage of faith in the infinite perfectibility of man and society through the growth of science and technology, and that had then been colored politically by association with Communism in the 1930s.

Sometimes, as in writing about Freud or Orwell, he might address himself directly to this heritage and this experience. But more often he did so indirectly. Thus, for example, when he wrote about *Huckleberry Finn,* he was not merely explicating the text in the fashion of an academic New Critic (although he did that too, and he did it, as always, brilliantly); he was challenging the standard liberal celebration of that novel as "a rejection of the notion of society and all the strains, difficulties, contradictions, of living a social life." (Those words come not from his essay on *Huckleberry Finn* but from the *Commentary* forum on culture where, with a directness unusual for him, he associated this rejection with "the promise of Marxist Communism as it was experienced by the Stalinists of my generation"—and, as he might easily have added, their liberal fellow travelers as well.) Even his essays on writers so apparently remote from the concerns of contemporary American liberalism as Keats (whom he used, among other things, to criticize certain liberal notions about proper child-rearing practice) and Jane Austen (in whose greatness he saw a living refutation of certain liberal assumptions about the proper relation between the artist and the surrounding society) reso-nated with political meaning and carried a political charge.

It was this very quality, indeed, that made Trilling so much more exciting to read than most literary critics even in the days when criticism in general was so exciting that the poet and critic Randall Jarrell named the entire age after it. Others were as good as and better than Trilling at the kind of interpretation against which Susan Sontag was later to inveigh; he was not, in fact, nearly so useful a guide to the difficult modern texts that inter-ested students of my own generation as critics like Cleanth Brooks or Edmund Wilson (to cite two who differed in every other possible respect). Nor did he especially excel in his critical judgments. Unlike T. S. Eliot and F. R. Leavis, who between them effected major changes in the accepted estimate of the writers of the past, and unlike Edmund Wilson, who found and promoted so many new young writers of his own day, Trilling did not contribute significantly to the demolition of inflated reputations or to the rediscovery of previously neglected classics or to the discovery of new ones. Nor, finally, did he rival such contempo-raries as I. A. Richards and Kenneth Burke in the significance of his contributions to literary theory.

Yet the political resonance of his writings made Trilling stand out with a salience no other American critic of his time managed to achieve. There were political undercurrents in the work of other critics too, but with some the politics were so indirect as to be nearly invisible, and with others they were so dominant as to violate the principle of the autonomy of art. In the case of Trill-ing's critical essays, the political charge was strong enough to electrify the mind and yet so subtle and muted that it never overwhelmed their independent value as literary criticism.

In short, Trilling's essays performed the high function Matthew Arnold (about whom Trilling himself had written a wonderful book in the late thirties) prescribed for the critic in Victorian England: they undertook a "criticism of life" by means of an effort "to see the object as in itself it really is." Trilling's essays, then, were political in exactly the same way literature itself could be said to be: as one element in a complex fullness of response to the time and place in which the writer finds himself.

But if being political in this way is what made him so exciting a writer, it was also what made him an influential one—far more influential than it is usually given to literary critics to be, or than it was even given to them to be in Jarrell's "Age of Criticism." He was influential because he was relevant—but as with the term "political" a distinction has to be introduced between the sense in which this word can be applied to Trilling's writings and the sense in which it came to be used in the sixties. Here again, Trilling's own writings resembled imaginative literature. That is, they were relevant not by virtue of their ability to capture the wandering attention of an easily bored audience, or by their usefulness to some transient extraliterary purpose, but rather in touching with great accuracy on the central concerns "of this time, of that place" (to borrow the altogether significant title of the only piece of fiction he ever wrote that could bear comparison with the best of his critical essays).

In one of the earliest symptoms of a backlash against the new influence of "New York" (that is, Jewish) writers and intellectuals that was to grow more open and more virulent, Trilling was once attacked by the novelist George P. Elliott for his constant use of the word "we." Who, demanded Elliott, was we? Trilling might, he went on to say, speak for a certain group of New York Jewish intellectuals, but he did not speak for anyone else and he therefore had no right to make the claim of representativeness implicit in the plural pronoun.

Elliott was wrong. It was true that Trilling spoke out of his experience as a member of a particular community. Yet he did so at a time when the great issue agitating that community had begun to affect the educated American middle class in general (including, on the evidence of his own novel *Parktilden Village,* George P. Elliott himself). This issue—the issue of alienation— had perhaps been marginal and exotic in the past, but like so much else that had once been confined to the intellectual community, it was beginning to be massified (or, if Daniel Bell's politer term is preferred, "democratized"). It was mainly because Jewish novelists like Saul Bellow understood it so well and not, as Truman Capote later charged, through any conspiracy, that their work now reached out far beyond the small circle of their fellow intellectuals to a very large audience (itself swelled in size by the simultaneous spread of higher education). And it was for the same reason that Jewish intellectuals like Trilling also began to be read by a commensurately larger audience (which was of course smaller than the audience for fiction).

Trilling was thus entitled to say "we"—and all the more in that he, in common with this larger audience, was searching for an honorable way out of the alienated attitudes it had inherited and into a state of greater self-acceptance as Americans and as members of a class they had been taught by their culture to despise. Trilling said at the forum on culture that the war between the culture of the middle class and the life of the middle class was "one of the most fascinating occurrences . . . in the history of the world." Like Bellow, who also found it endlessly fascinating, Trilling had long devoted himself to negotiating a peaceful settlement of this war at a time (roughly the first fifteen years after the Second World War) when prevailing sentiment was moving in the direction of reconciliation; and it was this that made him so relevant a writer and so much more influential than any other American critic of the age.

This being so, I suppose there was a certain rough justice in the fact that his influence began to decline when the war between the culture of the middle class and the life of the middle class heated up again in the sixties and actual hostilities erupted.

18

The moment for mediation or negotiation had passed. The barricades were now up, and the armies of the alienated were much larger than they had ever been before and those of the established order were weaker and less confident. In the past, the best the alienated could do was to conduct sporadic guerrilla warfare from tiny sanctuaries in the intellectual community. Now, however, those sanctuaries had grown to include all the major universities and were being supplied and sustained by allies in many of the most powerful media of communication. For example, the leading newspaper in the country, *The New York Times*, which had only recently regarded itself and been regarded as a pillar of the established order (it even supported Kennedy and Johnson in their Vietnam policy) had by the late sixties become so sympathetic to the cause of the alienated that its Op-Ed page often read like a slightly sanitized or bowdlerized version of such organs of the counterculture as *The Village Voice* and *Rolling Stone*.

The same thing happened to *The New Yorker*. In the late fifties, when I was reviewing books for them, the editor who dealt with my pieces once asked me whether there was a special typewriter at *Partisan Review* with the word "alienation" on a single key; there you had the authentic tone and spirit that had always marked *The New Yorker*. Ten years later, however, the magazine scored a great sensation by publishing almost the whole of *The Greening of America*, a book about the "youth" by a newly radicalized Yale professor named Charles Reich who carried the idea of alienation to lengths that must surely have embarrassed *Partisan*

Review alumni like Dwight Macdonald, Mary McCarthy, Hannah Arendt, and Harold Rosenberg, who were themselves now writing regularly for *The New Yorker*.

Rosenberg in particular had cause to be embarrassed. Long ago he had coined the phrase "the herd of independent minds" to describe the small group of self-proclaimed alienated intellectuals around *Partisan Review* (with which he had then been on the outs for personal rather than political reasons); they were, he said, merely being pretentious in calling themselves alienated. Now that the "herd" had broken out of its Greenwich Village confines and, gathering force as it moved along, was threatening to stampede the entire country, one might have expected that he would be inspired to even greater heights of derision. Yet Rosenberg, so quick to make fun of the culture of alienation when it was a tiny marginal movement, grew notably reticent as it grew notably large. In his case, the failure of nerve took the form of a benevolent neutrality—except when he dealt as *The New Yorker*'s regular art critic with developments in the art world of the sixties like Pop and Op which he criticized as illegitimate extensions of the modernist tradition ("the tradition of the new," in another of his memorable phrases); and even then he carefully refrained from any attempt to connect these phenomena with the broader cultural movement of which they were so integral a part.

An even greater measure of how powerful the armies of the alienated had become by the end of the sixties was the respectful treatment they received in the report of a presidential commission on campus unrest, the so-called Scranton Report:

A "new" culture is emerging primarily among students. . . . Most of its members have high ideals and great fears. They stress the need for humanity, equality, and the sacredness of life. . . . They see their elders as entrapped by materialism and competition and prisoners of outdated forms. They believe their own country has lost its sense of human purpose.

This language might easily have been lifted from the Port Huron Statement, and was indeed written mainly by Kenneth Keniston, a prominent academic apologist for the Movement since the early days of its existence. That the culture of alienation should have become powerful enough to wrest what a young writer named David Bromwich, himself a member of the generation in question, characterized as "diplomatic recognition" from the United States government—that is, the highest embodiment of the established order to whose destruction it was avowedly devoted—was remarkable enough. But that this should have been done by a government whose head was Richard Nixon could only be read as a sign that even the worst enemies of the alienated culture felt intimidated by it.

When the Scranton Report came out, I telephoned Pat Moynihan in the White House. "For this," I asked him, paraphrasing a mordant Yiddish joke, "we needed a Nixon administration?" In 1968 I had supported McCarthy and Moynihan had supported Kennedy, but we both wound up voting for Humphrey, which did not prevent Richard Nixon, the winner over Humphrey in that election, from offering Moynihan a job as chief domestic adviser and did not prevent me from urging him to take it. That he did take it said something about the course he as a liberal had followed since 1960; and that I approved said something about the road I as a radical had traveled during the same period. He still considered himself a liberal; indeed his main activity while working in the Nixon White House was to develop a program of welfare reform that amounted to a guaranteed annual income which he persuaded the president to sponsor by pointing to the way Disraeli the conservative had outfoxed Gladstone the liberal in pushing through some of his rival's most cherished reforms. (In the event, Nixon's attempt to emulate Disraeli in the matter of welfare reform was foiled by an alliance between his fellow conservatives, who opposed the measure as too liberal, and his liberal enemies, who said it was not liberal enough, but whose real objection was to its sponsorship by an opponent they hated even more than the Gladstone liberals hated Disraeli, intense as the hatred of Disraeli was in its own right.)

Still, Moynihan's authorship of the Family Assistance Program aside, he had developed doubts about the capacity of the federal government to deal with all the problems that he, like so many other liberals, had confidently thought it could solve in the early sixties. He had helped design Johnson's war on poverty, but now that he could see the disappointing results of some of the programs he himself had been instrumental in developing, he had become convinced that they would never succeed, either because the problems had turned out to be more intractable than anyone had originally thought or because the programs had been misconceived.

Moynihan was by no means the only liberal who had emerged from the experience of the sixties with a new appreciation of "the limits of social policy," as Nathan Glazer called them in an article for *Commentary* published just as the new decade got under way. Glazer (previously "a mild radical" rather than a liberal, but still a former believer in the power of the federal government to solve most social problems) was another, and so too were such prominent social scientists as Daniel Bell, Seymour Martin Lipset, and James Q. Wilson.

In 1965, together with Irving Kristol, these people had founded a magazine called *The Public Interest,* whose main purpose was to analyze public policy, and especially its limits and consequences. Before long, all of them were being denounced as conservatives. I say denounced not because the epithet "conservative" is in itself necessarily a term of abuse, but because in the climate of the times it was very widely taken to mean a person of stodgy tastes who cared mainly about the protection of his own privileges. No wonder, then, that it was resisted so fiercely by most members of *The Public Interest* group, several of whom indeed (Bell and Lipset, for example) still insisted on calling themselves socialists. The one great exception was Kristol, who would willingly have accepted the label "conservative" but settled more happily for "neoconservative" because it suggested that there was something new in this conservatism to distinguish it from the old. (The new element, of course, was an acceptance of the welfare state in opposition to which old-style conservatives had defined themselves in theory ever since Franklin Roosevelt had begun building the foundations for one in this country, however they may have behaved toward the welfare state in practice and in office.) Kristol even eventually took the step, extraordinary for an intellectual of his background, of joining the Republican party. Most of the others either remained loftily technocratic, concerned only with issues that transcended or did not engage partisan politics, or if they did participate in partisan politics at all, it was as Democrats.

But by 1970 it was not primarily the idea of the limits of social policy that kept these "liberals," "socialists," and "neoconservatives" together. More profoundly what now united them was a common decision to take a stand against the armies of the alienated. Most of them thought that the Scranton Report exaggerated wildly in comparing the campus uprisings of the late sixties to the Civil War. Yet they all shared the view that "the divisions of American society" were very deep and they agreed that "the nation as a whole" was in crisis and was being divided into "opposing camps." Where they differed from the Scranton Report, and from most of their fellow "liberals" and "socialists" in the intellectual community and beyond, was in their understanding of what each of the "opposing camps" stood for.

To begin with, they did not see the "new" culture as new. It was in their view the current expression of a tradition of hostility to bourgeois civilization going back in the American context at least to the 1870s; the only thing that was new about the contemporary variant was its unprecedented size and influence. Nor did they see it as a "youth" culture, either in the sense that most young people were part of it, or in the sense that all older people were excluded from it. Their argument (supported by the polls and later confirmed when McGovern, against all expectations, barely carried a majority of young voters against Nixon in the 1972 presidential election) was that American youth was divided very much along the same lines that divided their elders. We were dealing here, as I once put it, not with a generational conflict but rather with a political one cutting across all age groups on an axis of social class and ethnicity.

Nor, finally, did they accept the Scranton Report's version of the nature of this conflict as one in which the forces of "idealism," the believers in "humanity, equality, and the sacredness of life," were ranged against the forces of "materialism" entrapped by the competition for money and privilege and lacking in any "sense of human purpose." What they saw instead was a "New Class" of educated, prosperous people, members of the professional and technical intelligentsia, making a serious bid to dislodge and re-place the business and commercial class which had on the whole dominated the country for nearly a century now.

This New Class was hailed by sympathizers like Michael Har-rington as a "constituency of conscience," even though as a Marxist Harrington might have been expected to understand that such self-gratulatory talk about any social class was likely to be what Marx called a mystification—that is, an attractive ideological cover for the pursuit of self-interest. But Harrington himself was so caught up in this class and its ambitions that the job of demysti-fying it was ironically left to an anti-Marxist critic like Irving Kristol (making good use, however, of his education in Marxism as a young Trotskyist). The New Class, said Kristol, represented itself as concerned only with the general good, the good of others (especially the poor and the blacks), but what it really wanted was to aggrandize its own power.

Speculating on the relation between the New Class and the "youth," I myself liked to say that in trying to dislodge the old order, the New Class was using its own young people as comman-dos, sending them out into the streets to clash with the enemy's troops (the police and the National Guard) while the "elders" directed the grand strategy from behind the lines and engaged in less dangerous forms of political warfare against the established power. And not the least effective form of this warfare was to identify their side with the youth, thus implying that they were the fabled wave of the future.

I suppose I ought to emphasize that this was a fanciful, even a mischievously playful way of thinking about the relation between the young radicals of the Movement and their elders of the New Class. The "cultural revolution" in this country was not a case of direction from above, as its namesake was in China, where the young (the Red Guards) were sent out on a rampage by the authorities to squelch potential opposition among the intelligentsia. Here indeed it was the other way around. That is, our young radicals came out of the intelligentsia to challenge the authorities, and while they were applauded and even egged on by many of their elders—their parents and their teachers—for the most part it was they who took the initiative.

It is true that their activism sometimes went too far even for their admiring parents and teachers—Keniston, for example, could never bring himself to condone student violence, though he was rarely at a loss for exculpatory explanations. But it is equally true that the aggressions against the established order by the young radicals of the Movement did serve the political purposes of those of their elders and mentors who were maneuvering for control of the Democratic party and for whom the toppling of the regular leadership was an essential precondition. Getting rid of Johnson was the first step; beating Humphrey in the primaries would have been the second, but McCarthy's chances were spoiled by Kennedy, and Kennedy (who looked as though he might be turning into the instrument of this process) was murdered. At that point the Movement devoted itself to the defeat of Humphrey. Demonstrations to "Dump the Hump" were held in Chicago during the Democratic convention of 1968, and the resultant clashes with the police (deliberately provoked, as some of the radical leaders later admitted) had the desired effect. Humphrey did win the Democratic nomination, but the violence in Chicago contributed to his defeat in the general election.

I imagine that many of the elders and mentors of the Movement, horrified by the prospect of Richard Nixon as president, voted for Humphrey in the end, but many refused to vote at all, and very few exerted themselves on his behalf. The apparent reason was his continuing identification with the war in Vietnam. Yet in view of the fact that Nixon was even more hawkish, and that Humphrey was known to be moving—as far and as fast as the fear of Johnson's power to cut off a major source of his financial support permitted him to do—in a dovish direction, Vietnam could only have been an excuse. The truth was that so hungry were the forces of the New Class (now increasingly being identified with the "New Politics") for the opportunity Humphrey's defeat would give them to move in and take over the Democratic party that they were even willing to pay the price of Richard Nixon's accession to the presidency.

And indeed, from that point of view it turned out to be a price worth paying. By the time the next presidential campaign came along, the forces of the New Politics had taken sufficient control of the machinery of the Democratic party to succeed in nominating their own candidate, George McGovern, even over the fierce opposition of such previously unshakable bulwarks of the old system as the AFL-CIO.

Of course, in order to do this, the New Politics had to temper the ideas and attitudes it had inherited from the more radical Movement, which in certain respects went too far even for its most sympathetic fellow travelers within the established order and were in their unexpurgated state altogether repugnant to many voters who might be receptive to them if offered in more familiar and less pugnacious language. Thus, for example, on Vietnam, the Movement's by now explicit support of the Communist side and its undisguised wish for a defeat of the United States that would discredit the entire anti-Communist foreign policy of which Vietnam was a product, had to be downplayed. Thus too with the Movement's openly contemptuous view of the possibilities of peaceful progress under the present economic and political order, and its jubilant predictions of increasing racial tension and violence leading ultimately to the overthrow of the system. And thus finally with the Movement's belief that the American way of life in general, with its middle-class or bourgeois values and its relentless pursuit of economic and technological growth, was "dangerous to children and other living things." Just as the young radicals who decided to work for McCarthy's campaign had to be "Clean for Gene"—that is, they had to get rid of the beards and long hair that were offensive in themselves to many voters—so their ideas and attitudes had to be sanitized if they were to "work within the system."

And that is exactly what happened. The slogan of the McGovern campaign, "Come Home, America," referred to far more than a withdrawal from Vietnam. It represented a translation into respectable terms of the idea that the best thing the United States could do for the rest of the world—especially the underdeveloped or "third" world, where Communist-led revolutions were deemed both necessary and desirable—was to stop being "counterrevolutionary" (as the economist Robert L. Heilbroner called it in 1966 in one of the last expressions of *Commentary*'s by then diminishing commitment to the new radicalism). The fondest wish of all Movement radicals would have been to turn the United States around altogether—from a counterrevolutionary power into an active sponsor of the revolution—but in those days this seemed an unrealistic goal. Not so the next best thing, however, which was at least to remove the United States from the business of counterrevolution by neutralizing it. This was a realistic goal because it could appeal to the deep currents of isolationist feeling that flowed through all segments of the population and through the entire political spectrum from Right to Left; and it was to those currents that McGovern, as the standard-bearer of the New Politics, appealed in crying "Come Home, America."

The new isolationism, then, was what happened to the Movement's ideas about the American role in world affairs when they were cleaned up to "work within the system" under the auspices of the New Politics. Similarly with what America was supposed to do once it came home. On the issue of race, the Movement's idea was that racism ran as deep in the North as in the South and that outlawing discrimination would therefore not suffice to bring about integration of the black population into the middle class. For the Movement—most visibly represented in this area between 1968 and 1972 by the Black Panthers—this opened up the possibility of a revolution within the United States leading to the overthrow of an incorrigibly oppressive system. But despite the great popularity of the Panthers among fellow travelers of the Movement—it was for the Panthers that Leonard Bernstein threw a fund-raising cocktail party to which he made the mistake of inviting Tom Wolfe, who then wrote the devastating account of it he published under the title "Radical Chic"—their call for a violent revolution at home was understood to be even more unrealistic than the hope that the United States would become the sponsor of revolution abroad. Even Andrew Kopkind finally denied that the United States was quite ripe for revolution—or, to use the technical term, that the country was in a "revolutionary situation."

In this area the next best thing was to do away with a system based on the principle of equality of opportunity and replace it with one based on the notion of equality of results. Representing as it would an assault on what was perhaps the single most distinctive feature of the American tradition—its emphasis in law and to a considerable extent in practice on the individual as an individual, and the correlative idea that social justice is satisfied by the distribution of rewards on the basis of individual merit—this change in the system would be so radical as almost to be considered the functional equivalent of its overthrow. And yet it was no less realistic a goal than the neutralization of American power abroad, and for the same reason. For it too appealed to deep currents of feeling and interest flowing through important elements of the population, again including some (like the Ford

Foundation and many university administrators) who were by no means sympathetic to the Movement or the New Politics in general, but who saw an opportunity here for pacifying or even buying off a restive and unruly black community at a relatively low price. And again, too, it was to those various currents that McGovern and the New Politics movement in general appealed in championing the institution of racial quotas in all areas of American life.

Nor was this radically new conception of equality confined to the issue of race. It was also extended by the New Politics to cover the distribution of income within the populace as a whole. According to the traditional American idea, everyone had an equal right to "the pursuit of happiness" (meaning, above all, as the original draft of this phrase in the Declaration of Independence actually said, "property"), and the duty of the government was to eliminate as many obstacles as possible to the exercise of this right. For example, it was in the name of equal opportunity and free competition that laws forbidding discrimination against individuals on the basis of "race, creed, color," and later sex, were passed; and it was in the name of the same principle that efforts were constantly being made to prevent undue concentrations of economic power in the form of trusts and monopolies. That such laws were not entirely effective, especially with regard to the blacks, was true. But that did not alter the principle they were promulgated to express and protect, which was that everyone should be assured an opportunity to better himself in life.

Yet if establishing that right was the duty of the government, it was also, according to the traditional American idea, the duty of the government to get out of the way once the job had been done and to permit the operations of a free competition in which some (being by nature more energetic or talented or clever—or lucky) would inevitably get more and others would get less, in which some would succeed and others would fail. It was also entirely consistent with the American system that the losers in the "pursuit of happiness" should be provided for—that no one should be permitted to starve or to live below a certain minimum standard of material subsistence.

But it was inconsistent, radically inconsistent, to demand that no one should be permitted to lose at all—that any inequality in the distribution of income must be considered unjust and that the ultimate goal must be a society in which everyone ends up with roughly the same rewards.

In keeping with the need to reassure voters who would be put off by too radical an appeal, the New Politics tried very hard to deny the inconsistency here and to make preferential quotas for blacks and the closing of the gap between rich and poor seem an indigenous element of the American Dream. But this was like the claim of the early Christians that their new religion was the "fulfillment" of the Judaism from which it had originally derived instead of a rebellion against it.

The truth was that by 1970 the American Dream, far from having been perverted and distorted and turned, as was so often said, into a "nightmare," had come very close to realization, precisely in the sense that equal opportunity was now more widely and firmly established than ever before. If there was a "nightmare" it was the dream come true, not the dream destroyed. This was what the critic Eric Bentley, one of the elders and mentors of the Movement, had meant in saying that the radicalism of the sixties was born not out of a revulsion against the failures of American society (the persistence of poverty and discrimination) but against its successes in making the middle-class way of life available to an extraordinarily high proportion of the people.

And indeed, the egalitarianism of the New Politics, along with serving as a cleaned-up version of the Movement's ideas about racial and social justice, also did double duty in carrying the Movement's hostility toward bourgeois civilization into the respectable political mainstream. Under the new egalitarian banner, and in the name of justice, it was possible to denigrate the pursuit of success as well as the values traditionally associated with it (ambition, discipline, work). People who possessed these qualities could be stigmatized as exploiters and oppressors; or if they were not themselves especially successful, they could be looked down upon for the "meanness" of their aspirations.

19

When Lionel Trilling first read *Making It* in 1967, neither he nor I—nor, for that matter, anyone else—anticipated that the ideas and attitudes of the new radicalism would ever achieve this degree of currency in the world of electoral politics, let alone that it would do so in less than five years. Yet we both knew that these ideas and attitudes had already gone very far indeed in the academic and literary communities. Two years earlier, in 1965, he had called attention to the fact

> that the student today is at liberty to choose between two cultural environments. One of them. . . . we can take . . . to be philistine and dull, satisfied with its unexamined, unpromising beliefs. The other environment defines itself by its differences and its antagonism to the first, by its commitment to the "sources of life," by its adherence to the imagination of fullness, freedom, and potency. . . .

To the ideas and attitudes of this second environment Trilling gave the name the "adversary culture" and he was aware, long before most other intellectuals, that it was itself spreading into the first environment, "as witness the present ideational or ideological status of sex, violence, madness, and art itself." It was because he was so conscious of all this that Trilling advised me not to publish *Making It* at all, unless I were to add a new conclusion clearly repudiating the suggestion that the pursuit of success was not necessarily a corrupting force in American life.

That acting on this advice would be a cowardly thing for me to do I understood. But I did not understand until much later, and then only in the light of how Trilling would conduct himself in the coming years, how telling a sign it was of his own failure of nerve. Trilling had been through the antiradical wars as a young man in the thirties, and though (in contrast to many of his contemporaries) he was not in the least inclined to repent of his political past by switching sides in the latest outbreak of hostilities, neither did he have the stomach to enter the lists again. It was too hard—even harder than the last time. Then there had only been the Communists and their fellow travelers to fight, whereas now the whole phenomenon was so much more diffuse and elusive. Describing the group of intellectuals with whom he had been associated in the thirties (the group led by Elliot Cohen), Trilling once wrote that any member of it "would have been able to explain his disillusionment" with "radical politics" by "a precise enumeration of the errors and failures of the [Communist] party, both at home and abroad." But now radical politics offered no such precise target. Now "subjects and problems got presented in a way that made one's spirits fail."

In addition to being more difficult intellectually, the new struggle was also more dangerous than the first one had been. In the thirties, a young writer fighting the Stalinists could expect a good deal of punishment in the form of vilification (and despite the nursery rhyme, "names" can harm at least as much as "sticks and stones" and many people are with good cause more afraid of the former than the latter). Yet even though, as Trilling himself once put it, "Stalinism was established as sacrosanct among a large and influential part of the intellectual class" in the thirties, the part in question was not nearly so large or so influential as was the case with the radicalism of the sixties. In the thirties one risked being wounded; in the sixties— to borrow from an old joke about a soldier's explanation for refusing to leave his foxhole—one could get killed out there, or

anyway (as Trilling predicted would happen to me) incapac-
itated for the duration.

Finally, there was the problem of his own implication in the
spread of the adversary culture as a critic and a teacher of literature—and especially of modern literature, which had played "a
dominant part" in the formation of the adversary culture's "assumptions and preconceptions." Although he had been something of a Stalinist for a very short time in the early thirties, in
subsequently joining the fight against Stalinism he had never felt
personally responsible for having once contributed to its "sacrosanct" status within the intellectual class. By contrast, for all
that Philip Rahv and others accused him of having been a conservative all along, he could not easily dissociate himself from the
radicalism of the sixties. Allen Ginsberg had been a student of his,
even as I had been; and Ginsberg continued throughout the
sixties to treat him with high regard and to acknowledge a debt
of influence. Nor did Trilling deny this or attempt to disown
Ginsberg. Still less did he attempt to disown the many younger
students of his who became academic fellow travelers and apologists of the counterculture. Then, when Columbia erupted, not
only did he say that, contrary to his first expectations, he had
"great respect" for "the relatively moderate but still militant
students" and that their "demands" made sense to him, he also
said privately that he could not simply oppose them because they
were, after all, his own students.

Nevertheless he *was* opposed to the new radicalism, and he
tried to express this opposition in his writings of the late sixties
and early seventies. To the extent that Communism as such was
still, or had once again become, an issue, he could be as clear and
tough—and simple—as ever without losing his hold on the complexities that were the essence of his mind and style. Thus in his
introduction to a reissue of Tess Slesinger's novel of the thirties,
The Unpossessed (it is from that introduction that the passage
quoted earlier about the sacrosanct status of Stalinism comes), or
in his introduction to a new edition of his own novel, *The Middle*

of the Journey, where he defended the much-vilified Whittaker Chambers as "a man of honor," or in his brief contribution to the *Commentary* symposium on "Liberal Anti-Communism Revisited," where he testily and unequivocally reaffirmed his commitment to anti-Communism, he sounded like the Trilling of *The Liberal Imagination.* The prose of those pieces was a little fussier and more self-regarding, perhaps, than the prose of his best early essays, but the complexities and nuances and qualifications were still mainly there for the sake of precision, to sharpen and refine and enrich the point being made and to add plausibility and credibility to the stand being taken.

In criticizing the cultural radicalism of the sixties and its historical sources, on the other hand, Trilling increasingly seemed to use both the idea of complication and the prose embodying it not so much to clarify and deepen his own point of view as to disguise and hide it. Reading the series of lectures he gave at Harvard in 1970 and then gathered together in *Sincerity and Authenticity,* for example, one got the impression of a writer no longer trying "to see the object as in itself it really is" but trying instead to conceal as much as to reveal, to say something and to deny at the same time that he was really saying it, to take part in a battle while at the same time pretending to be above it.

To be sure, there had always been a touch of this tendency in Trilling. More than most writers, he hated being labeled, or even characterized; he thought—or rather he felt, since in theory he understood as well as anyone that universality can only be achieved through particularity—that it limited him intolerably. But this standing temptation to deny his own particularity was aroused more irresistibly by the effort to pin certain labels on him than others. Most of the time, for example, he did not object to being called a liberal and in his younger days he even used the term of himself. But almost always he fought against being called a conservative.

The first time I ever got a real sense of how strongly he felt on this point was at a party at the home of Richard Chase in the late fifties. Chase, a younger colleague of Trilling's at Columbia who had also been a devoted disciple, was then in the process of developing a new theory of American literature that implicitly involved a break with Trilling's general perspective. As everyone present that evening knew, and as anyone who did not know would have understood from the tension between Chase and Trilling, this apparently academic dispute was not in reality academic at all. Chase's work of that period—a book on American culture called *The Democratic Vista* and a study of the American novel and its tradition—was one of the first harbingers of the new radicalism, and like some of my own pieces of the late fifties, the case it made inevitably depended on a repudiation of certain basic assumptions behind the prevalent liberal temper of the day—and where literary criticism was concerned that meant Lionel Trilling. That Trilling should have resented and resisted what smacked to him of personal betrayal by a disciple was to be expected. But what astonished me was his refusal to admit that his work had any wider implications whatsoever: all he ever did, he kept insisting (as though he were a particularly disingenuous New Critic) was interpret texts.

For Trilling this was only the beginning of what would be a difficult time. For about ten years, from the late forties to the late fifties, his name had rarely been mentioned in print without admiration or at least great respect, but now he was often sniped at and sometimes subjected to full-scale attack. "I love being attacked," he once told me, "it gets my blood up." But in truth he no more loved being attacked than anyone else, and he responded with a testy defensiveness and with an irritability that often crept into his once perfectly poised prose.

Unlike many liberal academics, who knew how to handle criticism from the Right but were simply shattered by the eruption of thunder on the Left, Trilling was a specialist in how to deal with radical assaults on the liberal position. But underlying and exacerbating the difficulties I have already mentioned in trying to explain why he was inhibited in practicing this specialty, there was a great impatience in him, which grew greater as he grew older, to achieve what might be called a position of venerability.

If he had been English he would, like his friend Isaiah Berlin, have by now become Professor Sir Lionel Trilling, resting on his intellectual laurels, admired by all, and already in his own lifetime seeming to be not for the age but for the ages. The trouble was that there was also a side of Trilling—the New York or Jewish side —that did not wish to be above the battle; and as the example of Sidney Hook so vividly demonstrated, not even a record of distinguished work was enough to make an aging American intellectual venerable if he remained on the field of political and ideological combat. In sharp contrast to Isaiah Berlin, who kept his diplomatic distance from the fray, a benevolent friend to both sides (though a touch more benevolent to the radicals who, after all, were the dominant power in his world), Hook went on fighting the New Left and its liberal fellow travelers as vigorously as he had fought the Stalinists and their fellow travelers in the thirties and forties and fifties, giving no quarter and getting none. For Trilling, Hook was the cautionary figure of his own generation— the one who had gone too far in the rebellion against radicalism —just as Irving Kristol was of the generation below him and as I myself, ten years younger than Kristol, was rapidly becoming for the generation below that. Trilling's fear of the fate of Sidney Hook was not nearly so great as that of William Phillips, who would have done almost anything to avoid it. But Trilling did, I believe, grow fearful enough in the late sixties to shy away from too close an identification with the antiradical position.

Torn, then, between the exemplary roles of Isaiah Berlin and Sidney Hook, unable to become the one and afraid of becoming the other, Trilling exhausted himself in the last years of his life. It showed in most of the writing he did in those years, but never more than when he was chosen in 1972 to deliver the first of a series of Jefferson Lectures sponsored by the National Endowment for the Humanities. This was a moment that any novelist would have relished for the richness of its revelations. That Trilling should have been chosen meant that he had not altogether failed in his ambition for venerability; Hook would have been too controversial for such an honor. At the same time he decided to touch on the very theme—the mounting assault on the idea of "professional excellence" in the universities and the concomitant institutionalization of quota systems in hiring practices—that Hook himself was just then actively engaged in discussing on every possible occasion, and to take much the same position as Hook had been taking against this "liberal" outgrowth of the Movement's belief in the inability of the American system of equal opportunity to promote progress among blacks. Yet so long did he spend in getting to the point, and so heavily did he load it with academic baggage, that its power to impress—and to offend—was almost entirely dissipated.

That this point did in fact possess such power I discovered at first hand when around the same time Trilling was preparing his Jefferson Lecture I received an invitation from the then dean of admissions of Harvard College to talk to his staff on the subject of racial quotas. The reason he had invited me was that a series of articles had been appearing in *Commentary* warning against the tendency of "affirmative action"—that is, special efforts to find and admit blacks (and, later, women and certain other groups deemed to be oppressed minorities)—to turn in practice into a system of predetermined quotas involving preferential or reverse discrimination. When I accepted the dean's invitation I knew that his purpose was to persuade me that Harvard had no intention of doing what both of us knew it was in fact already doing, and that nothing I could say would have any real effect. Nevertheless I decided to fly up to Cambridge and speak my piece for whatever it might be worth.

Sitting around a table in an informal session, I told the group of admissions officers that I supported special efforts to recruit qualified blacks and that I also supported special efforts to help unqualified blacks compete on an equal footing. What I opposed

was the admission of unqualified persons in order to fill a predetermined quota. Such a system, meant to fight racism, was itself
implicitly racist in assuming that blacks would never be able to
compete with whites on an equal footing. I myself did not believe
this, and if I were black, I would feel insulted by it. But I was not
a black and I would not presume to talk to them as one. I would
talk rather as what I was—a liberal, a Jew, and an intellectual. In
each of these capacities, I said, I had a strong reason for opposing
quotas. As a liberal I believed in the traditional principle of treating individuals as individuals and not as members of a group; as
a Jew, I feared that a quota system designed to overcome discrimination against blacks would almost certainly result in discrimination against Jews—and I could not bring myself to believe
that the only way to achieve social justice in the United States was
to discriminate against my own children; and as an intellectual,
I worried about the lowering and erosion of standards entailed
by any system of reverse discrimination.

As I spoke—and I was speaking in a low-keyed and non-
provocative style—the eyes around me grew narrower and the
nostrils grew wider, and when I finished the questions were so
charged with hatred that I found myself wondering whether even
a public reading from *Mein Kampf* could have elicited greater
outrage. Almost everyone who took the antiquota position in
those days had similar tales to tell, and yet neither when he
delivered his Jefferson Lecture nor when he published it in a
small bound volume did Trilling elicit more than a polite yawn.

If, as I believe, clarity is courage, there was little courage in
such writing. But Trilling was also justified in refusing to plead
guilty to the charge of cowardice. "Fatigue" was his word, and it
was perhaps as precise a word as any to explain why he could
never summon up the will to go into "opposition" (his word too),
even at those moments when he was tempted to do so.

One such moment came in 1970, shortly after my growing
doubts about radicalism had coalesced and come to a head in a
conviction so blazing that it ignited an all-out offensive against

the Movement in *Commentary*. Trilling, just back from a stay in England (where, as also in France, Germany, Italy, and Japan, radicalism had once again become all the rage in the universities and among intellectuals in general, even without benefit of governments at war in Vietnam or societies torn by racial conflict), told me that he approved of what I had started to do. "I see," he said, "that it isn't all over yet."

"Will you help me then?" I asked. "I need you."

"You shall have me," he replied.

But I never did. He allowed me to publish a section of *Sincerity and Authenticity* which I featured even though I found it characteristically muffled in its attack on the idea of insanity as a species of rebellion against the spiritual oppressions of middle-class society. This idea had been from the beginning (in Allen Ginsberg's declaration that the "best minds" of his generation had gone mad and in Norman Mailer's celebration of the psychopath) a central element of the new radicalism, and it still figured in the work of serious thinkers like the psychologist R. D. Laing and in more popular form in a novel like Ken Kesey's *One Flew Over the Cuckoo's Nest* which, as a measure of its by-then mass appeal, was subsequently turned into a very successful movie. It was also an idea profoundly repugnant to Trilling, and yet, as in the case of his Jefferson Lecture, he could only bring himself to an expression of this repugnance by a route so convoluted and difficult to follow that many readers were lost on the way.

Except for his participation in the round-table discussion of culture in 1974, about a year before his death, this attenuated blast on an uncertain trumpet was all the good he ever made on his promise to join in the *Commentary* campaign against the Movement. In fact, his initial declaration of solidarity and approval turned out to be the impulse of a moment, when his blood was up, and it soon gave way to an unmistakable coldness toward the enterprise.

Ten years earlier we had quarreled bitterly over my radicalization. He had accused me then of going too far with the radical critique of American society and American foreign policy. A little later, I had in turn accused him of having been driven by a horror of Stalinism into extolling the virtues of American society and the values of the middle-class spirit and thereby abdicating the intellectual's proper role as a critic of society. Now our roles were reversed. Now it was he who accused me of overreacting to the excesses of the new radicalism and going too far in celebrating the virtues of American society and the values of the middle-class spirit, and it was I who accused him of excessive deference to the radicals and their ideas. But since we were both determined never to quarrel again, these accusations were never spoken bluntly by either of us to the other. Whether he knew how I felt about him in his current position, I cannot say for certain; probably he did. But for my part, I could certainly tell how he felt, and after the first flush of disappointment, I could see that I had been a little foolish to think that it would ever be otherwise. If, after all, even *Making It* had gone too far for him in its critique of the values of the Movement, how could he have been expected to identify himself with the no-holds-barred campaign *Commentary* was now conducting against the Movement?

20

Irving Howe was someone else about whom I was foolish in much the same way, though perhaps with greater encouragement from him. Like me, but unlike Trilling, Howe had welcomed the appearance of a new radicalism in the early sixties. Like me too, he had developed serious doubts about its attitudes toward democracy on the one side and Communism on the other, and he had expressed those doubts forcefully enough to provoke Philip Rahv and others into charging him with having deserted "genuine radicalism" altogether. When, therefore, my younger *Commentary* colleague Neal Kozodoy (who had long since seen through the pretensions of the Movement) and I decided that the time had come to declare full-scale war, we had good reason to expect Howe's enthusiastic cooperation, and we got it—for as long, that is, as he continued to worry about the Movement's claim to have supplanted "democratic socialists" like himself as the true heir of the radical tradition.

But knowing what I knew about his compulsive need to maintain his credentials as a radical and as a socialist, I should also have realized that the alliance he had entered into with *Commentary* would be tactical and temporary. Once the Movement had been discredited, he would lose no time in trying to reestablish his claim to leadership of the Left, not by moving to the Left himself but by turning his polemical guns on us for having moved to the Right.

In the early fifties he had used an attack on the intellectuals associated with *Commentary* to prove that he was still a radical and a socialist even though, exactly like them, he had been spending most of his time fighting other self-proclaimed radicals and socialists, and even though, exactly as with them, very little remained in his own political views that could be called socialist and still less that could be called radical. Now, twenty years later, he was still refusing to face up to the fact that he had long since ceased to be a radical and that he no longer believed in socialism either. The chances were thus good that he would once again use an attack on *Commentary* in the service of this refusal, and it was foolish of me to be disappointed when he finally did.

In the meantime, however, he was willing to join forces with us in the campaign against the Movement that began with the June 1970 issue and continued with great intensity for about three years. In the course of that time, the magazine ran articles critical of almost every important aspect of the radicalism of the sixties: its political ideas, its cultural attitudes, its institutional structures,

and its literary and intellectual heroes; and I myself participated
as a writer with a monthly column similar to the one I had done
ten years before.

In the issue that constituted the opening salvo alone, there was
a piece on several influential radical theorists of education called,
in the defiantly provocative style that would typify this phase of
Commentary's history, "Quackery in the Classroom." Another article dealt in equally harsh terms with "Literary Revolutionism,"
and there was also a devastating piece on Mary McCarthy's work
as a born-again radical. In the months that followed, there were
attacks on the Movement's ideas about the urban crisis and its
belief that the United States was on the brink of fascism. Its
leading organization within the black community, the Black Panthers, was taken on, as was its newest manifestation, Women's
Lib, and one of its oldest, "the radicalized professor." So too with
The New York Review, by now the most sophisticated exponent of
the Movement's perspective (the "chief theoretical organ of radical chic," Tom Wolfe had called it), as well as leading individual
apologists and apostles to the liberal community like Charles
Reich, Theodore Roszak, and Kenneth Keniston.

Nor did we spare such prominent liberal fellow travelers as
Ramsey Clark, such fellow-traveling institutions as the Op-Ed
page of *The New York Times,* and such radicalized liberal organizations as the American Civil Liberties Union. On questions rang-
ing from crime to the nature of art, from drugs to economic
growth, from ecology to the new egalitarianism, the dogmas of
the Movement—both in their unexpurgated state and in the sanitized versions that had by now become the conventional wisdom
of a fellow-traveling culture laying claim to the epithet "liberal"
—*Commentary* became perhaps the single most visible scourge of
the Movement within the intellectual community.

I could say that the reason for our effectiveness was a high
literary standard. But though necessary—if only to make the
point that opposition to the Movement was not confined to primi-
tives and provincials and obscurantists—this was not sufficient;

otherwise the highly literate *National Review,* which had fought the Movement all along from a position on the Right, or the intellectually irreproachable *Public Interest,* which had been critical of it from a "neoconservative" perspective, would have had a greater impact than they actually managed to achieve. What distinguished *Commentary* in this context was, of course, that it had itself been identified or associated with the Movement in the past and thus could and did speak with the authority of an insider. There was usually something off-center in the way *The National Review* talked about the New Left or the counterculture; it could get the doctrines right and could sometimes analyze them accurately, but it was so remote from the actualities of the Movement and so little in personal touch with the people involved that its criticisms were unable to draw blood. This was even true, though to a much lesser extent, of *The Public Interest,* which had in its opening statement of purpose proudly proclaimed itself middle-aged and was indeed a little too "square" to take a fully accurate measure of the political culture of the Movement.

Commentary suffered from no such disabilities. We knew the radical world of the sixties at first hand and in all its aspects. We knew the people and we knew the organizations; we knew what they really thought and felt, which did not always coincide with what they considered it expedient to say in public; and we knew how to penetrate their self-protective rhetoric. I myself, and many of the writers who now contributed regularly to the magazine— veterans like Nathan Glazer, Midge Decter, Dennis Wrong, Michael Novak, Jack Richardson, Walter Goodman, Joseph Epstein, and Bayard Rustin, as well as newer writers like Dorothy Rabinowitz, Samuel McCracken, Edward Grossman, Carl Gershman, Penn Kemble, Elliott Abrams, and Diane Ravitch—had also had some degree of experience with the Movement. Even Paul Goodman himself, appalled by the sight of a progeny so ignorant and intellectually incurious that they did not even recognize him as their spiritual father, was willing to cooperate in the last two years of his life by attacking the Movement's ideas about literature and the arts. (Of course his willingness also had a good deal to do with the principle he said he had always followed of never voluntarily breaking with anyone who controlled access to a printing press.)

In addition to the disenchanted, we also had the occasional or frequent help of writers who had never been identified with the Movement (except in most cases to the extent of opposing the war). Some—like Daniel P. Moynihan, Alexander M. Bickel, Irving Kristol, Hilton Kramer, Robert Alter, Seymour Martin Lipset, James Q. Wilson, Robert Nisbet, Leslie H. Farber, William Barrett, Joseph Adelson, Joseph W. Bishop, Jr., Paul Seabury, Charles Frankel, Jeane Kirkpatrick, Roger Starr, Daniel Bell, Paul Weaver, Suzanne Weaver, Edward Jay Epstein—wrote mainly on domestic or cultural issues; others—Walter Laqueur, Theodore Draper, Robert W. Tucker, and Edward Luttwak—mainly on international affairs.

What brought all these writers together into an identifiable group was not a positive political perspective. Ideologically, indeed, they were very diverse. Some thought of themselves as socialists, some as liberals, others as neoconservatives, and one or two simply as conservatives. In practice, moreover, they would have been unable to agree on a program of political action, or even on a presidential candidate. In 1972, for example, they were mostly divided between Muskie and Humphrey in the Democratic primary; in the general election, several—including Nathan Glazer and Daniel Bell—gave public support to McGovern, and several (including some who had never before voted for a Republican) to Nixon, but most of them supported neither.

What did unite them all, however, was the view that the single greatest threat to their own political values now came from the Movement and its ideas, and that nothing was now more important or more urgent than the job of exposing that threat and refuting those ideas. What Nathan Glazer, describing his own "deradicalization," said of himself in 1970 could have been said by all, whatever their past relation to the Movement might have been:

I for one . . . have by now come to feel that this radicalism is so beset with error and confusion that our main task, if we are ever to mount a successful assault on our problems, must be to argue with it and to strip it ultimately of the pretension that it understands the causes of our ills and how to set them right.

From this sense of things arose a new approach and a new tone in the discussion of these matters. Previously the tendency even among intellectuals critical of the Movement had been to give its supporters the benefit of almost every doubt. They were assumed to have the right values, to be well-intentioned, idealistic, "concerned," sincerely outraged by the sight of injustice, and so forth; if they had a fault, it was naïveté or inexperience or excessive zeal, and the best way to correct it was by a patient and respectful demonstration of how they could be more effective in satisfying their self-evidently "legitimate demands." Now, however, the tables were suddenly turned on the Movement and its ideas. For the first time in years, it was they who were put on the defensive. Their motives were subjected to a skeptical "demystifying" scrutiny and their ideas to a sustained critical analysis by writers who could not easily be discredited and would not be intimidated.

Here are a few samples:

Out of self-dramatization, self-indulgence, honest neurosis, idealism, and careful policy, the Movement's leaders have taken as their task the generating of passion, keeping the campuses and the streets in turmoil, exciting provocations and retaliation, recruiting bodies for new forays, and making middle-aged contributors feel young again. Such is the sum and substance of their policy. (Walter Goodman, "The Question of Repression")

The world of the Black Panther party might have been constructed by Kurt Vonnegut out of bits and pieces of Dostoevsky. It is a world of double and triple agents, radical rhetoric and reactionary consequences, mindless violence and breakfast-for-children programs, cop killers and killer cops, penny-ante stickups and Park Avenue fund-raising soirees, chiliastic impulse and unforgiving discipline. (Tom Milstein, "A Perspective on the Panthers")

If the ideology of relevance is potentially dangerous because it
provides a scheme for enforcing a new orthodoxy (which is, as
Sydney Smith defined it, "my doxy; heterodoxy is another man's")
there is yet another danger. Relevant subjects are often defined as
those subjects having immediate or prospective practical value,
but this neo-Babbitry is in some ways less troubling than another
definition—that relevant subjects are those subjects to which one
can relate. (Samuel McCracken, "Quackery in the Classroom")

The New York Review is guilty of having contributed to the present
prospect of a confrontation on all fronts between the Movement
at its arrogant mindless worst and the demagogic patrioteering
Right, a confrontation that will do little harm to the established
intellectuals and tenured academicians who produce *The NYR* but
which promises to hurt seriously the very groups whose interest
they claim to uphold. The first victim, however, has been the truth.
. . . (Dennis H. Wrong, "The Case of *The New York Review*")

Capitalism, imperialism, and colonialism had all undergone immense changes, but hatred of the free world (and I insist on using
that designation without quotation marks . . . , for despite the
combination of ignorance and intimidation which has forced its
abandonment in recent years, it still points to the largest *single*
distinction between the Communist and and the non-Communist
countries) was as fierce in 1970 as hatred of the unreformed capitalism of forty or eighty years ago. (Nathan Glazer, "On Being
Deradicalized")

This was strong stuff and its impact was immediate. Challenged
in this vigorous way, the Movement's supporters and sympathizers were unable to marshal any solid arguments; and with their
usually potent arsenal of abusive epithets suddenly rendered useless, they seemed incapable of finding anything else to say. It had
been so long since they had been faced with a serious and determined opposition that they—like their anti-Communist elders
when first confronted by them ten year earlier—had trouble
remembering the answers. Collectively they were like a fighter
gone soft after too many years of being matched against setups

BREAKING RANKS

for whom he had hardly bothered keeping in shape; now thrown without warning against a dangerous challenger, he could only cower and run.

Altogether, something curious seemed to have happened to the role of the Left—using this term in the broadest sense to embrace both radicals and their sympathizers within the liberal community —in American intellectual life. In the past, the assumption had been that reason and enlightenment were mainly to be found among liberals and radicals; everyone else lived in the shadows of obscurantism, superstition, and bigotry. The great symbolic event was the Scopes Trial of the 1920s in Tennessee, when Clarence Darrow defended the teaching of evolution in the schools and William Jennings Bryan argued against it. Portrayed by Spencer Tracy in a slightly fictionalized film version of the case, Darrow, as befitted the voice of reason and enlightenment, was collected and coherent, while Fredric March's Bryan, egged on by a howling mob of southern fundamentalists, was wild-eyed and nearly demented in his fanaticism. This sense of things was still sufficiently alive in the 1970s to warrant both a revival of the movie and a new documentary version of the story itself on television.

But as the ironies of history would have it, one could around the same time see another program on television that inadvertently showed how much things had changed. This was a debate, staged in the form of a mock trial, on the question of whether amnesty should be extended to the thousands of young men who had chosen exile over army service during the Vietnam war. Arguing on behalf of amnesty was Ramsey Clark, who had served as attorney general under Lyndon Johnson and who had then become radicalized—and in an unusual way. Some politicians were radicalized in the late sixties out of prudent deference to the old rule that the way to get ahead in politics is to find a crowd that is already going somewhere and put yourself at the head of it. They sided with the crowds demonstrating at the Pentagon, that is, not because they had decided to desert the "Establishment" and throw in their lot with "dissent," but on the contrary because they had become convinced that power was flowing out of the one and into the other, and they wanted to go where it now was or soon would be. Thus when George McGovern's poor showing in 1972 against Nixon even among the young convinced them that they had been mistaken, they quietly moved back again to wherever they thought the power was flowing now.

Clark was different. Like Tom Wicker of *The New York Times,* who in covering the riots during the Democratic convention in Chicago in 1968 had heard one of the demonstrators calling to him, "Join us, Mr. Wicker," and had suddenly realized that he belonged with them and not with the "Establishment," Clark seems to have experienced a genuine and lasting political conversion. He was like the husband in the old Jewish joke whose wife complains to the rabbi that he does nothing all day but sit and study the Talmud. "But that's wonderful," says the rabbi, "it's just what I do myself." "Yes," answers the wife, "but you do it for a living, whereas my husband, that fool, he really means it."

Clark, in any event, was pitted in the amnesty "trial" on television against a lawyer named Jason C. Hill whose accent was clearly redolent of the Deep South (and who came, in fact, from Atlanta). But this time it was the Leftist in the person of Clark who seemed the fanatical zealot (he really did mean it), while his opponent from the Deep South was all sweetness and light; and this time the howling mob was made up not of illiterate rednecks but of students from Harvard and Radcliffe who screamed their approval at every word their champion said and looked for all the world as though they were ready to lynch the lawyer on the other side.

Nor was it only on a strictly political issue like amnesty that this reversal of roles could be observed. Indeed, exactly the same reversal had taken place by the seventies on the issue of evolution itself. "It is a remarkable fact," wrote the biologist Edward O. Wilson in 1978, that in recent years the most effective opposition to the study of human evolution has come not from the religious fundamentalists and the political Right, but from biologists and other scientists who identify themselves with the radical Left. The focus of these critics was initially on the inheritance of intelligence, but more recently, and significantly, it has broadened to include virtually any kind of study that touches on the genetic evolution of human behavior.

What was even more marked than the weakness of the response to our offensive from within the precincts of the Movement itself was the amount of attention paid to it by the liberal press. An extraordinary number of articles on the new turn in *Commentary* appeared—extraordinary both because there were so many of them and because papers like *The Washington Post, The New York Times,* and *The Boston Globe* were not normally given to treating debates within the intellectual community as newsworthy or indeed as anything more than the eccentric antics of a strange and incomprehensible tribe to be looked upon with puzzled amusement. But with one or two exceptions the articles on *Commentary*'s violent break with the Movement were earnest in tone and made a serious effort to explain what the issues were and why they had arisen.

Obviously the editors who decided to get such pieces and the reporters assigned to write them had learned from the experience of the sixties that changes within the intellectual community were as likely as not to foreshadow changes in the country at large and eventually even in the balance of political forces. Indeed one of the points all these pieces made was that the rise of the New Left and the counterculture had been foreshadowed in *Commentary*'s turn toward radicalism exactly ten years before, and that the new turn away from radicalism might well be a portent of what the cultural and political atmosphere of the decade ahead would be like.

But why was *Commentary* doing this? What had happened to explain our defection? That experience, and continued reflection on it, could by themselves lead to a change of mind—that in other words, seeing how one's ideas worked out in practice might force one to abandon those ideas as mistaken and even as stealthily pernicious—did not seem a good enough explanation. There had to be something else.

Traditionally the radical Left had always accused defectors from its ranks of "selling out" for money or for some other kind of bribe; and in this, as in so many other ways, the Movement was a true carrier of the radical heritage. Thus in my case it was said that in turning against the Movement, the author of *Making It* was obviously acting on his own self-confessed hunger for success. But the problem with this explanation was that I had enjoyed much more worldly success as a radical than I was now enjoying as an opponent of radicalism. As a radical I had been sought after both professionally and socially; rarely had there been an important conference to which I had not been invited, and my evenings as often as not were spent entertaining or being entertained by the fashionable and/or famous. It was as a radical, not as a critic of radicalism, that I had been picked up by a White House limousine on the field of the Washington airport. Now there were no limousines and very few invitations. Indeed, I found myself shunned by most of my former friends.

The most dramatic instance was Jason Epstein. He was so outraged by the political course I was taking that he not only cut me off but said abusive things about me to Merle Miller, who duly quoted some of them in a piece in *The New York Times Magazine* entitled "Why Norman and Jason Don't Speak." Of course the fact that *Commentary* had run an article attacking *The New York Review,* and another (by Alexander M. Bickel) attacking a book Jason himself had written on the trial of seven Movement celebrities charged with having conspired to incite the riots in Chicago in 1968, added personal fuel to his radical fires. Yet given how brightly those fires had come to rage in Jason just when they were dying out in me, I think that he would have behaved in much the same way in the absence of any narrowly personal grievances.

But even those of my old friends and acquaintances on the Left who out of personal loyalty and affection stayed in touch gradually became distant because the strain on both sides, mine as well as theirs, was so great. In the case of Norman Mailer, it was I and not he who eventually found the strain intolerable. He insisted on seeing me and he demanded that I explain myself. Yet whenever I did he would grow willfully obtuse, and on the one occasion when he allowed himself to enter into my terms enough to understand what I was saying, he became so upset that he said he was unable to go on with the conversation. There was no pleasure for me, then, and less profit in being alone with him; and whenever I accepted an invitation to one of his parties, I would run into so many people who no longer wished to speak to someone they considered a turncoat, or to whom I could no longer speak without either having to hold my tongue or get into a useless quarrel, that I would spend the evening avoiding and being avoided—no easy thing to do in that surprisingly small apartment with its spectacular view of the harbor in Brooklyn Heights. And so I stayed away from Mailer, who accused me in consequence of being a "foul-weather friend," only to be depended upon when he was down on his luck. It was a loving accusation, but what he really thought was that I had never forgiven him for his article about *Making It*; and for that he forgave *me*.

Lillian Hellman (at whose home I had met Mailer for the first time so many years before) was another old friend who would have preferred to remain on warm terms if it had been possible for us to do so. Like Mailer, she took the initiative, calling me more often than I called her, even though she felt as uncomfortable as I did whenever we got together. We had once been easy and open with each other, but there was something literally clandestine about our relationship now. Not only did many things have to be hidden away and left unspoken if we were to avoid a nasty quarrel, but we ourselves were more and more able to meet only if each of us was alone—she without her old friends, so many of whom had once also been mine, and I without my new ones, so many of whom were equally hostile to her. Under these impossible circumstances we drifted further and further apart, to the point where neither of us any longer regarded the other as a friend.

Yet even if we had managed to remain friends during the heated years of the *Commentary* campaign against the Movement, I doubt that our friendship would have survived the appearance in 1976 of her little book *Scoundrel Time.* For there, in the course of telling the story of her appearance in 1952 before a congressional committee investigating Communist influence in American life, she offended me both by representing herself as a hero and a martyr, and by accusing the anti-Communist intellectuals who had been writing in those days for *Partisan Review* and *Commentary* of cowardice in failing to oppose McCarthyism.

In most quarters, *Scoundrel Time* was received with even greater enthusiasm than Lillian's other autobiographical books, *An Unfinished Woman* and *Pentimento,* which had in their turn been greeted with greater enthusiasm than almost anything she had written since such early plays of the thirties as *The Children's Hour* and *The Little Foxes.* F. Scott Fitzgerald, whom Lillian had known—as she had known everyone and still did—once famously said that there were no second acts in American lives, but he would have been forced to change his mind had he lived long enough to watch the development of her career. Lillian had a second act, as a memoirist, and in this new literary incarnation she was even more successful than she had been in her old one as a playwright.

Certainly in the thirties and forties, as the author of one Broadway hit after another and then as a Hollywood screenwriter, she had made a great deal of money. She had also become a celebrity. But the only critics who had ever praised her were those she referred to contemptuously as "Broadway intellectuals." In the serious literary world—the "quality lit. biz," as Terry Southern once called it—she had never been regarded as anything more than a competent "middlebrow" playwright. Now, however, with her sure commercial touch, she was producing hit books the way she had once produced hit plays, but the books were also establishing her as an important literary figure among the very highbrow critics who would once assuredly have snubbed the plays. Some of these critics might have snubbed the books as well if not for the fact that they knew and admired her personally. Indeed, she herself was so much more interesting and amusing and intelligent than anything she ever wrote, and so gifted a hostess, that being acquainted with her was bound to sharpen one's disappointment in reading her work while at the same time increasing one's readiness to find a reason to praise it.

But for Lillian's natural middlebrow audience—now swollen by the rising tide of feminists who saw her, somewhat to her own discomfort, as a kind of founding mother—no such qualifications or reservations applied. Once again, then, she found herself becoming the darling of the current crop of Broadway intellectuals (most of whom, now that the movies had taken over from the theater as the leading middlebrow art form, had moved to Hollywood). Her prose style—an imitation of Hammett's imitation of Hemingway, and already so corrupted by affectation and falsity in the original that only a miracle could have rendered it capable of anything genuine at this third remove—was to them the essence of honesty and distilled candor.

And if this were not enough, there was also the fact that she had been blacklisted in the McCarthy period for refusing to name names to the House Un-American Activities Committee. Naming names was what the "scoundrels" of *Scoundrel Time* had done; and when the people they named were punished, said Lillian, *"Commentary* didn't do anything" and *"Partisan Review,* although through the years it had published many, many pieces protesting the punishment of dissidents in Eastern Europe, made no protest when people in this country were jailed or ruined."

To the Broadway and Hollywood intellectuals of the seventies, the story Lillian told in *Scoundrel Time* was as true as the prose in which she told it, and her heroism and martyrdom were as real as the ostentatiously understated manner in which she subtly laid claim to them. Thus when she appeared on the stage at an Academy Awards celebration in the mid-seventies, she received a standing ovation before an audience of fifty million Americans watching on television; and it was altogether appropriate that in *Julia,* the film subsequently made of one of the stories in *Pentimento,* the role of Lillian Hellman in the thirties should have been played by the First Lady of the Hollywood radicalism of the sixties, Jane Fonda (now married to Tom Hayden, formerly of SDS but now "working within the system" and soon to run for the United States Senate in the Democratic primary in California), and that Lillian herself should have been virtually apotheosized by the film as a great writer, a great woman, and a great political heroine.

To me, however, *Scoundrel Time* was so outrageous in itself, and so pernicious in its potential effect on young and innocent readers, that it very nearly destroyed whatever regard I still had for Lillian. The outrage began with the title: so far as I was concerned, the true scoundrels of her story were not the ex-Communists who had repented of their support for Stalin and his monstrous crimes but the Communists and the fellow travelers who had persisted in defending Stalin and apologizing for those crimes. It was true that some of these people had suffered for this by going to jail or losing work, but that did not justify their ideas or make their political activities any less reprehensible. It was also true that combatting those ideas and activities through demagogic congressional investigations, and by sending people to jail or throwing them out of work, was disgraceful and disgusting, but to me it seemed nothing short of blasphemous to compare the fate of "dissidents in Eastern Europe" whose "punishment" consisted of execution, torture, or long years of imprisonment under conditions of hardship scarcely imaginable to Lillian Hellman with, say, the six months Dashiell Hammett spent in jail cleaning bathrooms, let alone the luxury in which she herself lived on the East Side of Manhattan or Martha's Vineyard even when she could no longer command million-dollar contracts for writing Hollywood films. If this was martyrdom, it was so mild a form that laying claim to it was ridiculous at best, just as was her claim to have shown "guts" in her testimony before HUAC when all she did was follow the legally safe course of pleading the Fifth Amendment.

Nor, finally, was there any truth in her charge that the anti-Communist intellectuals of *Partisan Review* and *Commentary* never "protested against McCarthy." Nathan Glazer, who had himself written a piece attacking McCarthyism for *Commentary* in the early fifties, gave the lie to this charge in "An Answer to Lillian Hellman" and he also pointed out that opposition to McCarthyism had been so taken for granted by both magazines "that the main intellectual contribution they could make was to examine and clarify the many questions surrounding the phenomenon"—including the question of why Communism represented a threat to liberty and democracy and how that threat could best be countered:

> . . . Our own preference was to expose Communism in the pages of *The New Leader* and *Commentary,* rather than before congressmen for whom we had no political or any other kind of sympathy. Indeed the fact that the committees made exposure of Communist connections and sympathizers so damaging often inhibited us in describing Communists and Communist sympathizers for what they were.

Despite her belated acknowledgment in *Scoundrel Time* of "the sins of Stalin Communism" and her equally tardy admission that she had closed her eyes to them for a long time, Lillian Hellman was still unwilling to recognize that Stalinism could exert no legitimate claim on the sympathies of anyone like herself who professed to believe in and value freedom and democracy.

21

But whether it was I who broke with them or they who broke with me, the fact remained that becoming an opponent of radicalism effectively cut me off from most of my old friends and acquaintances on the Left—which for all practical purposes meant being cut off from the most fashionable and in some ways most influential circles in New York. I do not emphasize this in order to follow Lillian Hellman's example by representing myself as a victim of political persecution. For far from feeling persecuted in those days, I experienced the special happiness that comes from breaking out of a false position and giving free rein to previously inhibited sentiments and ideas. Because everyone who knew anything about the situation recognized that my turn against radicalism was costing me more in the worldly sense than I seemed to be gaining, the theory that I was "selling out" never quite took; and because everyone who knew me or who was paying any attention to the tone of my monthly column in *Commentary* also recognized that I was nevertheless having such a good and happy time, a different theory began to circulate to the effect that I had literally lost my mind.

Outlandish though it may seem, this theory actually served as a way of excusing my political behavior in the eyes of certain old friends who were reluctant to write me off altogether or to join in vilifying my name. But the plea of insanity entered on my behalf was based on more than mere speculation. There was also evidence in the form of a rumor that my new political turn had come about as the result of some kind of religious experience—

and for certain people within the intellectual community that in itself was enough to establish a presumption of madness.

As it happens, there was an element of truth in these rumors. After my long contention with radicalism and all the questions it raised, I had indeed come to a new clarity in my thinking about first things and last. But there was no truth at all in the accompanying idea that this new clarity had turned me into a political zealot. On the contrary, it left me not with a religious certainty about my own political views, but precisely with a new appreciation of the dangers of confusing politics and religion. I also emerged with a new understanding of how central this confusion had always been to the radicalism of the sixties.

It was no secret to anyone who had studied these matters or who had read scholars like Norman Cohn that political radicalism in general drew on energies and appealed to aspirations that were more religious than political, and I for one knew that the radicalism of the sixties had come more directly and explicitly out of such energies and aspirations than out of its often advertised concern for reform and social change. What I now began to see much more fully was how this "pursuit of the millennium"—to borrow the title of a book by Cohn about several remarkably similar eruptions of such movements in medieval Europe—had worked to produce not the millennium but the nihilism into which the Movement had sunk by the end of the decade: a nihilism that expressed itself in the terrorism practiced by the Weather Underground, in the ideology of "revolutionary suicide" preached by the Black Panthers, and in the spread of drug addiction among the affluent young.

In thinking about the connection between the secularized messianism out of which the Movement came and the nihilism into which it was now degenerating, I found myself remembering a couplet by Dr. Johnson:

> How small of all that human hearts endure
> That part which laws or kings can cause or cure.

There was an illuminating negative clue here, for in exact anti-
thetical contrast to Dr. Johnson's skeptical eighteenth-century
view of the power of politics, the underlying belief of American
radicalism in the 1960s was that all the sufferings of the human
heart were caused and could therefore be cured by laws and
kings. This was a comforting belief not only because it held out
the messianic hope of a perfect world and a painless life, but also
because it absolved the individual of all responsibility for his own
predicament. No wonder, then, that it spread, and along with it,
the disposition to blame every conceivable trouble on society and
to demand remedial action by the state, whether or not the trouble actually was social in its causes and whether or not the state
actually possessed either the wisdom or the power to heal and to
cure. When the state responded and the trouble remained, or
when the state, not knowing what to do, did not respond at all,
the sense of oppression deepened, giving greater and greater
impetus to a suicidal drive toward the violent destruction of "the
system."

What then was the alternative? I was often asked this question
in the early days of the campaign against the Movement, and
almost always I resisted answering it with the help of the philosopher Morris Raphael Cohen's quip that nobody ever asked Her-
cules to refill the Augean stables. I took this tack because I believed that an essential element of any healthy alternative to the
soured messianism of the Movement was a skeptical attitude toward the power of any political program—including my own—to
"solve" most of the problems of the human condition. Having
become a radical ten years before out of the hope that the
spiritual ailments of the age could be reached through political
action, and having seen with my own eyes how acting upon this
hope had led again, as it so often had led in the past, either to
nihilism or to what the French writer Jean-François Revel would
later call "the totalitarian temptation," I thought the most important order of intellectual business was to expose the illusion on
which it was ultimately based. Hence my reluctance to cooperate

in keeping that illusion alive by feeding it yet another "program" promising to succeed where the Movement had failed.

This was a perspective that could easily have led to political quietism, to giving up on politics altogether, but it led me instead into the arms of the social democrats. As the name suggests, the social democrats were socialists, but, as the name also suggests, they were democrats too. In fact most of them were even Democrats—members, that is, of the Democratic party—who, long before their rivals and enemies of the New Left decided to do so, had been working "within the system." In their case, however, working within the system represented an act of commitment to keeping it alive, not a tactic in a continuing effort to destroy it. So committed were they to the American system, indeed, that many of them, especially those affiliated with the organized labor movement, the AFL-CIO, even supported the Kennedy-Johnson policy in Vietnam. In domestic affairs they also supported the entire range of liberal legislation—the great civil-rights acts and the programs making up the war on poverty—sponsored by the Johnson administration, which they looked upon as a vindication of their faith in the ability of the American political system to achieve a degree of social justice that some of them had once thought possible only in a socialist country.

What I admired about the social democrats in general, and the labor movement in particular, was precisely this willingness to respect the limits of political action and to do what could be done. Samuel Gompers, the founder of the American labor movement, had said that what the American worker wanted was "more," and yet by pursuing that homely objective it had succeeded not only in improving the lives of millions of ordinary people beyond even the utopian imaginings of more radical socialists who denounced them as traitors to the true interests of the working class; it had also brought benefits to everyone else in the form of a more stable society and a generally more prosperous one. Surely it was no accident that the frank pursuit of its own material interest by the labor movement had resulted in so much good, while the supposedly selfless "idealism" of so many radical activists, both in the United States and elsewhere, had issued in so much evil, both to themselves and to everyone else.

To me it seemed that there was a lesson here in the nature of healthy political activity—and it was a lesson I pressed upon myself as a guide to my own political activity. In order to act responsibly within the political realm, I was obligated to shed the pretense, so dear to all intellectuals, that I had no interests of my own, that I spoke as a disembodied mind on behalf of the common good. This pretense was in itself a "mystification," in the sense that it concealed a claim to superior political wisdom and therefore a presumptive right to political leadership. Yet if the experience of the sixties proved anything, it proved that intellectuals as a class possessed no such wisdom. They did not know what was best for others, and to judge by the way so many of them had acted in the face of an onslaught on their own home territory, the universities, they did not even know what was best for themselves. While I was not prepared to go as far as William F. Buckley, who said that he would rather be ruled by the first two thousand names in the Boston telephone book than by the combined faculties of Harvard and MIT, I was ready to agree with the Catholic theologian James Hitchcock, who argued in a piece for *Commentary* that in the decade just past it had more often been "the general populace which preserved its sanity in the face of the peculiar hysteria of the highly educated" than the other way around.

This had been shown over and over again in the contrast between the attitudes of the general populace and those of the intellectuals on all the major issues of the period. Thus, for example, on the issue of race, the great majority of Americans, so often denounced as bigots and racists, nevertheless opposed both discrimination against blacks and the kind of "affirmative action" which involved reverse discrimination against whites and which most intellectuals tended to support. On the issue of poverty, similarly, most people in America, so often denounced as selfish and mean-spirited, nevertheless supported federal spending to increase the economic opportunities of the poor while simultaneously opposing the kind of radical redistribution of income favored by so many intellectuals.

Even on the issue of Vietnam, the general populace had a far better record than the intellectuals. The psychologist Robert Jay Lifton, a prominent fellow traveler of the Movement, said in 1972 that the American people as a whole not only shared in "a moral or criminal culpability" for the war but lacked the "moral sensitivity" and the courage to acknowledge their guilt. Yet even if one agreed with Lifton's view that the war was an American crime rather than an American blunder, it made no sense to point to the American people as the guilty party. None of the major decisions concerning the war—neither Kennedy's decision to enter it, nor Johnson's decision to escalate it, nor Nixon's decision to withdraw from it gradually rather than all at once—owed much to popular pressure. The people went along, but they were never enthusiastic; the war had after all been conceived and executed by "the best and the brightest," who later —and with exactly the same dogmatic assurance—opposed and denounced what they alone had wrought. And just as the people had been skeptical about the judgment of "the best and the brightest" regarding the strategic necessity of American military intervention to begin with, so they were now skeptical over the revised judgment of "the best and the brightest" as to the moral necessity of a humiliating American defeat. By 1968 most people in America had, according to all the polls, come to believe that the American intervention in Vietnam had been a mistake, but they also refused to accept the view of so many of their "betters" (some of whom, as Pat Moynihan quipped, were now pleading innocence on the ground that they had only been *giving* orders, and others of whom were claiming vindication of their original and ongoing support of the Communist side) that it was a crime.

It seemed to me that what had led the intellectuals astray on all these issues was a mistaken conception of their own political responsibilities. In my early days as a radical, I had written an admiring essay on Edmund Wilson which, however, had ended by criticizing him for advising his fellow writers and intellectuals to give up (in his words) "trying to improve the world or make a public impression," to forget about "transforming human society"—or "realizing the Kingdom of God on earth"—and to concentrate instead on the ideal of "touching the superlative" in their own work. "I have to say in reaction to all this," I wrote, "that I find myself a little resentful at being told . . . that there is no longer any point in trying to change the world and that we might as well settle down to the business of pursuing a private salvation. . . ."

Now, ten years later, it had become as clear to me as it had once been to Wilson that by acting politically as "citizens of a human society gone wrong" instead of as citizens of the Republic of Letters, intellectuals were as likely to make things worse for the world as to make them better. Having, moreover, seen the interests of the Republic of Letters denigrated and sacrificed over and over again in the sixties to the presumed requirements of establishing the Kingdom of God on earth—just as Wilson had seen happen in the thirties—I was much more inclined to accept his prescription of a "high-minded egoism" as the intellectual's best protection against the temptations and corruptions of the radical spirit.

I have already described how, under the influence of that spirit, a community which had once been committed to a belief in the values of high culture, in the importance of art, and in the importance of mind, had been unable or unwilling to defend this belief and protect those values from attack as "irrelevant" or as "elitist" or as "counterrevolutionary." Yet even when the fevers of radicalism subsided in the mid-seventies, the intellectual community was still unable or unwilling to defend itself against the radical assault on culture which—in exact parallel to what happened in the case of the more strictly political ideas of the Movement as they were cleaned up by the New Politics in order to work within the system—had now been sanitized and taken over by the federal government itself. Thus, for example, when the government demanded that they abandon their own criteria of excellence in hiring and admissions in order to satisfy the requirements of an egalitarian idea which had itself derived from the radicalism of the sixties, very few universities resisted. They did not say, as a "high-minded egoism" would have led them to say, that their primary responsibility was to maintain the standards without which there could never be any hope of "touching the superlative." Nor did they try to show the rest of the country that they could make a far greater contribution to the general welfare by pursuing their special interests than by abandoning them—especially when these interests were being abandoned for the sake of ideas about equality and social justice that were themselves dubious in principle and dangerous in practice. Indeed far from using their special talents for analysis and argument to dispel a major public confusion, and thereby helping not only themselves but everyone else, many members of the academic community spent their time elaborating ingenious justifications for these dangerous practices and dubious ideas.

Yet even in the absence of such external support from Washington, the radical spirit of the sixties still would have retained enough influence in the seventies to subvert the values of the academic community. I have described how during the heyday of the Movement the booing and heckling of speakers whose views differed from the accepted radical line of the moment had become a common practice. It had only been a minority who actually behaved in this way, but to the astonishment of many of us outside the universities who had always regarded them as sanctuaries of free inquiry and unfettered speculation, there was a considerable degree of tacit acquiescence among the liberal majority in what was perhaps the most fundamental challenge that could have been mounted to its way of life. Yet even now, when the New Left had disappeared as an organized force, the principle of free discussion was still being sacrificed to the demands of the radical spirit. "In the last two or three years," James Q. Wilson reported in 1972 of Harvard, the university at which he taught (and the same might have been said of many other universities as well), "the list of subjects that cannot be publicly discussed there in a free and open forum has grown steadily, and now includes the war in Vietnam, public policy toward urban ghettos, the relationship between intelligence and heredity, and the role of American corporations in certain overseas regimes." (Within another year, several new items were added to the list—Richard Nixon, ecology, the condition of women, and the moral and medical character of homosexuality.) That is, people who held the "wrong" views on these subjects were, as Wilson put it, "harassed and in some cases forcibly denied an opportunity to speak"—and, he added, also denied an opportunity to help the rest of us think more clearly and make up our minds.

In devoting itself, then, to the aim of "transforming human society," the intellectual community had not only failed to make things better for everyone else; it had also betrayed its responsibilities to culture and to the life of the mind. In anticipating this, Edmund Wilson had been right, and I had been wrong. But we had both been wrong in thinking that the course of "high-minded egoism" (or "jobbism," as he also called it) necessarily involved a withdrawal from politics altogether. Indeed, merely in order to keep going, a healthy intellectual community—one taking a self-respecting stand on behalf of its own interests—would be forced into political activity. On the one hand, it would have to make the case for the financial support it needed to exist, and on the other hand it would have to fight against the government's use of this support to interfere with cultural and academic freedom. But that would be political activity guided by what intellectuals really were capable of knowing better than anyone else—not what was good for others but what was good for themselves. And it would be political activity directed toward an objective that intellectuals really did have the power to reach—not the transformation of human society but a deepening of the society's sense of things, the refinement of its consciousness, the enhancement of its cultural life.

This, then, was the lesson in the nature of healthy political activity that I pressed upon myself as a member of the intellectual community, and that I tried to press upon the community as a whole. Underlying it was the conviction that intellectuals as intellectuals had a far greater stake in the maintenance of a liberal democratic order than they had ever realized, and that they themselves were mortally threatened by the radical effort to undermine and ultimately destroy that order as it existed in the United States.

But if this was true of the intellectual community, it applied with perhaps even greater force to the other community of which I was a member, the Jewish community. As I now felt obligated to declare my interest as an intellectual, I also felt obligated to declare my interest as a Jew; and as I tried to persuade my fellow intellectuals that radicalism was their enemy and not their friend, I tried to make the same point in addressing my fellow Jews.

If the anti-intellectualism of the Movement—reflected politically in its hostility to freedom of speech and inquiry, and culturally in the vogue of irrationalist doctrines and practices within the counterculture—gave plausibility in arguing with the intellectuals to the idea that radicalism was an enemy rather than a friend, so too did the hostility to Jews and Jewish interests within the Movement. By 1970 almost everyone knew that the radical Left was antagonistic to Israel; and even though opposition to the state of Israel was in theory not necessarily a form of anti-Semitism, the "anti-Zionism" of the radical Left was becoming increasingly difficult to distinguish from anti-Semitism in the more familiar sense. Ever since Israel's victory in the Six-Day War of 1967, propaganda emanating from both the Arab world and the Soviet Union had literally portrayed the Israelis as the new Nazis, and far from repudiating this breathtaking inversion, certain elements on the radical Left in America (and in Europe as well) had cooperated in propagating it.

But the portrayal of Israel as the latter-day incarnation of the spirit of Nazism enjoyed less success than another theme of the anti-Zionism of the radical Left, which was to represent the Jews of Israel as white imperialists living on stolen land and oppressing the dark-skinned natives to whom it properly belonged. All this was so reminiscent of the charges of exclusivism and of exploitation of the native populace which anti-Semites had traditionally made against the Jewish communities living in countries dominated by other religions and ethnic groups that it could be seen as a translation of the old anti-Semitism into terms suitable to the new problem of dealing with the phenomenon of a Jewish state living among states dominated by other political and cultural values. Yet the spread of this new internationalized version of anti-Semitism, with a Jewish state as its main target, by no means entailed the disappearance of the old "domestic" expression of the same ideas. On the contrary: it stimulated and legitimized their revival. Thus around the same time that Israel was being portrayed as a nation of imperialist white settlers oppressing a dark-skinned native populace, American radicals, both black and white, began pointing more and more openly to American Jews as the principal oppressors of American blacks: Jewish landlords and Jewish storekeepers were, they said, exploiting them economically while Jewish social workers and Jewish schoolteachers were oppressing them culturally.

So openly, indeed, had these charges come to be made, and so vicious were the terms in which they had come to be expressed that by the late sixties a certain number of Jewish radicals found themselves forced to leave the Movement altogether. Others, however, remained. Some of these Jewish radicals—or rather radicals of Jewish origin—like most of their forebears beginning with Karl Marx himself, looked upon Jewishness as a form of reactionary bourgeois nationalism and had no trouble swallowing or even peddling the anti-Semitic canards which had once again become, if not exactly respectable, then at least thinkable and sayable. But there were some radical loyalists of Jewish origin who denied that there was any anti-Semitism in the new radicalism and even had the *chutzpah*—in this at least remaining authentically Jewish—to argue that the Jewish religion itself commanded support of the Movement and its ideas.

The leading exponent of this new gospel (the Christian word seems appropriate here) was my old acquaintance Arthur Waskow of the Institute for Policy Studies in Washington. Looking now more like a cross between a hippie and a Hasidic *rebbe* than like the marine drill sergeant in civilian dress he had resembled as a congressional assistant in the early sixties when I had first met him, Waskow began preaching the new gospel in a series of articles and books (including a version of the Passover Haggadah in which the words of such heroes of the Movement as Allen Ginsberg, Bob Dylan, A. J. Muste, and Eldridge Cleaver supplemented or replaced biblical and rabbinical passages of the original text), and through an equally prolific series of organizations calling themselves Jewish but in reality committed to the religion of Abraham, Isaac, and Jacob only to the extent that it could be thought to confirm the religion of the "Prophet Abraham Johannes Muste."

It was amazing to me—and would have been altogether incredible if I had not grown so accustomed to similar developments everywhere else—that Waskow had managed to get the financial backing of various Jewish organizations and the support of a good many religious leaders for his work, and especially for a theologically grotesque and ignorant document like the "Freedom Seder." But beyond the egregious taste and the low level of Jewish knowledge this travesty of the Haggadah revealed, there was also its political message, which could be summarized in the doctrine that Jewish interests, whether in America or in Israel, were illegitimate and must be sacrificed "on behalf of Mankind." If the Freedom Seder had been written some years later, the word "Personkind" would undoubtedly have been used instead of

"Mankind," but the grand abstraction would still have turned out on closer inspection to mean not the entire world but only the Third World and, more specifically yet, the Arabs in the Middle East and the blacks in the United States. A poem included in the Waskow Haggadah thus spoke of "our brothers our cousins/our black our brown family" and ended with the prayer that we be "next year in the THIRD WORLD."

It was perhaps understandable, if ominous, that blacks and other non-Jews should have felt that Jewish interests were illegitimate. It was also to be expected that radical Jews who were as frank as their forebear Rosa Luxemburg had been in 1917 in disavowing any concern for "special Jewish sorrows" as compared with those of the "wretched Indian victims in Putamayo [and] the Negroes in Africa" should feel the same way. Nor, in the light of several historical precedents, was it really surprising to find such sentiments among radical Jews pretending to a concern for Jews and Jewishness and Judaism. But it was extraordinary that leaders of the organized Jewish community—rabbis, teachers, officials of the defense organizations—should lend their support to a movement which believed that Jews represented the major obstacle to the achievement of justice in the Middle East and were one of the major obstacles to the achievement of justice in the United States.

To make matters worse, this view—as with so many other ideas and attitudes of the Movement—had by the early seventies found its way in various sanitized versions into the mainstream of respectable American opinion in general. Thus one could now hear grumblings in presumably liberal circles and indeed throughout polite political society that Jews were "overrepresented" in the universities, in the professions, in business, and even in the literary world: they only constituted three percent of the population and yet as a group they occupied far higher percentages of the best positions in these areas and far more than their "fair" share of wealth and income.

These grumblings were sometimes accompanied by the suggestion (offered, for example, by Truman Capote and Gore Vidal in speaking of the Jewish role in American letters and by others in speaking of the merit system as a Jewish invention) that Jewish success had been achieved and was being maintained by a conspiracy of mutual help and promotion. No matter that Jewish writers and critics were more often at one another's throats than in one another's pockets; no matter that Jews had played no part in establishing the system of apportioning jobs in the teaching profession and other branches of the civil service by competitive examination (it had been instituted by reformers seeking to undermine the "spoils system" of political patronage which had existed before); no matter that Jews could take no credit for the extension of the merit system to the colleges and universities (it had been done mainly in order to enhance the capacity of the United States in competing against Soviet science and technology). Such facts as these had never stood in the way of the conspiracy theory of Jewish success in the past, and they were not permitted to stand in the way now.

Yet even many people who resisted the conspiracy theory now seemed to feel that the Jews had perhaps grown too rich and too powerful and that their wealth and their power, if not acquired at the expense of blacks, was somehow holding back black advancement. For such people the new system of racial quotas seemed not only a quick but (by comparison with vast training programs, which were in any case of dubious effectiveness) a relatively inexpensive way to do something about both sides of a troublesome social imbalance.

I did not believe that the main purpose of this new system of racial quotas that began gaining so much favor within the liberal establishment toward the end of the sixties was to cut the Jewish position in America down to size. Obviously the main purpose, and in the minds of some, the only purpose, was to help blacks. What I did believe, however, was that, whatever its purpose, a system based on proportional representation according to race or ethnic origin would inevitably lead to the forcing out of Jews from areas in which they were now "overrepresented" and to discrimination against them in the future to make sure that the same "overrepresentation" did not occur again.

The acquiescence of many Jews in this assault on their own interests came out of the same conception of political responsibility that had also afflicted the intellectual community—the conception according to which one was supposed to act not as a member of a particular community but as "the citizen of a human society gone wrong" and not on behalf of the interests of that community but "on behalf of Mankind" as a whole. Since the conception was the same, its consequences were similar as well: the further spread of false ideas about social justice to the detriment of all, and the institutionalization of dangerous practices to the detriment of the particular community in question.

And the converse applied here too. If the Jewish community were to act, as I was, controversially, urging it to do, on the basis of the old question "Is it good for the Jews?" it would soon find itself defending the traditional liberal idea according to which justice is best served when individuals are treated as individuals and not as members of a group. There were those who thought that because Jews had flourished under this system, they were disqualified from testifying in its behalf. I took the opposite view —that it was precisely the urgency of their own stake in the system that obligated Jews to defend it as a better way of achieving social justice than the system now being set up in its place.

But if it was difficult to persuade many Jews that the radical position on domestic issues was a serious threat to their interests, and more difficult still to convince them that this imposed a moral obligation on them—an obligation both to themselves and to the nation—to oppose it, there was no such difficulty where Israel was concerned. Before 1947, there had been various pockets of opposition within the American Jewish community to the Zionist movement, but once the state of Israel was founded, most Jews made their peace with the idea of a sovereign Jewish state in the Middle East. After the Six-Day War of 1967, however, it became clear that the vast majority of American Jews had moved in twenty years far beyond even the previous enthusiastic support of Israel among those who had always regarded themselves as Zionists. Israel, said Nathan Glazer, was now the religion of the American Jews, and as usual he was right. Whatever else the Jews of America may or may not have cared about, they all (or anyway very nearly all) cared about Israel; and whatever they may or may not have done about being Jewish, they all gave their support to Israel. Those who had money to give gave it; those who had arguments to make made them; those who had votes to cast cast them.

Under these conditions, the anti-Zionist position which had come to prevail within the Movement by 1967 was bound to alienate Jewish sympathy, and it did. When the National Conference on New Politics met that year in Chicago and adopted a series of resolutions condemning Zionist aggression and expressing solidarity with the Arabs at a time when all Arab states were sworn to the destruction of Israel, the effect on a few Jewish radicals like Martin Peretz (the future editor of *The New Republic*) and on a much larger number of Jewish sympathizers was traumatic. As for the Jewish community in general, it became more receptive to the argument that the Movement and its apologists were, at a minimum, no friends of Israel and therefore had no claim on the support of American Jews.

In making this argument, then, I was to encounter less resistance than when making the case against Jewish support for the new egalitarianism. Nor was the Jewish community as reluctant to take a public stand on behalf of Israel as it was to defend its own social and economic position in American life. With a degree of forthrightness that surprised some and offended others, American Jews did everything they could to ensure American support for Israel. They lobbied, they demonstrated, they made political contributions, and, of course, they voted and kept on voting.

22

There was, to be sure, one thing that many of even the most passionately committed American Zionists were reluctant to do, and that was to face up to the fact that continued American support for Israel depended upon continued American involvement in international affairs—from which it followed that an American withdrawal into the kind of isolationist mood that had prevailed most recently between the two world wars, and that now looked as though it might soon prevail again, represented a direct threat to the security of Israel.

The main cause of this isolationist resurgence was of course Vietnam, which ended by doing more to give American interventionism—meaning for all practical purposes anti-Communist interventionism—a bad name than its worst enemies could ever have hoped. Vietnam brought discredit on the old idea that American intervention in world affairs must always be successful or at least effective; and it also brought discredit on the idea that American intervention must always be morally benevolent. These new feelings came in various shades, but they all flowed together into a swelling current of disgust with what anti-Communist interventionism had led the country to do abroad and with all the trouble it had caused at home. It was a disgust that was most visible among liberals of the New Politics variety who tended to see Vietnam not as proof of American folly (though they were not averse to using that argument whenever it suited their political or polemical convenience) but of American immorality—an immorality sometimes ascribed to the very nature of the country and sometimes to the anti-Communist policies it had permitted itself to follow. Yet even many self-styled conservatives who wanted the United States to continue in its efforts to check the spread of Soviet power and Communist influence now began wondering aloud whether the country still had the stamina and the will to do so, knowing that it might lead again, as it had led before, into war and the threat of war.

As had been the case with me on the issue of Vietnam from the beginning, I found myself toward the end in an unusual position. I have described how in the early sixties I had become part of a small group (led intellectually by Hans J. Morgenthau) who opposed American intervention not because we thought there was anything wrong with trying to prevent a Communist takeover in Vietnam but because we thought that there was very little chance of succeeding in this particular case. To oppose American policy on these grounds in the early days was of course to be against the liberal Establishment—that is, the Kennedy administration together with most of the great centers of liberal opinion outside the government itself, including *The New York Times, The Washington Post,* and the Council on Foreign Relations. But the position we held also differed from the one that prevailed in the peace movement, where opposition to American intervention was for the most part based on the hope that the Communists would win.

Later, and again because I thought that neither taking over command from the South Vietnamese, nor sending in more and more American troops, nor sending B-52s to bomb the North would ultimately do any good, I opposed the Johnson administration and those members of the liberal Establishment still on board when they decided to escalate the American role in the war. At the same time I found myself unable to stomach the main arguments against these policies being made by my fellow opponents, who now included not only pro-Communist elements but, increasingly, former supporters of the intervention within the liberal Establishment and large numbers of college students who were neither pro-Communist nor anti-Communist but could see no good reason for the United States to be fighting a war in Vietnam.

As the American role escalated, then, and as the opposition to it escalated in response, I remained in a somewhat isolated position. If anything, indeed, my position in the mid-sixties was more isolated than it had been a few years earlier, since even Hans Morgenthau had now joined in the moralistic clamor. And the moralistic clamor itself had almost inevitably led to the idea that the entire policy of trying to check the spread of Communism was and always had been morally wrong as well. This was not an idea I could accept. I could not accept it in relation to the past, when that policy had saved Western Europe from the barbarism and misery which had become the lot of every country in the world with the misfortune to fall under Communist rule. And I could not accept it in relation to the future, when I believed that in the absence of active American resistance, this tide of barbarism and misery would almost certainly sweep over the entire world, and might even ultimately engulf the United States itself.

By the early seventies there were few opponents of the war, whether early or late, who shared this perspective. In fact, almost the only allies I could find were diehard supporters of the Kennedy-Johnson policies who still thought it had been right to go into Vietnam and who believed that the South could still be saved from Communism even after the withdrawal of American forces (begun by Richard Nixon when he became president in 1969 and scheduled to be completed by 1973).

I was in truth uneasy about entering into a political alliance with people who had backed so disastrous a policy, but no more uneasy than I had been ten years earlier about associating politically with people who supported the Vietcong. Then the most important consideration had been to take a stand against the dangers of an indiscriminate act of American intervention in the fight against Communism; but now that the war was winding down, the most important consideration was to take a stand against the dangers of an equally indiscriminate American withdrawal from the fight against Communism in the future. I had swallowed my uneasiness then in joining the peace movement, and I now did the same thing on the other side when I joined with a group which included a number of unrepentant hawks in founding a new organization called the Coalition for a Democratic Majority, or CDM.

Stated in practical terms, the purpose of CDM was to challenge the influence of the New Politics movement within the Democratic party. Robert Kennedy having been assassinated and Eugene McCarthy having faded away—mainly, I have always suspected, because he had come to despise his followers as an upper-middle-class rabble—the New Politics had become a movement in search of a leader. The last of the Kennedy brothers, Edward, would in all probability have picked up the banner and run with it in 1972, but when, after a party on Martha's Vineyard, he drove his car off the bridge at Chappaquiddick, killing the girl who was with him and then telling a story of very doubtful credibility about the entire episode, his chances of undertaking a race for the presidency were (for the time being anyway) destroyed. With the field thus open, George McGovern had stepped in and succeeded first in staking his claim as the legitimate leader of the New Politics constituency and then, to everyone's amazement, in beating out all the other candidates—the front-runner Edmund Muskie, who had the support of most of the party leaders, as well as Hubert Humphrey and Henry Jackson—for the nomination.

In the four years since I had first committed myself to Eugene McCarthy, I had grown so hostile to the New Politics that I offered my help to Muskie. I felt no great enthusiasm for him, but Humphrey and Jackson were more visibly compromised by their record on Vietnam, and in any case neither seemed likely to win. Muskie, then, was the man to stop McGovern—and unlike a great many other people, who gave McGovern no chance when the primary season began, I thought his chances of getting the nomination were very good indeed. For one thing, as chairman of a commission established after 1968 to "open up" the Democratic party, he had pushed through new rules designed precisely to give certain advantages to an insurgent candidacy like his own over a candidacy based, as Muskie's was, on the "old" politics of relying on the regular party organization.

But what was from my point of view even more important, the New Politics carried with it a charge of energy, of enthusiasm, and of ideological conviction that stood in the sharpest possible contrast to the demoralized tone of the Muskie campaign. It seemed to me that Muskie himself and many of the people around him had in their turn begun suffering from the same failure of nerve which had first afflicted so many intellectuals in the mid- and late sixties as they watched the new radicalism grow from a marginal force into a huge and powerful Movement. Thus instead of defending the old liberal heritage of the Democratic party which he was presumably claiming to represent as against the new liberalism represented by McGovern, Muskie more often seemed to compete with McGovern in denouncing it.

One might perhaps have expected this in the field of foreign affairs, where Muskie's own record and that of the party faction of which he was the candidate suffered from the taint of Vietnam —though one might also have expected a confident and self-respecting leader of the regular Democratic party to find a better way of overcoming the disability of Vietnam than by playing into the isolationist mood of the insurgents. But what was altogether unexpected, and clearly indicative of a failure of nerve, was the adoption by Muskie of a position on the domestic record of the Democrats, from Roosevelt to Lyndon Johnson, that was even closer to the party line of the Movement than the position of the New Politics itself. Thus in an amazing speech to the Liberal party in New York, Muskie declared: "We meet tonight in a time of failure of American liberalism. . . . The blunt truth is that liberals have achieved virtually no fundamental change in our society since the end of the New Deal." So much for the civil-right acts of the mid-sixties and so much for the war on poverty. Both of these great achievements of the old liberalism had been denounced by the Movement as a fraud and then by the New Politics as grossly inadequate, and here was the heir of the liberal tradition out of which they had come echoing the unexpurgated as well as the sanitized versions of the attack.

It was the same with the issue of growth. As nothing had been more central to the old liberalism of the Democrats—the liberalism of Kennedy and Johnson—than a belief in growth as the key to general prosperity and as the only way to lift the poor out of poverty without dispossessing the prosperous, so nothing had been more important to the new radicalism than its hostility to growth as the means by which a hated system was kept alive. Within the Movement this hostility had been directed not primarily at the idea of growth as such but against the technological advances through which it was achieved, and sometimes even against industrialism itself. But an attitude so close to Luddism being much too extreme to "work within the system," a translation into more respectable terms was needed; and it soon appeared in the form of a new concern over the "environment." Under the influence of this concern, technology could now be portrayed as a kind of carcinogenic agent and the growth it produced as the cancer of the body politic. In the late sixties Susan Sontag had once made the connection altogether explicit:

> The white race *is* the cancer of human history; it is the white race and it alone—its ideologies and inventions—which eradicates autonomous civilizations wherever it spreads, which has upset the ecological balance of the planet, which now threatens the very existence of life itself.

Some years later, after falling victim to cancer herself, Susan Sontag would repent of the metaphoric use of cancer in this passage. But by that time a sanitized version of the same idea had gained widespread currency through the theory (which, by the way, she did not repudiate) that the literal, not the metaphorical, cause of cancer was those very technological and industrial "inventions" of our civilization which were allegedly—and again literally, not metaphorically—upsetting "the ecological balance of the planet."

But in addition to upsetting the ecological balance of the planet by polluting the air and the water and the food supply, growth was also charged with exhausting the planet's resources. Prophets disguised as scientists and waving computer projections instead of scriptural texts now began warning that unless a halt were called to growth, the world would soon—again literally, not metaphorically—come to an end. This was the message of a report, sponsored by a business group known as the Club of Rome, and entitled *The Limits to Growth,* whose influence was so great that even after its pretensions as a scientific analysis had been destroyed by a host of critics, the case it made against growth was still widely believed to be based on reliable data and irrefutable mathematical projections.

In truth, however, this theory no more deserved to be called scientific than Marx's theory of history, which had also claimed to be scientific and for which, indeed, the anti-growth doctrine served as a replacement in the continuing campaign to prove that Western civilization was doomed by its own internal contradictions. In the Marxist scheme, the survival of bourgeois civilization depended upon continued growth, but this could only be achieved by impoverishing the working class which would at some point arise to destroy it; history (whose inexorable laws had now been scientifically discovered by Marx) thus decreed that bourgeois civilization was unviable. Now according to the new scheme, it was the laws not of History but of Nature which decreed that bourgeois civilization was doomed—that it could not go on existing without either poisoning itself or running out of the raw materials it needed to feed its insatiable machines.

Armed with such ideas, the New Politics movement took a position that amounted to so complete a reversal of the theme of John F. Kennedy's New Frontier that it might have campaigned under the slogan "Let's Stop the Country from Moving Again." Yet here too, Muskie failed to uphold the old liberal tradition against the New Politics assault. He did not challenge the scientific pretensions of the New Politics' hostility to growth; he did not identify that hostility as the product of a political ideology; and he did not seize on the opportunity to demystify the "liberalism" of the New Politics by showing how a no-growth policy must lead to continued poverty for the poor and (as one of its own advocates, Robert L. Heilbroner, had the honesty to acknowledge) the virtual abolition of political liberty for all. Instead Muskie tried to show that he was just as convinced of these ideas as anyone, just as worried about overcrowding and pollution, just as determined to do something about the problem of growth.

Working in the Muskie campaign, I was perhaps more aware than I might have been from the outside of how badly the candidate himself and his advisers were suffering from a failure of nerve in the face of the New Politics, and I was therefore less surprised than many other people when the tide began turning toward McGovern. But the fact that the New Politics had now become strong enough to take over the Democratic party did not mean that it was strong enough to take over the country. There were those who thought that McGovern could beat Nixon by forging a "new coalition" of "the young, the poor, and the black," but I was not among them. Neither were Jackson supporters like Ben Wattenberg, who had worked in the Johnson White House and was now making a name for himself as an analyst of public opinion, or Humphrey people like the Washington attorney Max Kampelman and the political scientist Jeane Kirkpatrick. We did not believe that the New Politics commanded overwhelming support even among those groups in whose name it presumed to speak, and we also believed that, in thus presuming, it was alienating many normally Democratic voters. Being, as Wattenberg put it, "unyoung, unpoor, and unblack," these voters would either sit the election out in protest against the barely concealed hostility of the McGovernites to them and their base "middle-class" concerns, or they would vote the Republican ticket—many of them for the first time in their lives and even though it meant voting for someone they disliked and distrusted. McGovern in our opinion was to the Democrats what Barry Goldwater had been to the Republicans in 1964. He was the candidate of an ideologically fervent constituency drawn from the extreme end of the party's spectrum (Right in the case of the Republicans, Left in the case of the Democrats), with little appeal to the moderate majority within each party itself and still less to the electorate as a whole. As the Goldwater of the Left, McGovern, we believed, was bound to be defeated in a landslide, just as Goldwater had been—and it was with this expectation that we decided to found the organization which became CDM.

In giving it that name, we really did believe that our political position reflected the ideas of the majority of Democratic voters and—since registered Democrats far outnumbered Republicans —the majority of the American people. We stood, we said, for the liberal tradition as embodied in the Democratic party of Roosevelt, Truman, Kennedy, and Johnson. As against the isolationism of the New Politics, we believed that the United States should continue to play an active role in the defense of freedom throughout the world, and we supported maintaining the military capability required by such a role. As against the New Politics ideal of a society based on equality of condition, we believed in a society based on equality of opportunity, and we supported government action to eliminate all forms of discrimination including the deceptively benign one of racial quotas. And as against the "neo-Malthusianism" of the New Politics, we believed that further economic growth was possible and that it was also necessary to ensure the continued prosperity of the already prosperous and the future prosperity of the presently poor.

In the most general terms, what CDM was trying to say was that the much-abused American "system" was a precious thing and that it needed and deserved to be defended. For me personally the decision to do what I could to defend it represented yet another aspect of the lesson in the nature of healthy political activity that had guided me toward a frank defense of my own interests as an intellectual and as a Jew. Because there was so much anti-Americanism within America itself, speaking as an

American in defense of America meant in the first place addressing myself to other Americans; and this I tried to do not in terms of abstract political theory but through the running critique in *Commentary* of the assumptions of the anti-American position in domestic affairs.

Then, suddenly, a great event occurred that simultaneously internationalized the context of this debate about America and showed that the centers of Republican conservatism now governing the country were no more immune from the failure of nerve than their counterparts in the old liberal Establishment. In 1973, the Organization of Petroleum Exporting Countries (OPEC), led by Saudi Arabia, announced that it was raising the price of oil by four hundred percent.

"We know," wrote the political analyst Robert W. Tucker in an article for *Commentary* entitled "Oil: The Issue of American Intervention," "how the oil crisis would have been resolved until quite recently. Indeed, until quite recently it seems safe to say that it would never have arisen because of the prevailing expectation that it would have led to armed intervention." Yet despite the fact that throughout history threats to a nation's sources of raw materials had been a cause of war, and despite the fact that the aggressors in this case were infinitely weaker than their victims, the United States neither used force nor even seriously threatened to use it. More remarkable still, most of the leading centers of opinion, inside the government and out, nodded in agreement at arguments in justification of the OPEC cartel that amounted to little more than the charge that the prosperity of the West in general and the United States in particular had been achieved not by their own productive energies but by exploiting the peoples of the Third World and plundering their resources. No doubt there were good reasons for refraining from the use of military force in response to the action of OPEC, but what good reason could there be for allowing such accusations to go unanswered? Clearly what we were seeing here was the most vivid instance yet of what Pat Moynihan, in another *Commentary* piece entitled "The United States in Opposition," also called "patterns of appeasement so profound as to seem wholly normal." What might happen, he wondered, if these patterns were reversed—if, that is, the United States were to "cease to apologize for an imperfect democracy" and were to begin speaking forcefully out of its own traditions of economic, political, and civil liberty? "We are," he wrote, "of the liberty party, and it might surprise us what energies might be released were we to unfurl those banners."

After reading that article, Henry Kissinger gave Moynihan an opportunity to put its precepts into practice by appointing him ambassador to the UN. Yet Kissinger, as secretary of state, first under Richard Nixon and now under Gerald Ford, had himself been contributing to the pattern of appeasement that Moynihan wanted to reverse. Kissinger had a habit of making strong statements, but so weak and uncertain were his actions that he, too, seemed to have reversed Theodore Roosevelt's dictum; or to put it another way, he often sounded like Winston Churchill while behaving like Neville Chamberlain. Thus he had made a series of threatening noises in response to OPEC's act of economic aggression against the vital interests of the United States, but that was all he was ever to do.

What was much more serious, however, he had presided over a policy of "détente" under cover of which, as Theodore Draper, Walter Laqueur, and others would soon demonstrate, the Soviet Union was being permitted to strengthen its military power to the point where its leaders could brag of an imminent and irreversible shift in "the balance of forces." Already the Russians were stronger than we were in conventional military capability, and they were now pushing toward a position of strategic nuclear superiority as well. This did not, however, disturb Kissinger. "What in the name of God," he asked, "is strategic superiority? What do you do with it?" By this he meant that so long as we still had the power to destroy the Soviet Union after a surprise nuclear attack, the fact that they might have a larger arsenal of missiles was of no great importance. But the Russians evidently disagreed with this theory. They seemed to know very well both what strategic superiority was and what you did with it—you intimidated other nuclear powers who might wish to stand in your way when you started to move ahead.

That the Russians were in fact moving ahead, the Churchill side of Kissinger acknowledged. They were, he said, in a period of imperialist expansionism (a judgment they would soon confirm by continuing their own military buildup and by sending Cuban proxies into Africa). But while he was in office at least, his Chamberlain side prevailed, and he did not press on to the necessary conclusion, which was that in the absence of determined resistance by the United States, the Russians would go as far as their ideological and imperial ambitions could carry them—and possibly even to the ends of the earth.

I did not believe that the Russians were planning to launch a nuclear strike against the United States. What I did believe, along with Laqueur and others, was that their medium-term objective was to control the whole of Western Europe in the way they now controlled Finland—which was not one of their satellites but was permitted a certain degree of freedom at the price of political subservience—and that this process required the neutralizing of American power. There were those for whom the prospect of "Finlandization," while unpleasant, did not seem especially threatening to the United States; astonishingly, the great theorist of containment, George F. Kennan himself, the choicest convert of all to the new isolationism, was now among them. In my judgment, however, the United States would be unable to survive as a free democratic society in a Finlandized world. For even if we were safe from Soviet military domination, we would be extremely vulnerable to the pull of their political culture: we would, in Jean-François Revel's term, find ourselves becoming "self-Finlandized." Indeed, there were signs that this was happening already, the main one being a new tendency to dismiss liberty—

always held by our own political culture to be the highest of all values—as unimportant in comparison with rival values like equality and community which the political culture of Communism honored more highly (in principle if not in practice). It therefore remained as true as ever that the fundamental interests of the United States—its very survival as a democratic society— dictated a commitment to the defense of Western Europe, as well as of the few democratic countries that existed in other parts of the world.

One afternoon in 1976, before developing these ideas into an article that would be called "Making the World Safe for Communism," I tried them out in a talk at the Council on Foreign Relations. Up until recently, the Council had been perhaps the most powerful center of opposition to isolationism in the United States and, correlatively, one of the most influential sources of support for the policies of anti-Communist interventionism grouped under the rubric of "containment." But things had been changing in the Council. To follow George Kennan's example by going all the way over to a frank isolationism would have been too much for most members of the Council, but they were very receptive to ideas which, while seeming to prescribe a continued American role in world affairs, actually served to rationalize a greater withdrawal of American power than the Council could have countenanced if it were described too openly in those terms.

The main such idea was that the conflict between the United States and the Soviet Union no longer stood at the center of international life; what now mattered most was the conflict between the developed nations of the "North" and the underdeveloped countries of the "South," and in this new international order, military power was as irrelevant as the East-West conflict was becoming obsolete. So far had this notion progressed toward the status of a new revelation that when in my talk before the Council I argued that, far from being obsolete, the case for containment was even stronger now that the Soviet Union had become powerful enough to pose a serious threat to the democratic world than it had been in the days when we were so much more powerful than they, my audience responded the way a congregation of recent converts to a new religion might have done if a preacher of the faith they had just deserted suddenly appeared before them. One member of the congregation, Theodore Sorensen, was particularly outraged when I quoted the promise he himself had supposedly written into John F. Kennedy's inaugural address that the United States would "pay any price, bear any burden, meet any hardship . . . to assure the survival and the success of liberty." But this did not surprise me. What did come as a surprise was the discovery during the question period that my position was being interpreted by at least some people as a piece of elaborate special pleading in the interests not of the United States but of Israel.

To say that I was unaware of the implications of my position for American policy toward Israel, or that I was indifferent to them, would have been untrue. I knew very well that an American foreign policy dedicated to "the survival and the success of liberty" was good for Israel, one of the few democratic countries in the world and the only one in the Middle East. Conversely, I also understood that an American foreign policy dedicated to the construction of "a new international order" would lead at the very least to a tilt toward the Arabs and at the worst to an abandonment of Israel as the price of a secure and affordable supply of oil. Nevertheless, the truth was that my position did not arise out of a concern for the survival of Israel. It arose out of a concern for the survival of the United States.

Nor was it because of hypocrisy, as my critics insinuated, that I had failed even to mention Israel in my talk. It was because I was speaking that day as an American in defense of America, in defense of the liberal democratic system under which the country lived, and in defense of its right and its duty to ensure the survival of that system against all who wished to discredit or destroy it. The fact that I as an individual, and the ethnic group of which I was a member, had experienced the blessings of the liberal democratic system in such abundance certainly inclined me to speak in its defense. Similarly with the fact that Israel depended for its own ability to survive on the willingness of the United States to do what was necessary to "assure the survival and the success of liberty." To me, certainly—though again not to a good many of my fellow Jews—this was all the more reason for taking the position I did on American foreign policy.

Conversely, my antipathy toward the Soviet Union did not primarily arise, as my critics implied, from the fact that the Russians were enemies of the state of Israel or that they had become the single most powerful source of anti-Semitism since the fall of the Nazi regime in Germany. I loathed the Soviet Union because I loathed the system of Communist totalitarianism by which it was ruled, and the fact that this system included a hatred of Jews among its many sins and crimes only intensified the obligation I felt to take a stand against it.

But to take a stand against Communist totalitarianism involved more than conducting an ideological battle in the world of ideas. There was also the problem of responding to the Soviet military buildup and the expansionist actions it was beginning to make possible. Here too *Commentary* became involved, first through a series of articles by writers like Edward Luttwak and Richard Pipes demonstrating that the Soviets really were on the move and not—as the neo-isolationists and the appeasers argued—merely trying to catch up with us or imitating our own bad example in maintaining a bloated military establishment; and then in demonstrating the need for an American military budget adequate not only to deter an attack on the United States but to discourage Soviet adventurism in other parts of the world.

One of these parts of the world was of course the Middle East, where the Russians had only recently played an essential role in helping the Egyptians launch the surprise attack on Israel that set off the Yom Kippur war. What had saved Israel from being overrun by the Arab armies was an airlift of American arms; and what had prevented the Russians from intervening when they threatened to do so at a certain point was the American nuclear deterrent. Nothing could have more vividly demonstrated the inextricable connection between the survival of Israel and the military adequacy of the United States. Nevertheless, even after the Yom Kippur war, many members of the American Jewish community and many self-proclaimed friends of Israel in the general liberal community continued to act as though the one had nothing to do with the other. They were loud in calling for a continued American commitment to the security of Israel, but they simultaneously favored cuts in the defense budget which, if implemented, would make such a commitment impossible to carry out.

It was in this contradiction that one could see the most dramatic evidence of the reluctance of the American Jewish community to face up to the unpleasant truth that the hostility to anti-Communist interventionism was as dangerous to Israel as the anti-Zionism of the Movement.

23

The inextricable connection between the survival of Israel and American military strength was an idea I would soon also have the opportunity to lend strong support to during Pat Moynihan's race against Bella Abzug and Ramsey Clark for the Democratic nomination for the United States Senate in New York in 1976.

Although by 1976 Moynihan had held high appointive positions under the last four presidents, he had only run for elective office once before—as the Democratic candidate for president of the New York city council in 1965—and he had done badly enough to discourage the idea that he might have a future in electoral politics. But almost overnight, after only a few months of putting the ideas he had expressed in his *Commentary* article into practice at the UN, he had to his own and everyone else's amazement become one of the most popular public figures in the United States. Walking the streets of New York, he would be stopped by passersby and slapped on the back; in restaurants, his table would be surrounded by people congratulating and thanking him; in a theater or concert hall, the mere sight of him was likely to set off a standing ovation. According to the public-opinion polls, it was the same everywhere in America: his approval ratings ran to an astonishing seventy percent in every region of the country and among every group in the population.

Americans loved him because he was the first public figure in a long time to assert, in language that was simultaneously blunt, eloquent, and credible, that the United States, as leader of the "liberty party," stood for something precious in the world. They loved him too because not only did he refuse to be put on the defensive by the lies and the slanders regularly hurled against the United States by the Communists and by representatives of the Third World; he also managed, just as he had prescribed in "The United States in Opposition," to put them on the defensive by the truths he had the undiplomatic clarity to speak (as, for example, when with literal accuracy he called Idi Amin of Uganda a "racist murderer").

Most Jews shared in this general American enthusiasm for Moynihan's stance, but they also had a special reason for looking up to him as their champion, and that was the way he behaved when the Arabs and the Soviet bloc introduced a resolution at the UN condemning Zionism as a form of racism and thereby in effect branding Israel a criminal state. Together with his UN colleague Leonard Garment—who was perhaps the only close associate of Richard Nixon to have emerged from the Watergate investigations with his reputation enhanced—Moynihan responded with a denunciation of the resolution the like of which had not been heard either in the UN or anywhere else for a very long time indeed. The United States was not the only country that voted against the resolution, but most of the others did so—as their representatives all hastened to the rostrum to explain—because they thought the resolution politically unwise. Moynihan, by contrast, declared that the United States opposed it because it was wrong in principle, and because it represented a perversion of language as well as a distortion of the historical record. He used words like "obscenity" and "lies" and he did not hesitate to warn that by approving this egregiously anti-Semitic resolution (which it eventually did) the UN would disgrace itself and make a mockery of everything for which it pretended to stand.

What very few people understood about Moynihan's response to the Zionism/racism resolution was that it arose not out of any special feeling for Israel or the Jews as such, but out of the conviction that the resolution represented an attack by the totalitarian world and its satellites and allies against the democratic world of which Israel happened for the moment to be the most vulnerable member. It was, in other words, on behalf of the liberty party rather than for the sake of the Jewish people that he sprang to the defense of Israel and because he believed that the campaign to delegitimize the state of Israel was aimed ultimately at the democratic world in general and the United States in particular. The ideological defense of Zionism was therefore dictated not only by moral considerations but by the American national interest.

I understood this because I knew Moynihan well and because he and I and Garment had discussed all these matters for many long hours while drafting the speeches they were to make in explanation of the American vote. But to most Jews this was, or would have been, had they been conscious of it, a distinction without a difference: what they heard was an official American spokesman standing up for a besieged and increasingly isolated Jewish state and doing so in a way that lifted the spirits and gladdened the heart.

For their part, what the Arabs and the Russians—and those Americans sunk in the "patterns of appeasement" Moynihan was trying to reverse—heard was an appeal for Jewish support in the upcoming senatorial campaign. So worried was Moynihan that this explanation of his motives might discredit his entire position that he disclaimed any intention of running for the Senate, and in the strongest possible terms. He could afford to do this because he really had no intention of running, and it was only after being forced out of his job at the UN and then being worked on relentlessly by people like Bayard Rustin, Lane Kirkland of the AFL-CIO, and me that he agreed to enter the Democratic primary.

In sixteen years of personal friendship and professional collaboration, Pat Moynihan and I had had our differences and disagreements, but both of us had emerged from the experience of the sixties with the same general perspective. It was often said that we had moved to the Right, but neither of us was satisfied with that description. In one sense, of course, it was true: anyone moving away from the Left had to move to the Right. But the Right, as we understood the term, stood for a position that was in its own way no less radical than the position of the Left against which we had so decisively turned (I from a starting point much closer to it than he had ever been even in the early sixties). What was radical about the Left was that it regarded the liberal welfare state established by Roosevelt and his successors as a sham and a fraud and an obstacle to the social goals it pretended to serve; and what was radical about the Right was that it regarded that same liberal welfare state as an intolerable infringement on individual liberty. These were both radical positions in the sense that they both stood outside the majority consensus in favor of the liberal welfare state—the Left opposing it because it did not (and could not without being fundamentally altered) go far enough, the Right opposing it because it had already gone too far and threatened to go further still. Moynihan and I, however, believed in the liberal welfare state, we supported it, and we wanted to preserve and defend it—increasing its social benefits to the poor and the handicapped without violating its *liberal* character as a system in which government control over the individual was kept within jealously guarded limits and in which initiative and enterprise were still encouraged and rewarded.

This individualist emphasis had once been taken for granted as the essence of liberalism, but in recent years the word "liberal" had come to be used so insistently as a euphemism for "socialist" that even people who called themselves socialists were referred to in the media as liberals. Nevertheless, neither Moynihan nor I was willing to acquiesce in this theft of an epithet that we thought belonged by right of historical title and philosophical pedigree to the position we held rather than to the position held by the New Politics or the Old Left.

By the same token we were both reluctant to accept the label "neoconservative" even though almost everyone else was beginning to use it of us and of our political friends, some of whom were also using it of themselves. As I have said, what in the authoritative view of Irving Kristol distinguished the "neo" or "new" conservatives from the older variety was precisely their acceptance of the welfare state; instead of working to dismantle it, as the "old" conservatives (or the Right) wanted to do, the neoconservatives wanted to make sure that it remained consistent with traditional American principles. If this was what defined a neoconservative, then Moynihan and I could legitimately be included. And yet, and yet. In a *Commentary* symposium on the question "What Is a Liberal—Who Is a Conservative?," Midge Decter said she had come to recognize that she owed "her very existence" to the idea historically associated with liberalism "that no person may be forcibly imprisoned within the class or clan or even family into which he was born," and that "had conservatism been dominant among my precursors, they would have ruled *me* out." Consequently, even though there were nowadays many more things she wished to conserve than to improve upon, and even though life would be simpler and more peaceful if she submitted to the title "conservative" now so commonly used of people with her political views, she could not yield without betraying her obligation to contend with those enemies of the liberalism to which she owed her life who were now seeking to "abscond with its good name."

I felt very much the same way, and I think Moynihan did too: as the child of an Irish slum in New York he also owed his existence to the traditional liberal idea. Others might call us conservatives or neoconservatives, and we certainly had no desire to be identified with the views of many of the people usually known as liberals today. In looking for convenient alternatives to use in public, we would say that we were "centrists." But privately, when we wondered what to call ourselves *to* ourselves, the invariable answer was: a liberal.

But all this was bound to remain relatively abstract until it could be translated into the concrete terms of actual candidacies for political office. Like everyone else in the CDM circle, I believed that popular support for our point of view was there, waiting to be appealed to and mobilized, and I also believed that the race for the United States Senate in New York in 1976 presented a perfect opportunity to do just that. The leading candidates in the Democratic primary, Bella Abzug and Ramsey Clark, were both "liberals," she by way of the Old Left and he by way of the New. As for the Republican incumbent, James Buckley (brother of William F. Buckley of *The National Review* and as such a member of the first family of American conservatism), he was exactly the kind of conservative who might more properly have been called a radical of the Right. After all, he and his fellow organizers of the Conservative party had originally broken with the Republican party in protest against the latter's decision, when it finally came to power in 1953 under Eisenhower, to ratify the welfare-state reforms of the New Deal instead of trying to repeal them; now he had brought a sanitized version of this position into the Republican party itself, much as the New Politics people had done on their side in carrying the ideas and attitudes of the radical Left into the Democratic party.

Running against Abzug and Clark in the Democratic party, and then against Buckley in the general election, was therefore an opportunity to define a liberal alternative first to the Left and then to the Right and to prove that this alternative commanded more popular support than either. Something else Midge Decter said around that time—"Between the Left and the Right there's nowhere to go but down"—may well have provided the ultimate stimulus in persuading Moynihan to run. Now that his great popularity had turned him into a promising candidate, we all had another chance to go forward instead of down.

Moynihan's campaign against Abzug and Clark accordingly focused on the theme of "a society worth defending." In contrast to the New Politics "liberalism" of his opponents, he asserted his conviction that the old liberal tradition running from Roosevelt through Truman, Kennedy, and Johnson (and closely identified with the political culture of New York State itself) remained vital and viable. In contrast to the hostility shown by the New Politics to "middle-class" values, he affirmed the enduring importance of social institutions like the family (often accused in those days of being the source of all evil) and equally abused cultural values like the "work ethic" and the idea of individual responsibility. And in the sharpest contrast of all, he countered the calls of Abzug and Clark for deep cuts in military spending with the argument that a society worth defending also needed to be defended by an adequate military budget. It was in the course of raising this issue that Moynihan was able to demonstrate more vividly than anyone had done before that there was a direct contradiction between caring about the survival of Israel—as both Abzug and Clark professed to do—and opposing, as they both did, the defense appropriations out of which aid to Israel had to come.

Though this campaign against the Left resulted in a less decisive victory than I had expected, Moynihan did nevertheless win. He then went on to win—and much more decisively—against Buckley on an issue that gave sharp definition to the difference between the old liberal tradition he represented and the rightist tradition out of which Buckley came: the issue of federal intervention to help the economically deprived or disadvantaged. In this case, the victim was not a class or an ethnic or racial group but an entire city—New York—and just as Buckley's political forebears had opposed federal intervention in the past where earlier victims were concerned, so he now opposed similar action to rescue New York City from bankruptcy and financial ruin. In making the case for federal help, Moynihan was thus simultaneously able to mount a general defense of the liberal welfare state against its enemies on the Right.

The alternative to going down between the Left and the Right had now been marked out: having already shown that it could win in the world of ideas, it now showed that it could win in the world of electoral politics as well. With this—and at least for me—one phase in the long and ongoing contention with radicalism had come to a happy end.

POSTSCRIPT

There you have it, John, the story of how I came to believe "all that stuff," how I came to hate and fear it, and how it both acquired and lost an amazing amount of power within the space of twenty years. Not that its power is entirely gone; far from it. But I don't have to tell you that. From listening to your teachers and your friends and their parents, you know better than I how many of the things I used to believe when I was part of a tiny group of radicals in the early sixties have become the conventional wisdom of the seventies. You know from your own experience that if the Movement is dead, which in a formal sense it certainly is, it died as much because it won as because it lost. Its ideas and attitudes are now everywhere.

But when I say that radicalism is still alive, I have in mind something deeper and more general than the particular doctrines of the New Left and the counterculture and the habits and the mores and the tastes and the fashions to which they gave rise. To the extent that these doctrines have become an orthodoxy in so many American circles, they have inevitably lost their radical bite; and to the extent that the American way of life has undergone a marked change under their influence, the "counter" culture no longer has anything to be counter to.

Where then does radicalism now live? Exactly where it has always lived: not primarily in doctrines and not in the outward signs of manner and dress, but in self-hatred and self-contempt. It was out of an infection of self-hatred and self-contempt—disguised, to be sure, by the various gospels of expanding human possibility preached by early prophets like Norman O. Brown, Norman Mailer, and Paul Goodman—that the radicalism of the sixties was born; and as it grew and spread, the infection grew and spread until it reached the proportions of an epidemic. The young were especially vulnerable. They had been inoculated against almost every one of the physical diseases which in times past had literally made it impossible for so many to reach adulthood. But against a spiritual plague like this one they were entirely helpless. Indeed, so spiritually illiterate had the culture become that parents were unable even to recognize the disease when it struck their own children, and so confused were they that they went on insisting, even when the evidence of sickness and incapacity stared them full in the face, that the children were models of superior health.

In the case of the white young, the contemptuous repudiation of everything American and middle-class was mistaken for a form of idealism when it really represented a refusal to be who they were and to assume responsibility for themselves by taking their place in a world of adults. The case of the black young was more complicated because unlike their white counterparts they had real external oppressions to contend with. But this only made it easier to mistake the plague for health when it struck them in the form of a refusal to accept any responsibility whatever for their own condition—to trace its ills entirely to the actions of whites and to look entirely to external forces for the cure. In the case, finally, of the intellectuals, the third major group that proved especially vulnerable, self-hatred took the form of a repudiation not so much of who as of what they were. To be an intellectual—a scholar, a thinker, an artist, a writer—was not good enough. Not even "the production of literary masterpieces" was good enough: one had to change the world. Nor was it even good enough to be, as Shelley had said the poets were, the unacknowledged legislators of the world: they had to be acknowledged, they had to exercise actual political power.

After sweeping so many away, the plague seems to have run its course among the young, among the blacks, and among the intellectuals. People of your own generation seem to be growing up reasonably well and seem eager rather than bitterly unwilling to take their places in the world; in the black community, leaders like Jesse Jackson have begun to preach an ethic of self-help and individual responsibility; and in the universities there is a new emphasis on intellectual activity as its own justification and its own reward.

But if the plague seems for the moment to have run its course among these groups, it rages as fiercely as ever among others: among the kind of women who do not wish to be women and among those men who do not wish to be men. The same spiritual illiteracy that made it so easy for so many to mistake the self-hatred into which their own children or they themselves had fallen in the sixties for political idealism now makes it easy to misread the female self-hatred so evident in elements of the women's movement or the male self-hatred pervading the gay-rights campaign as self-acceptance expressing itself politically in the demand for acceptance by others. Yet there can be no more radical refusal of self-acceptance than the repudiation of one's own biological nature; and there can be no abdication of responsibility more fundamental than the refusal of a man to become, and to be, a father, or the refusal of a woman to become, and be, a mother.

In an individual the ultimate expression of self-hatred is suicide —the murder by its own hand of the hated self. Thus it was that the sixties saw a huge rise in the number of suicides among the young, both white and black, and an untold increase in the number of unrecorded suicides through drugs and other "accidents" —all taking place in the context of a culture in which suicide was virtually encouraged by being romanticized (in, for example, the cult of Sylvia Plath) as an expression of superior sensitivity and therefore as an affirmation of life. "Whom the gods wish to destroy," wrote Euripides, "they first make mad"—mad enough, in this application of the rule, to mistake death for life and life for death.

But if the plague, unchecked, causes death by suicide in individuals, it can also attack the vital organs of the entire species, preventing men from fathering children and women from mothering them. Here the disease, unchecked, leads not to the destruction of the individual's will to live (though it may) but to the destruction of the individual's will to propagate and reproduce. Thus it was that when the plague invaded women as women and men as men, the birth rate began to fall precipitously and the number of abortions soon exceeded the number of births. There was a message in the fact that in an age when contraception had become so easily available and so effective, abortion should have remained so prevalent a form of birth control: it was almost as though the species were trying to force itself to recognize the symptoms of the plague behind the cunning deceptions by which it had been tempted into the service of sterility. And just as the rise in the number of individual suicides before had been accompanied and further encouraged by the rise of a veritable cult of suicide, so now sterility was promoted in ways both direct and devious: through warnings about overpopulation; through a harping on the difficulties and miseries of raising a family as compared with the pleasures and excitements of the unencumbered life; through the rise of new therapies like est and "self-help" books which elevated selfishness into the single most important of all moral imperatives. This identification of sterility with vitality is what links the new narcissism of the Me Decade to Women's Lib and the gay-rights movement, and it is what links all of them to the radicalism of the sixties.

By the same token, it is what distinguishes them from the politics of interest that I have come to see as the only antidote to the plague and the only effective protection against ever catching it again. The politics of interest promises neither salvation nor the experience of spiritual transcendence that radicalism pretends to offer. It promises only the satisfactions that come from acting out of respect for oneself and out of responsibility toward those extensions of oneself—one's family and the groups and communities to which one belongs, whether by birth or by voluntary choice —that an openness to life inevitably creates. That this is all the transcendence of self that mortal beings can hope to achieve through action in the public realm, I now believe with all my heart. But is it, for all that, a politics of selfishness? Not if it is pursued in the context of a pluralistic society like our own. In this society the assumption is that the politics of interest not only serves the purpose of civil peace by providing the best way to resolve conflicting claims; it also works to preserve and protect political liberty itself. For as James Madison explained in the best statement of the case for the American Constitution ever made, *it is only where liberty exists that the politics of interest can flourish and only where the politics of interest flourishes that liberty can exist.*

What I am trying to say is that if the politics of interest goes beyond individual selfishness in embracing the claims of family, community, and group, it also embodies and simultaneously broadens into an instrument of political liberty. At least it does in the American constitutional system, and for those of us who are determined to keep faith with the men who ordained that system "in order to form a more perfect Union, establish Justice, insure domestic Tranquility, provide for the common defense, promote the general Welfare, and secure the Blessings of Liberty to ourselves and our Posterity."

Ourselves—*the summons is to me.* Posterity—*the summons is to you.*

Index